CW01431824

# Ludicrously Inappropriate Magic

**Books by Clayton Taylor Wood:**

## The Runic Series

Runic Awakening

Runic Revelation

Runic Vengeance

Runic Revolt

## The Fate of Legends Series

Hunter of Legends

Seeker of Legends

Destroyer of Legends

Avenger of Legends

## Magic of Havenwood Series

The Magic Collector

The Lost Gemini

The Magic Redeemer

## The Magic of Magic Series

Inappropriate Magic

Ridiculously Inappropriate Magic

Ludicrously Inappropriate Magic

# Ludicrously Inappropriate Magic

**Book III of the Magic of Magic Series**

Clayton Taylor Wood

Copyright ©2021 by Clayton Taylor Wood.

All rights reserved.

This book or any portion thereof may not be reproduced or used in any manner whatsoever without the express written permission of the publisher except for the use of brief quotations in a book review.

This is a work of fiction. Names, characters, businesses, places, events and incidents are either the products of the author's imagination or used in a fictitious manner. Any resemblance to actual persons, living or dead, or actual events is purely coincidental.

Published by Clayton T. Wood.

ISBN: 978-1-948497-18-3

Cover designed by James T. Egan, Bookfly Design, LLC

Printed in the United States of America.

Special thanks to Howie and Nancy, who have a kind of inappropriate magic all their own. And to the hidden magic within each of us, waiting patiently to be found.

DISCLAIMER:

This book contains (ludicrously) inappropriate depictions of (ludicrously) inappropriate people doing (ludicrously) inappropriate things. Including, but certainly not limited to, inappropriate language and veiled connotations of the naughty variety. Although not *nearly* as veiled as the first and second books.

And of course, (ludicrously) inappropriate magic.

## Table of Contents

# Ludicrously Inappropriate Magic

# Prologue

When destiny knocked on Chauncy Little's door, it was long overdue that *he* be the one to answer it.

He happened to be rather depressed at the time, mechanically making the usual breakfast of eggs and sausage on the kitchen stove for his fiancée Valtora. A breakfast he usually made with an oversized helping of love, but on this particular morning, he made with no helping at all. The specifics of why will have to wait a bit, for destiny, having been delayed on several occasions, was more than a little impatient. So, dear reader, please bear with it and let destiny have its way with you, at least for the moment. Destiny deferred is a dangerous thing, after all…as Chauncy himself would surely attest to.

So sizzle he did, nudging the sausages and eggs on the pan glumly, until the moment came to pass. Then came destiny's fateful knock on the door, and Chauncy turned to answer it at last.

And promptly turned right back to what he was doing, the thought of interacting with anyone else utterly unbearable. For at the moment, he didn't even want to be with himself, so disgusted was he with this particular subject.

The knock came again, and Chauncy ignored it, hoping that whoever it was would assume he wasn't home. But his hopes were in vain, for when destiny knocked upon one's door, it rarely did so just once.

"For crying out loud!" he blurted out, picking up the pan and slamming it down on the stovetop. He stomped toward the door, grabbing the knob and twisting it, then yanking the door open viciously. "What do you want?" he snapped.

And then froze.

For there, standing at his doorstep, was a terribly familiar man. A terribly *elderly* man, tall and slender, with a stooped back and big, knobby hands. His face was the oldest face Chauncy had ever seen, and his long white beard had hairs that, to be blunt, were embarrassingly thin. But his blue robes and his long blue pointed

1

hat were quite marvelous, particularly in comparison to that which they contained. And his tall staff – with just the most impressively perfect amount of twisty – was most glorious of all.

It was none other than Imperius Fanning, perhaps the greatest wizard in all the land. And he who'd doled out destinies to Chosen Ones since antiquity.

"Oh," Chauncy blurted out, freezing in place.

"I see that rudeness is a family trait," the man stated, glaring at Chauncy indignantly. Chauncy grimaced.

"Sorry," he apologized. "I just…you caught me at a bad moment is all."

"So I see," Imperius replied, his gaze dropping. Not to Chauncy's chest, or his belly, to but matters a bit further below. Chauncy followed Imperius's gaze, and realized that he was quite naked.

He *shrieked.*

Chauncy fled back into the house, slamming the door behind him. If he'd had any presence of mind, he'd have bounded up the stairs to the second floor, then gone into the bedroom to get dressed. Instead, he ran into the kitchen, grabbing the nearest pan from the stove and hiding his particulars with it.

Unfortunately, it was the pan he'd been using to sizzle Valtora's sausage and eggs…and now it was sizzling *his.*

Chauncy *screamed.*

He dropped the pan, grabbing his blistering bits and yelling a word that, to be frank, he would not be enacting any time soon. Then he slid down onto his buttocks on the cold kitchen floor, and promptly wept.

"Honey?" he heard Valtora call out from upstairs. "Are you okay?"

He wasn't. But his attempt to communicate this ended up as a kind of pathetic mewling sound.

To Chauncy's horror, the front door opened, and Imperius came into the house…just as Valtora limped downstairs.

"Impy!" she gasped as she spotted the old man. "OhmygodI *missed* you!"

"And I you," Imperius admitted, giving her a warm smile. She reached the bottom of the stairs, leaning in and giving him a hug. Then they both turned to Chauncy.

"Oh," Valtora blurted out, putting a hand to her mouth. "Chauncy, you're *nude!*"

"Fuck," Chauncy gasped, covering his grilled genitals with his hands. But he accidently brushed his hand against them, sending a truly exquisite pain lancing through his groin.

A sound came out of him then. One that was precisely the opposite of brave and masculine.

"Chauncy!" Valtora gasped, rushing up to him as best she could. "What happened?"

"Pan," he gasped, rocking back and forth. "Hot."

She grabbed one of his hands, pulling it away from his injuries, then gasped, her eyes widening.

"Oh," she blurted out.

"What is it?" Imperius inquired, joining them in the kitchen.

"Um..." Valtora replied, gesturing at Chauncy's sausage and eggs. Imperius's eyebrows rose.

"Oh," he blurted out. "Oh my."

"Did you see the size of that blister?" Valtora asked him. "It's like, *huge*."

"I did," Imperius confirmed, seeming not at all pleased with this fact.

"Right on the tip too," Valtora noted.

"Fuck," Chauncy repeated. And to his horror, he was crying.

"It's okay," Valtora reassured Chauncy. "Everything is going to be all right, you'll see."

"Mmfff," he replied, continuing to cry.

"Guess both of our happy places aren't very happy right now, huh?" she pressed with a rueful smile. Which will take some explaining, dear reader, but rest assured it'll all make sense soon enough.

"It seems that catching you at a bad time was precisely the right time to catch you," Imperius mused, patting his gut. "My gut is never wrong, after all."

"Why *are* you here?" Valtora asked, standing up and facing the wizard.

"Your world is in grave danger," Imperius warned, his tone darkening dramatically. Valtora rolled her eyes.

"Here we go again," she muttered. Then she frowned. "Wait, you're supposed to say 'our world' not 'your world,'" she protested.

"I'm supposed to say whatever I say," Imperius said. "Now if you'll let me say it..."

Valtora sighed, gesturing for him to continue.

"Your world is in grave danger," Imperius repeated, to slightly less effect than before. "Before you were born, Chauncy, your father made a very powerful wizard his enemy. A wizard that will stop at nothing to get revenge on your father." His scowl deepened. "Soon this wizard will come for you, and destroy everything you know and…well, just you, really." He paused. "Which would destroy everything you know, technically."

"Huh?" Chauncy mumbled, still hunched over on the floor.

"I'll get your robe," Valtora offered. She left the kitchen and went back upstairs, returning shortly with Chauncy's purple, glittery, wizardly robe. She draped it over his pan-seared particulars, and he screeched in anticipation of horrible pain. But the robe's silky white inner lining bothered his blistered bits not one bit. Which in that moment, seemed like potent magic indeed.

"So…huh?" Chauncy repeated, staring at Imperius uncomprehendingly.

"A wizard named Zella Trek is dead-set on getting revenge on your father," Imperius explained. "And as she cannot harm him directly, he's determined to do it indirectly."

"Oh…kay," Chauncy replied.

"By killing you," Imperius concluded.

"Oh," Chauncy stated with a grimace. "Shit," he added, rather appropriately, considering the circumstances.

"Well, at least it's not the end of the world," Valtora offered, smiling at Chauncy. "Kidding," she added.

"Not of ours, but his," Imperius countered. "For the end of *you* is the end of *your* world," he explained. "In the end, that's all there is."

Thus, destiny having quite literally caught Chauncy not just with his pants down, but with no pants at all, it was at long last no longer deferred. And that was fortuitous indeed, for Imperius had arrived just in time to provide Chauncy with a most timely tip…one even more important than the one he'd burned.

So at this point, dear reader, you've become quite the expert in how these things go. Old hat and all that, you know. But in the interest of being interesting – and in not lacking consistency – we've said it before and we'll (approximately) say it again:

And that, dear reader, was how the end of Chauncy's world began.

# Chapter 1

Now, dear reader, that destiny has no longer been deferred, we'll return you to what *has* been: the story of how poor Chauncy came to be in this blistery pickle in the first place. It all began approximately one day earlier, in a different *when* but the same *where*.

Chauncy found himself busy cooking breakfast that fine, sunny morning, clad only in his chef's apron, as per his routine. His fiancée Valtora sat at their little kitchen table…a much further distance away from that table than she'd sat the last time destiny had knocked, of course. For destiny hadn't been the only thing doing the knocking…and having been knocked up, Valtora was a full nine months pregnant, her belly looking for all the world as if it were ready to burst.

"What about 'Wesley,'" Chauncy offered as he scrambled some eggs and sizzled some sausage. It was Valtora's favorite breakfast, and he simply loved to cook it. For it made her smile every time to eat it, and bringing her joy brought *him* joy.

This, he suspected, was one of the secrets of life. The Republic of Borrin had tricked him into a life consumed with production for the purposes of future consumption, with money serving as the promise that the former would lead to the latter. Having had most of his life consumed by this cycle, Chauncy had quite definitively determined that it wasn't for him. For happiness – and magic – was one's relationship with the world. And relationships were happiest not when they were transactional, but when they were generous.

Valtora made a face.

"*Wesley?*" she replied. "Ew."

"What's wrong with Wesley?" Chauncy pressed.

"Too wimpy," she answered. "I want something *epic.*"

"Um…Chester?" he proposed. Lamely.

"Gag," she replied, sticking a finger down her throat. A disturbing distance, at least to some. But Valtora didn't gag, as it was a reflex she'd apparently been born without. A fact that wasn't nearly as disturbing to him as it might be to others.

"Chauncy junior?" he offered.

"Fuck no."

Chauncy frowned, waiting for her to add "no offense" or an equivalent apology. But she didn't, so offense was taken.

"Well you try then," he decided, feeling a bit irritated. Probably because he was still hungry. It was common knowledge that Chauncy was, in Valtora's words, a little bitch when he was hungry.

"How about...MAGNUS!" she boomed, spreading her arms out wide rather dramatically.

"Eh."

"Okay," she stated. "How about...PIERCE!"

"Too stabby," he opined. She frowned prettily, leaning forward as much as she could and tapping her fingers on the table. And given that it was her left hand – one made entirely of diamond – each tap left little dents in the wood. He frowned, irritated at this; for it was Grandma Little's table, and he preferred to preserve it.

"How about...BRAWLEY!" she exclaimed. Also dramatically. For Valtora did everything dramatically, though not intentionally. She was perhaps the most explosively colorful person Chauncy had ever met, which was one reason he adored her. With Valtora, life was never boring...even the parts that were supposed to be. As a wizard, she made life magical...merely by being in his.

"Too punchy," Chauncy argued.

"Well shoot," Valtora said, pouting prettily. She crossed her arms under her bosom, which would've been quite bedazzling to Chauncy even if bedazzling hadn't been her magical power. But seeing as it was, he found himself doubly bedazzled. "What're we gonna *name* this bastard?"

Chauncy grimaced, not at all fond of the term. But technically, she was correct. Unless they got hitched soon, the baby *would* be a bastard. And in fact, Valtora had refused to get married for that very reason. So she could call the kid a bastard...and have plausible deniability as to whether it was an insult or merely factual.

"How about some girl names?" he proposed, struggling to keep his gaze northward. With little success.

"Eh," Valtora replied, making a face. For she'd made it quite clear that she wanted a boy, and wouldn't entertain the possibility of any other gender.

Chauncy sighed, turning off the stovetop. With that, he doled out portions of sausage and egg to each of their plates, then sat down opposite her to enjoy them. Valtora gobbled them down eagerly, hardly caring that they were piping hot. For, having spent two and a half decades on a live volcano, hot was a relative thing. "Mmm," Valtora gushed as she gobbled, finishing it up with shocking speed. Pregnancy had given her a voracious – and vicious – appetite, particularly for sausage. It was only by virtue of her powers of bedazzling that she maintained her usual gorgeous figure. One that pregnancy had seen fit to enhance in particular places. "It's good," she said between gobbles.

"Mmmf," he agreed, blowing his sausage a bit, then nibbling the tip cautiously. At length he finished his meal, while Valtora watched happily. For happiness was her default disposition, a fact that made her a joy to be around. "Love you poopy-dooz," Chauncy cooed, giving her a smile. Then he heard purring, and blinked, looking down at his lap. There was, to his surprise, a very large cat sitting on it. One with gold and black hair, and purple glowing eyes that stared up at him.

Sexily.

He realized that he was petting her with his free hand…and that he had absolutely no idea how long he'd been doing it for.

"Geez!" he blurted out. While still petting quite involuntarily. It was ZoMonsterz, a minion of The Dark One…and Valtora's favorite pet hellcat.

"Aww," Valtora said. "She loves you, you know."

"I got that," Chauncy grumbled. And it was true. ZoMonsterz was constantly appearing out of nowhere for a good petting. She was everywhere his free hand was, it seemed. One of her magical powers, according to Valtora. Her other power was a bit more disturbing. For if ZoMonsterz were to scratch a person – something she had never done to Chauncy – that person would be rendered utterly terrified of the hellcat for precisely two years.

ZoMonsterz continued to purr, licking Chauncy's petting hand. A bit too sexily for Chauncy's liking. For the cat's tongue was not rough in the way of normal cats, and – combined with her longing gazes – her feline kisses were at times a bit too suggestive for Chauncy's tastes.

"Okay," Valtora stated, pushing her plate aside and eyeing him eagerly. "How about…"

"…we go to the shop, and *then* think of more baby names," Chauncy interrupted. It was getting a bit late, and if they didn't hurry, they'd annoy their earliest customers.

"Aww."

"Let's go," he prompted. And with that, he took off his chef's apron – giving Valtora an eyeful of his eggs and sausage – and pranced out of the kitchen and made his way upstairs. He almost slipped on a sock halfway up, another consequence of having a hellcat in the house. For ZoMonsterz was possessed of the strange compulsion to strew socks and underwear all over the house. Particularly on the stairs, where the odds of them committing murder were highest.

"Put on the special underwear!" she called out after him. Chauncy grimaced, knowing she was referring to the…miniscule underwear that she'd insisted he wear ever since they'd traveled to defeat The Dark One about nine months ago. Underwear that he found profoundly uncomfortable to wear in public, hidden though it was by his wizardly robe. Still, he did as he was told, going to the "special" drawer beside their bed and finding one to put on. That done, he hid the evidence under his wizard's robe, one that was white and sinfully silky on the inside, and purple and outstandingly sparkly on the outside. A robe that screamed "wizard," among other things. That done, he hurried downstairs, eager to get on with his day.

"Ready?" he called out. Valtora waddled out of the kitchen and down the hallway to the front door, the Staff of Wind in her hand. A thick tree branch with just the right amount of twisty, it was Chauncy's signature weapon…and the first magical item he'd ever made.

"Thanks poopy-dooz," he said, leaning over to give her a kiss. Then he opened the door, gesturing through it valiantly. "After you, m'Lady."

"My *hero*," she gushed, batting her eyes prettily.

And with that, they stepped onto the porch, and Chauncy locked the door. Then, arm-in-arm, he helped Valtora down the front steps to the sidewalk, then turned right to make the mile-long walk to the city center…and toward the beginning of their workday.

"Oof," Valtora complained, grabbing her lower belly.

"Too quick?" he asked.

"Too pregnant," Valtora countered, making a face. "Can't wait to shove this thing outta me."

"It's not a thing," he corrected. "It's a baby."

"But you just said 'it's a baby,' which means it's an 'it,'" she pointed out.

"What I mean is it's a person," he argued.

8

"You said it was an 'it' again," she shot back. "You can't stop saying it."

"You know what I mean," he told her.

"No I don't," she retorted. Chauncy was about to reply when he realized they'd entered into an argument…and arguments were one of Valtora's favorite things. Particularly now that she was pregnant, and rather uncomfortably so. She'd been picking more arguments as of late, to the point where sometimes Chauncy wondered if it was for play or because she was actually upset. The only clue that she *wasn't* upset was that she hadn't committed any extreme acts of violence. Yet.

"I'm not arguing with you," he told her.

"Yes you are," she countered.

"No I'm…" he began, then snapped his mouth shut. She pouted. "Aww."

"You're sure you're okay?" he pressed, putting a hand over her hand on her belly. She gave him a radiant smile.

"I'm *way* better than okay."

"That's for sure," he agreed, smiling back.

"Kisses," she demanded, puckering up. He leaned over to kiss her, and was delighted to find that her kiss was precisely as it'd always been. Passionate, mind-blowing, and rather inappropriate for public spaces. But inappropriate was Valtora's way, and to his delight, she hadn't changed a bit since he'd fallen in love with her. Other than her belly and bosom, of course.

They continued forward then, and Valtora made another face, grabbing her belly.

"Are you sure you don't want me to get a carriage?" he asked. For the umpteenth time that week.

"Pffft," Valtora replied, waddling faster. "I'm gonna walk this baby right outta me!"

"Oh," Chauncy said, picking up his pace. He hardly needed to hurry up to keep up with her, however. She really was quite pregnant. He shook his head at her determined expression, smiling to himself…and finding his gaze dropping to her left hand. Her diamond hand…with a diamond ring on her ring finger. It glittered prettily, even more so since Valtora had bedazzled it. Which'd been about ten seconds after he'd proposed. Also about eight months ago, on the very day she'd revealed that she was pregnant. By barfing all over a rather rude customer. Twice.

9

At length they made it to the center of Southwick. This consisted of a large circular courtyard with fine benches and ornamental trees and such, bordered by a main street that went 'round the courtyard's perimeter. In the center of the courtyard stood the statue of Archibald Merrick, the founder of the city…and of the Evermore Trading Company.

"Fucker," Valtora spat as she walked past it…and threw a vicious left hook at its leg. A leg that'd endured one too many blows over the last year or so, they soon discovered. For on impact, the limb shattered.

"Oh!" Chauncy blurted out, horrified at this turn of events. For defacing a beloved public statue was certain to be illegal, and carry a hefty fine, if not a jail sentence. He glanced around furtively, but found no witnesses present for the crime, to his profound relief. Valtora cackled.

"Bitch-ass bitch," she said, clearly satisfied with her handiwork. For now the statue was standing on one leg.

"Valtora!" Chauncy complained, pulling her along a bit quicker. "You're going to get us in trouble!"

"Pfft," she replied. "We're wizards. What're they gonna do?"

"I don't want to find out," Chauncy replied. And it was true. For while they were technically wizards, in actuality neither of them were particularly powerful. If an army of Southwick's finest soldiers – bedecked in some magical armor and weapons of their own – attacked Chauncy and Valtora…

"Pussy," Valtora shot back, inappropriately.

"Am not," Chauncy argued.

"Mmm*hmm.*"

"I'm not," he insisted. To his irritation, she didn't respond, choosing to continue on their journey in silence. Which forced him into the unenviable position of not being able to defend his masculinity. Or at least his lack of femininity.

At length, they reached the street at the far end of the courtyard, crossing it to end up at the front door of a narrow three-story building. "A Little Magic," read the sign on the front of the first floor. And on the second floor, another sign: "Time to Learn," in the process of being painted atop the first.

Chauncy gazed up at the latter sign, feeling a swell of pride. For it'd been his dream to found a magic school, and next month he'd make his dream – and the dream of many other would-be wizards – come true. After living most of his life without magic, and serving customers who'd spent their whole lives coming to his shop searching for it – Chauncy would finally give to others what Harry and Nettie had given to him. Why, if he could do so for just *one* person, he'd be more than content.

For magic was like color in a black-and-white world, and a black-and-white world was what Borrin had become. And as Chauncy had learned in his first foray into the Cave of Wonder, *he* was a source of magic…in those fleeting moments when he remembered that fact, anyway. If he could teach others to see that color, and realize that they could be a source of it too, then the black-and-white world they'd been fooled into settling for would…well, it'd be settled for no more.

Chauncy planned on charging not a copper for his lessons, preferring to give them away for free. After all, magic was one's relationship with the world…and giving for the purposes of getting was business, not magic. As one Gavin Merrick had learned a bit too late.

So it was that, filled with the boundless vigor of selfless pride, Chauncy unlocked the front door, then put his shoulder into it, popping it open with a *dong*.

"After you m'Lady," he stated, gesturing for Valtora to enter first. She batted her eyes again.

"M'Lord," she murmured coyly, waddling into the shop. She went for the broom closet then, as per their routine, but Chauncy beat her to it, retrieving his broom.

"You sit," he commanded, pointing to her stool behind the counter. "Your job is to watch your man work."

"Ooo," Valtora replied, clearly impressed with this bit of bravado. She did as she was told, eyeing him rather vigorously from behind the counter. He made a show of sweeping, attacking the dust-bunnies that inevitably accrued overnight and dumping their puffy bodies into the wastebasket. The shop's floor, as a result, shone spectacularly. Why, the mere sight of it would've brought a tear to Grandma Little's eye.

"It is done," he gasped, fully into the drama now. He slumped over the broom as if sorely tested by this feat.

"My *hero*," Valtora breathed. "Come, cast thy weapon aside and claim thine reward!"

Chauncy did just that, returning the broom to its closet, then going to sit beside her on his usual stool. She immediately

11

commenced with the rewarding, which involved an act not at all appropriate for the workplace.

"Oh," he blurted out. "Um…"

"Shhh," she scolded, not stopping.

"But a customer might come," he protested, eyeing the door nervously.

"Not before you do," she countered. With that, she resorted to a technique that guaranteed the accuracy of her statement. And to Chauncy's chagrin, he found himself utterly powerless to stop her from proving herself right.

"Wait!" he cried. But it was too late. And also, to Chauncy's horror, a tie. For at the very moment of claiming his reward, the first customer of the day burst through the front door with a *dong*.

"Ghhh…Welcome to A Little..nngggg…Magic!" Chauncy gasped.

"Oh!" their customer blurted out. To Chauncy's dismay, it was a woman. And to his horror, that woman was none other than Addie, his former lifelong crush…and widow to the town grocer.

"Ahh…nng….hi," Chauncy added, ending with an involuntary shudder. And a giggle.

"Oh hi Addie!" Valtora greeted, waving at her. With her rewarding hand, to Chauncy's chagrin.

"Hi," Addie replied, doing a little wave back. She stepped further into the shop. "Um…are you okay?" she asked Chauncy, regarding him with sweet concern.

"Uhhh-yep," he lied, doing his best not to die of shame.

"You looked flushed," Addie told him. "And sweaty."

"Did some pushups before the ol' shift," he offered, giving her the fakest A Little Magic smile he could muster. Which was pretty damn believable, especially after twenty-five years of Grandma Little's tutelage. Despite having never owned a cow, he was perhaps the world's foremost expert on bullshit.

"Oh," Addie replied, looking relieved. "Very healthy." Then she paused, eyeing Valtora's hand. "Making more lotion?" she inquired.

"Um…yes," Valtora replied. "We're thinking of renewing the 'Lotions & Potions' promotion, for old time's sake."

"Oh, nice!" Addie exclaimed. "It was very popular."

"Chauncy's lotion is second-to-none," Valtora declared proudly, patting her belly.

"Can I try some?" Addie inquired. Chauncy glanced at Valtora, shaking his head no.

"No," he mouthed to her silently, in case body language wasn't sufficient to the task.

"It's not ready yet," Valtora apologized. "Still working on the…um, fragrance."

"Oh," Addie replied, clearly disappointed.

"Anyway, what can I get for you Addie?" Chauncy interjected, eager to put this awful moment into his past as quickly as possible.

"Well, it's about your magic school," Addie answered. "My oldest daughter is sixteen, and well, I heard that the youngest age for your students was sixteen. So…"

"So you'd like to enroll her in A Little Magic School?" Chauncy guessed. Addie nodded. "Why, I'd…uh, we'd be delighted to have her, wouldn't we Valtora?"

"I guess that would depend," Valtora replied. Chauncy gave her a look.

"Nonsense," he retorted. "We'd be happy to have her. Sign her up!" he prompted, grabbing one of the signup forms from under the countertop. He handed this to Addie, and an inkwell and quill pen to boot. "Just fill out her name here, and her birthday," he instructed.

"Birthday?" Addie inquired. Chauncy smiled.

"So we can make it magical," he explained. "When it comes."

She smiled back, her cheeks flushing a bit. For it seemed that, no matter how much time had passed – and who Chauncy was with – he was still magical to her. And she to him, albeit less so than before. But while Chauncy had Valtora, Addie had only her businesses and her children. And Chauncy was an honest-to-gosh wizard to boot. So in Addie's view, his magic had only grown, not diminished, with time.

"Thank you," she murmured, finishing up the form. "When can she start?"

"Well, we don't open until next month," Chauncy answered. That was when the second floor dance studio's lease expired. "She can come on the evening of the first, at five o'clock."

"She'll be there," Addie promised.

"I can't wait," Chauncy declared, beaming at her. She blushed.

"Thanks again Chauncy," she told him. "For everything."

"You're most welcome."

With that, Addie did a little wave, then turned and left the shop with a *dong*. Chauncy watched her go, then realized Valtora was staring at him. While shaking her head. With her arms crossed over

13

her chest, as opposed to under it. Which meant she wasn't happy with him.

"What?" he asked.

"You and her," Valtora replied. "She's like, still totally in love with you."

"Not in love," Chauncy countered. "Maybe smitten."

"Crushing hard," Valtora retorted. "*Totally* wants you."

"Nah," Chauncy protested, waving the accusation away.

"You're oblivious."

"It doesn't matter," he decided, crossing his arms over his chest. "I'm with you, and that's that."

"Well that's true," Valtora conceded, breaking out into a smile. She patted his leg with her fleshy hand.

"Love you poopy-dooz," he cooed, leaning in for a kiss. She kissed him back...inappropriately, to his delight. Then she pulled away.

"Besides, I'd totally kill her if she tried to take you from me," Valtora said.

"Um..."

"I could totally do it, too," she pressed.

"I know," he replied. "But you're not going to."

"Not if it's just physical," she conceded.

"Huh?"

"I mean, if she just wants to jump your bones and get some, that's one thing," Valtora reasoned. "But if she wants to take you from me? Hell *fucking* no."

"Uh...?"

"You can totally screw her if you want," she told him. "I mean, it'd probably make her day. Just don't make any babies with her. And like, come back to me and shit afterward so I can reclaim you."

"Honey, I'm not going to..."

"I'll get a babysitter," Valtora interjected. Chauncy frowned, now utterly confused.

"We don't have any babies to sit on," he pointed out. Then he glanced at her belly. "Yet."

"Not for us," Valtora retorted. "For Addie."

Chauncy blinked. Then his jaw worked on trying to find some way to respond to this. Then he settled on leaving it hanging open.

"How about tonight?" Valtora offered.

"No!" Chauncy protested. "I'm not having...relations with Addie!"

14

"Why not?"

"Because I don't want to!" he exclaimed exasperatedly.

"Sure you do," Valtora argued.

"No I don't!"

"You wanted to since you were like, a teenager," she reminded him.

"Before I met you," he retorted.

"Pfft," she scoffed. "You don't stop wanting to bang people just because you're in a relationship."

He blinked, eyeing her suspiciously.

"Really?"

"Hell yeah," she confirmed. "I'll go talk to her and tell her it's okay. I'll babysit her kids at our house so you won't be interrupted."

"Honey!"

"Come on baby," Valtora insisted, patting him on the cheek and giving him a gorgeous smile. "Do it for me…and tell me *everything* when you get home tomorrow afternoon."

"Tomorrow after…*what?*"

"Well you're not just gonna bang and leave her, are you?" Valtora asked. "Gotta at least stay for breakfast. Morning sex is the *best*."

Chauncy gave up on trying to talk, realizing it wasn't doing him a bit of good. Valtora got up from her seat, waddling toward the door.

"What are you doing?" he demanded.

"Going to Addie's store," Valtora answered.

"Why?"

"Duh," was all Valtora said.

"No!" Chauncy blurted out in horror, bursting from his seat and rushing to the door to block her way. "You can't!"

"Really?"

"Really!" he insisted. "Go back to your chair this instant," he added rather paternalistically, pointing at her stool behind the counter. She sighed.

"Fine," she grumbled. And go back to her chair she did. They both sat down, neither one of them saying much for a while. For the whole conversation had gone down a very strange and disturbing path, and Chauncy didn't quite know how to handle it. Luckily their rather awkward silence was penetrated by a fortuitous *dong*.

"Welcome to A Little Magic!" Chauncy blurted out, bolting upright from his stool to greet their customer. A profoundly elderly woman named Mrs. Thimblethorp, who was inexplicably still alive.

15

Valtora had in fact made bets against the poor old lady every week, that she wouldn't last 'til the end of it. And every week, she'd lost the bet, to Chauncy's profit.

"Hmm?" Mrs. Thimblethorp inquired, being quite hard of hearing. Her ears had gone rather quickly over the last eight months, at a rate that, according to her doctor, was unheard of.

"WELCOME TO A LITTLE MAGIC," Valtora boomed.

"Oh," Mrs. Thimblethorp replied. "Good morning Chauncy. Still not a father?"

"Not yet," Chauncy replied. "Getting close now."

"Hopefully today," Valtora piped in, patting her belly.

"Oh, that'd be *wonderful*," the old woman declared, clutching her chest with both hands. At first Chauncy thought she was having an overdue heart attack, but the lack of a pained expression – and gasping and widening of the eyes and such – argued against it.

"It certainly would," Chauncy agreed with a smile. "I can't wait to meet it!"

"Him," Valtora corrected. "He's not an 'it,'" she added. "He's a human being, not a thing." Which was, of course, the exact opposite of her previous opinion.

"Hmm?" Mrs. Thimblethorp inquired, cupping a hand behind her ear.

"WHAT DO YOU WANT?" Valtora shouted.

"Just to say hello," Mrs. Thimblethorp replied. "I was hoping to see your baby before I, well…you know."

"Croak?" Valtora asked. Chauncy's eyes widened in horror.

"Honey!" he gasped.

"You said it," Mrs. Thimblethorp replied with a chuckle. "Relax Chauncy," she added. "Some people die wishing they could live, and some live wishing to die. Outliving your friends and family is nothing to hope for. When death comes," she added happily, "…I'll be happy to see him."

"Now now," Chauncy countered. "Don't talk like that Mrs. Thimblethorp. We want you around for years to come!"

She gave him an irritated look.

"Well it's not what *you* want, it's what *I* want," she stated resolutely. "So I'll talk however I like." She leaned over the counter. "Death isn't the worst thing that can happen to you, you know."

Chauncy grimaced, for he did know that. He'd had a near-death experience while battling The Dark One, having had his right arm cut off and been boiled alive to boot. Dying *wasn't* the worst thing

16

that could happen, considering that in the end, everyone was going to do it. Not living while you were living, he'd learned, was a far worse fate.

"In any case, I hope you enjoy your little one," Mrs. Thimblethorp added, her smile returning.

"We certainly will," Chauncy replied.

"…I wish I'd enjoyed mine," she continued, clearly not having heard him. Her expression soured. "She was an awful infant, never satisfied. And never got any better," she added. "Just an ungrateful, mean, vindictive little bitch. I kicked her out," she added proudly. "She died a year ago."

"My…um…condolences?" Chauncy replied.

"I'm glad she's gone," she declared. "And I wish she'd never lived."

Both Chauncy and Valtora stared at the old woman, neither of them knowing quite what to say. Which, at least for Valtora, was unheard of. For, having spent much of her life suffering the awful musings of The Dark One, she'd heard just about everything there was to hear. But a kindly old woman wishing that her child hadn't been born apparently wasn't one of them.

"But anyway, I hope yours is someone you can love," Mrs. Thimblethorp concluded merrily, with a twinkle in her eyes. "And I hope I get to see them!"

"You will," Chauncy promised, not quite sure if it was a lie or the truth. Mrs. Thimblethorp waved, and then turned about in the tottering way the very elderly did, making her way slowly out of the shop. She left as she'd come, in the way every customer they serviced came: with a *dong*.

"Guess I owe you another silver coin," Valtora stated. "Man, I was *sure* she'd be dead today!"

"I mean, there's still time," Chauncy pointed out. And felt just the slightest bit horrible for having said it. But inappropriate humor was something they both engaged in, being engaged to each other. And as long as no one else was listening, inappropriateness was something they very much enjoyed. For as he'd learned after defeating The Dark One, evil lived within everyone. Coming to terms with it – and balancing it with a fair amount of good – was the key.

"It *is* only morning," Valtora agreed, flashing him a wicked grin. Chauncy chuckled – and Valtora cackled – and then they sat there contentedly, waiting for the next customer.

17

"So about Addie," Valtora began.

"Not happening," Chauncy replied instantly.

"Not yet," she conceded.

"Not ever," he retorted.

"Spoilsport," she muttered. She set her jaw firmly, so that it jutted out. "It's *totally* happening."

"Let's talk baby names," he offered. She lit up, easily distracted by this. She'd already memorized the baby names book they'd gotten, much as she'd memorized the dictionary and thesaurus. For the sole purpose of winning arguments, naturally.

"How about…FUCK!" she boomed. Chauncy blinked.

"Pardon?"

"Gah!" Valtora blurted out, clutching her belly and leaning over.

"Honestly, I don't like either of them," Chauncy admitted.

"Baby!" she gasped.

"Too generic," Chauncy pointed out. "But I'm okay with calling it that until we have a name."

"I mean I'm having a baby!" Valtora all-but-shouted. And then she groaned, and started panting, all whilst clutching her belly. A little waterfall of clear fluid spilled onto the floor from her stool, and Chauncy's eyes widened, his hand shooting to his mouth.

"Oh," he murmured.

And that, dear reader, was how Chauncy and Valtora introduced a new member to their clan, and one boy's – or girl's – life began.

# Chapter 2

It is common knowledge that in an emergency, there are essentially two options: to run away from danger, or run toward it. Heroes face danger head-on, remaining calm in the face of terror. The rest have the good sense to run away, though by definition this makes them prey. A third type of person, however, faces danger not by fighting or fleeing, but by freezing. And faced with Valtora's impending parturition, Chauncy did just that.

"Urrgghhnnn," Valtora moaned, gripping the edge of the counter with both hands. And cracking the counter a bit with her diamond hand. Chauncy – still with his hand at his mouth – observed this rather numbly.

"Um…" he began. And stopped there, because he wasn't quite sure what to do next.

"Do something!" Valtora blurted out. Followed by another moan, and more cracking of the counter, to Chauncy's dismay.

"The counter," he pointed out, pointing out the crack. Valtora shot him an incredulous look.

"The baby!" she shot back. She appeared to have recovered from whatever was going on in her belly, and stood up from her seat, putting her hands on her hips and narrowing her eyes. To his horror, she executed a perfect, sphincter-spasming jawline-ripple. "I said do something!" she snapped.

"Um…"

"Get the doctor!" she commanded.

"Now?" he pressed.

"Yes now!"

"Okay," he agreed. And with that, he stayed where he was. "Will you be…okay?"

"I won't if you don't get me a damn doctor," she argued. Then she raised a fist. Her diamond one. "And neither will you…hhhnngg!" she gasped, bending over again and clutching her belly. A bit more fluid dripped out, and suddenly it occurred to

19

Chauncy that this was it. Their little bastard was coming, like it or not.

And he should really do something. Like, right now.

"Going!" Chauncy blurted out, leaping from his stool and grabbing his Staff of Wind. He burst out of the front door of the shop, spotting the doctor's office on the other side of the city center, beyond the courtyard. He was about to start running when he skid to a halt, remembering that, in fact, he was a wizard.

Which changed *everything*.

"Soaring Leap!" he cried, thrusting the butt of his staff downward and backward.

It struck the sidewalk, sending powerful blast of air down at it…and launching Chauncy upward and forward into the air. Pedestrians gasped as Chauncy flew high over the courtyard, reaching his peak directly above the newly-handicapped statue of Archibald Merrick. At first he assumed it was his display of wizardly power that captivated them, but then he saw a bit of pointing and laughing, and realized suddenly that he was wearing a wizard's robe. One that gave those below a special view of his special underwear.

"Crap!" he blurted out, bringing his knees together. But it was too late, judging by the chorus of laughter coming from a growing crowd below. He felt himself falling, and only the thought of Valtora in terrible pain stopped him from letting himself slam into the ground for a quick, easy death. He guided his flight with a few expert thrusts, landing on the far edge of the courtyard and sprinting across the street to the doctor's office. He reached the front door, knocking on it rather vigorously. Then he remembered that the door was unlocked, and he could just open it and speak to the receptionist.

So, feeling like a complete idiot, he did.

Chauncy stepped into a small lobby, the receptionist – he couldn't quite remember her name – sitting behind a desk. She immediately recognized him, of course. For despite the fact that he was a complete idiot, he was also a wizard.

"She's giving birth!" he declared.

"Valtora?" the receptionist inquired.

"Um, yes."

"I'll get the doctor," she told him. And proceeded to finish up with whatever paperwork she'd been doing. After which she stood up quite a bit more leisurely than Chauncy was comfortable with, making her way down the hallway to one of the doors of the patient rooms. She knocked on the door, and moments later cracked it open. "Sorry doc. Valtora's having contractions."

"Eh," Chauncy heard the doctor reply. "Baby out yet?"

The receptionist turned to Chauncy.

"Baby out yet?" she asked.

"Erm…no," he answered, fidgeting more than a little. "Um, we'd prefer the doctor be there before that."

"They want you there before that," the receptionist told the doctor.

"Why?" the doctor's muffled voice inquired. Rather irritably, Chauncy might add.

"First time," the receptionist explained.

"Oh for crying out…" the doctor began. Then Chauncy heard a heavy sigh. "Fine. Where is she?"

"Where…" the receptionist began.

"At the shop," Chauncy interrupted. She relayed this bit of information. Which was getting rather annoying, considering the entire conversation could've happened without an intermediary. But pointless inefficiency was a time-honored tradition of the medical profession, Chauncy knew. Or at least that's what Grandma Little had told him.

"Ten minutes," the doctor grumbled.

"Bye!" Chauncy blurted out before the receptionist could repeat this, exiting the shop as quickly as he'd come. He thought about flying over the courtyard, then remembered his special underwear. *Then* he remembered the reception his special underwear had gotten him, and decided he'd suffer the indignity of people seeing his dirty laundry rather than the indignity of facing their response.

"Arcing Flight!" he cried, executing the same maneuver as before. Whilst keeping one hand on the hem of his robe to pull it tightly around his legs. He landed a few yards from A Little Magic, running up to the door and ramming his shoulder into it. Tumbling into the shop, his eyes went right to Valtora, still hunched over the counter. "Poopy-dooz!" he cried. "Are you okay?"

"The doctor's…ngggh!...coming?" she gasped.

"Ten minutes," he replied. She blinked.

"Ten minutes?" she blurted out incredulously.

"That's what he said," Chauncy replied.

"I'm giving birth!"

"That's what I said," Chauncy noted.

21

"Son of a bbaarrggghhh," she gasped, breathing rapidly through pursed lips. "Oooo, crapcrapcrap."

"Tell me what to do," Chauncy pleaded, feeling utterly helpless to…well, to help her. It was a truly awful feeling, to see the love of his life in pain and not be able to do a damn thing about it.

"Get the damn doctor!"

"I mean besides that," he replied. She glared at him.

"Have this baby for me!"

"Um…I mean I would if I could," he offered lamely. She gasped, clutching her belly again and riding out another round of awfulness. Then her eyes got crazy.

*Scary* crazy.

"If you don't get this little *fucker* out of me now, I'm gonna rip him out and stuff him all the way up your ass and make *you* push him out!" she screamed.

And then, to Chauncy's immense relief, there came a *dong*. And to Valtora's peace of mind, it was the doctor. As it turned out, providing peace of mind appeared to be the limit of the doctor's capabilities, for Valtora was forced to do almost all of the work by herself. Which she managed only with a truly extraordinary vocabulary of ridiculously inappropriate language, in keeping with her personality…and her habit of reading the dictionary. Even the doctor was impressed and a bit taken aback, for while he'd attended countless births, Valtora's was – at least linguistically – by far his most memorable.

Still, at the end of the day, what had been created with a little bedroom magic was ushered into A Little Magic with a shrill, kitty-cat cry, and Chauncy found himself the proud – and rather terrified – father of a brand-new member of the family. A boy, to Valtora's delight.

But delight, like any other emotion, was a temporary thing, and it wouldn't be long before it faded. As life had shown Chauncy on several occasions, for every up there was a down, every moment of delight a prelude to misery. And while the doctor's *dong* had been a prelude to ecstasy, life was about to take a turn for the worse, yes sirree.

For it was only a matter of time before Chauncy would have to face the fateful *dong* of destiny.

# Chapter 3

Having successfully ushered a baby boy into the world, Valtora ended her day at A Little Magic, and Chauncy closed up shop. They returned home, taking a carriage there for the first time since…well, since Chauncy could remember. For, having been stretched and furthermore a bit torn up by the whole process, Valtora found walking a rather unpleasant process.

"Ugh," she complained as they exited the carriage, waddling toward the house. "It feels like my coochie's gonna fall out."

"Want me to hold the baby?" Chauncy asked, for Valtora had the baby boy cradled to her bosom.

"Get the door."

"Yes my sweet," Chauncy cooed. He lent her his arm until they were standing before the front door, then opened it for her, gesturing for her to walk inside. "After you, m'Lady," he purred, bowing grandly.

Valtora did step through, but without her usual reply. Being left thusly high and dry, Chauncy couldn't help but feel a slight dismay. But he could hardly blame Valtora for her mood, given the limits she'd been stretched to, both figuratively and literally.

"What can I do for you?" he inquired, stepping into the house and closing – and locking – the door. Valtora eyed him critically.

"I'd ask you to carry me to bed," she replied, "…but…"

She gestured at his arms, which were not particularly up to the task. For he'd spent most of the last year developing magic at the expense of muscle, and like most wizards, his constitution was sorely lacking.

"Ah," he mumbled.

Having insulted Chauncy's manhood, Valtora set forth in the grim, painful task of ascending the stairs, reaching the top in a symphony of grunts and muffled swears. Then she went right into the bedroom, Chauncy following behind, and eased herself – baby still on bosom – to their spectacularly pink bed. With another series of grunts – and swears, not so muffled – she got herself into a position of least discomfort, lying back on a pile of pink pillows with a sigh.

"Do you need anything?" Chauncy inquired, eager to help.

"No," she replied.

"Are you okay?"

"No."

"What's wrong, poopy-dooz?" he pressed. She arched an eyebrow.

"My coochie exploded," she explained.

"Oh," Chauncy replied. "Right."

The baby stirred, giving a cute little mewling cry, and Valtora shushed him gently, rocking him a bit. Chauncy stood there, a familiar feeling returning to him. One of being utterly useless. Helpless. Powerless. A third wheel. A…

"I'm hungry," Valtora told him. Chauncy perked up. For when Valtora ate, *she* usually perked up.

"I'll make dinner!" he exclaimed at once, making the baby flinch. And cry, to his dismay. Valtora shot him a glare, and Chauncy took the opportunity to escape. He bounded down the stairs and rushed into the kitchen, filled with vim and vigor. For a mission was just what Chauncy needed, and providing for his fiancée – no, his *family* – was job number one. He set out to make the best, tastiest, most impressively-presented dinner he could imagine. It was Valtora's favorite: the ol' frank and beans. He cooked them to absolute perfection, then rushed her plate upstairs, finding Valtora snorting their little son's neck.

"Your dinner m'Lady," he announced, posing in grand butler-y fashion.

"God he smells good," she gushed, snorting again. "On the bed," she added as an aside. Chauncy deflated a bit, unaccustomed to his theatrics being ignored. Still, he complied, then stood there, watching them. At length – after more neck-snorting – Valtora turned to frown at Chauncy. "What?" she asked.

"Um…just making sure you like it," he answered. "I made it just the way you like," he added. "Your favorite," he also added, for good-boyfriend points.

"I know," she replied. He stood there a bit longer. "Thanks?" she added.

"You're most welcome," he replied, bowing with an extra flourish. That got a smile out of her. She dug in, and it wasn't long before Valtora was…well, Valtora again. Effervescence required refreshments, at least in Valtora's case.

"Thanks m'Lord," she told him, squeezing her eyes shut and giving him smoochy-lips. He leaned in, kissing her with gusto. And to his delight, she kissed him back…in a way that most would find inappropriate to do in front of children. In fact, it wasn't long before she *really* got into it, and added a bit of…

"Oh," Chauncy murmured, pulling away and glancing at the baby nervously.

"What?" Valtora asked.

"The baby," he told her. "He's watching." And indeed he was.

"He's an infant," Valtora retorted. "He's like, practically brain-dead."

"Honey!"

"It's true," she insisted. "He won't remember a thing." And continued to do the thing she'd started doing that'd prompted his anxiety. Followed by something entirely else.

"Poopy-dooz!" he gasped, pulling away. But despite the fact that she'd had a *very* long day – and that both of their lives had quite permanently and rapidly changed – her habit of non-consent had not. So Chauncy found himself pulled quite firmly back into the act of permanently scarring his child. And despite his better judgement, he soon found himself submitting to said act, until the terrible deed was done…under the awful, unblinking gaze of his son.

"Oh my," Chauncy breathed. Then he grimaced. "Sorry son."

"Pfftt," she scoffed. "Little bastard better get used to it. I'm not stopping our fun just to be all proper and shit."

"You never do," he conceded. "Speaking of which, um…can we *not* call him a little bastard all the time?"

"Why not?" she inquired. "That's what he is."

"I know, but…"

"I mean, that's the whole point of not getting married until he was born," she argued. "So we *could* call him a bastard."

"So *you* could call him one," he corrected.

"Like you don't enjoy it," she retorted.

"I don't," he replied. "It's demeaning."

"It's funny."

"No it…" he began, then frowned. For he realized he was walking into yet another attempt at an argument. Valtora immediately sensed his realization, and her face fell.

"Aww," she pouted.

"Well, maybe we should think of some more names," he offered. She brightened up instantly.

"Ooo, we could go on the porch!" she exclaimed. "Like old people!"

"I'll make tea," he offered.

With that, they made their way downstairs, and Valtora went with the baby to the porch. Chauncy went to the kitchen, preparing some tea. Grandma Little's favorite tea, in fact…which she'd made every morning, sipping it while Chauncy ate. He smiled as the familiar scent greeted him, a scent that meant he was home.

He turned to gaze at the small kitchen table, at the chair she'd used to sit at, imagining her there. Why, how proud she would be of her grandson, that he'd found a wife and made a child…and that he was a gosh-darn wizard to boot.

Chauncy's smile broadened, and he was struck with a sudden sense of *arriving*. That he was right where he'd always wanted to be…and that his dreams had become his destiny.

*I'm a father,* he thought, filled with a sudden feeling of utter joy.

The tea began to shriek, and he finished up, pouring it into teacups and going outside. Valtora was seated on the long rocking bench he'd bought a few months ago, and she patted the spot next to her. He sat down, snuggling up with her, with the baby swaddled – in a bright pink blanket, of course – on Valtora's still-aching lap. The night sky was absolutely bejeweled with stars, as if the heavens themselves were celebrating the birth of their son. And the moon was a narrow crescent that seemed to wink at him from the heavens. Or perhaps it was a smile, slightly rotated. Either way, it was a magical night indeed. Not just because he was now a father, but because he was *here* and *now*.

In this moment, he was completely, utterly present. And as an old wizard named Harry had once taught him, this was as good as it got.

"How about…STONE!" Valtora declared in her best epic voice, scrunching her face up in a badass scowl. And startling the baby. Chauncy shook his head.

"Too close to Rocky," he replied.

"Hmm," Valtora said, tapping her lower lip. "How about…TALON!"

"Like a bird?"

"Well yeah," she replied. "A bird of prey."

"I don't know…"

26

"Fine," she grumbled. "How about…BLADE!"

"Too violent," he told her. "What if he doesn't like swords?"

"Good point," she conceded. Then she sighed. "Fine. Your turn."

Chauncy frowned, eyeing the baby. His face was all smooshed and swollen, and honestly, though Chauncy hated to admit it, he was kind of ugly. Like, *really* ugly. The doctor had convinced Valtora not to bedazzle the poor kid on the spot, assuring her that in a week or so things would sort themselves out. Nothing good would come out of naming the child after the way he looked, Chauncy realized. So instead, he lifted his gaze to the heavens. Specifically, to the crescent moon. It, along with the stars, represented a kind of order. A cycle of day and night, of space and light, with stars that served as an ever-reliable guide for navigators the world over. The affairs of humans seemed precisely the opposite…scattered and random and unpredictable. Gloriously so, for it was precisely what he found so mysterious and magical about Valtora. That he never quite knew what she would do next. And mystery was where magic lived.

"How about…Chaos?" he offered.

Valtora's eyes widened, and then she broke out into a huge smile, thrusting her free arm in the air.

"CHAOS!" she proclaimed, her voice echoing through the night air. She gasped, looking down at her ugly baby. "OhmygodI *love* it!" she exclaimed, clutching her hand to her heart. "It's perfect!"

"Um…" he said, suddenly having second thoughts. For "Chaos" had merely come to him in the spur of the moment, and on reflection, it was a terrible name to put on a child. But the damage had been done. Valtora was clearly in love with the name.

"Chaos Little," she said to herself, her smile broadening even more, if it was possible. "I frickin' *love* it."

"Actually, I think…" he began.

"Here," she told him, handing him the baby. He took him, clutching the child nervously to his chest. Then she got up from the rocking bench, waddling into the house whilst clutching at her groin.

"Where are you going?" he asked. But she was clearly in mission mode, and vanished into the house. Nearly a minute later, she returned, a piece of paper in her hand. "What's that?" he asked.

"The birth certificate," she answered.

"We should think of some more names first," he told her.

"Already filled it out," she replied, thrusting the paper in his face. There, written – in ink, not pencil – was Chaos Little.

"Oh god," he moaned. And would have lowered his face into his hands if he could have. But he was terrified to hold the baby with only one hand, for fear he'd drop the poor kid.

"Aww," she cooed, making smoochy faces at the baby. "He has the same initials as my widdle Chauncy-poo!"

"I'll pick up another certificate," Chauncy decided. She frowned. "Why?"

"Because we're not naming our son Chaos," Chauncy explained.

"Yes we are," she countered.

"No, we're really not."

"That's the name I want," she declared, putting her hands on her hips and glaring at him. A posture that usually forced him to back down. But on the matter of his firstborn son's moniker, Chauncy simply had to take a stand.

"We'll find another," he reassured her. Or at least, he *tried* to reassure. For she didn't seem reassured at all, he could be assured of that. For in addition to the hands-on-hips and glare, Valtora added her most potent weapon of all: the jawline-ripple. And despite everything, it made Chauncy's sphincter spasm just to see it.

"Who carried him in their belly for the last nine months again?" she inquired. Chauncy grimaced.

"Um...you," he answered.

"Who puked every day for like, half of those months?" she pressed, clearly sensing her advantage.

"You," he mumbled. "Darling," he added, in hopes of gaining points. To his dismay, it didn't work.

"And who just tore her coochie into a bloody mess shoving our baby out of her bleeding womb?"

Chauncy grimaced again, feeling a twinge in his testicles. For any mention of bleeding groins made him want to cross his legs. So he did...and she clearly noticed.

"So you're telling me," she concluded, her face growing pale and her pupils growing disturbingly large, "...that after all I've suffered, I *can't* name my son what I want?" She clenched her diamond fist rather menacingly, and Chauncy shrank away from her, holding the baby between them as a shield. A fact he wasn't proud of, but on balance, he'd grown up without a father, and didn't want poor Chaos to suffer a similar fate.

"Eeep," Chauncy eeped, not quite knowing what else to say.

"That's what I thought," Valtora declared triumphantly, crossing her arms over her chest and executing an equally triumphant chin-thrust. "Chaos it is."

And so it was. For it seemed that a little Chaos was necessary if Chauncy hoped to maintain order within his relationship. He supposed it was fitting, for chaos wasn't necessarily a bad thing. It was merely the opposite of order, and a bit of chaos could make life more interesting. Heck, his life had been a bit *too* orderly for a good quarter century, wiling his days away with Grandma Little at the shop. The chaos he'd endured in his two adventures with Harry and Nettie had been unpleasant at times, but in the end, he'd enjoyed it…and it'd made him the wizard – and man – he was today. Not to mention that he never would've had a baby with perhaps the most chaotic person he'd ever met…Valtora herself.

Perhaps a little chaos…or rather, a Chaos Little…was exactly what they needed in their life.

"Chaos Little," he mumbled, gazing down at his son. Who'd slept through the whole heated exchange. "I suppose it'll have to do."

# Chapter 4

King Pravus the Eighth gripped the hilt of his ridiculously long and broad sword, his tight black and gold royal uniform hugging every curve of his fantastically muscular body. He was a vision, why, the very *figure* of a heroic monarch. As he was well aware, having practiced his current pose in the mirror earlier that morning. He faced his opponent in his throne room. An opponent who was all-too-familiar to him.

None other than Templeton, his very cousin.

"How dare you betray me!" he shouted, holding his sword before him.

"You betray yourself," Templeton retorted coolly, holding his own blade at the ready. A long, slender blade, similar to a fencing coil. Pravus knew not to judge the weapon on the merits of its size. For Templeton had the uncanny knack of thrusting in and out of any holes in a man's defenses in a veritable blink of an eye. And unlike Pravus, Templeton created new holes in the men he penetrated, instead of utilizing the ones that were already there.

"We're family," Pravus protested.

"Correct," Templeton agreed. "Which is why I shall soon be king!"

With that, Templeton darted forward, thrusting his slender blade at Pravus!

Pravus dodged backward in the nick of time, then dodged to the side as Templeton continued with thrust after thrust. The bastard was relentless, his little blade nearly gutting Pravus a half-dozen times.

"Ha!" Pravus cried, swinging his own sword. It's formidable length made his reach far longer than Templeton's. But the villain merely ducked the blow, charging forward again with a vicious thrust to Pravus's exposed chest. It was only by virtue of Pravus's magical uniform that the blade was deflected without harm; Pravus swung his sword at Templeton's neck, but the man merely dodged backward, smirking at Pravus.

"Next time, I won't aim for your heart, cousin," he warned.

"You can't break it any more than you already have," Pravus retorted.

Templeton lunged at him, and Pravus readied himself to block. But it was a feint; Templeton followed up almost instantly with a thrust right between Pravus's eyes.

"Gah!" Pravus cried, his head jerking back reflexively. He dropped his sword, clutching at his face.

"Cousin!" Templeton gasped, dropping his sword and rushing to Pravus's side. Pravus lowered his hands, flashing the man a devilish grin.

"Got you again," he teased. For Templeton's sword had merely bounced off his flesh, without any pain or injury whatsoever.

"Ah, thank goodness," Templeton replied with a sheepish smile of his own. "Well played, my liege."

"And well fought, Templeton," Pravus replied. "You're still too quick for me."

"You're getting better," Templeton pointed out, retrieving his sword. A wooden replica of his magical fencing blade, it was utterly harmless. Particularly considering that, with Pravus's crown and magical uniform and whatnot, Pravus was practically impervious to bodily harm.

"I suppose I am," Pravus agreed.

"Again?" Templeton inquired, raising his sword. Pravus hesitated. For as much as he enjoyed the prospect of crossing swords with his dashing cousin – something he would far prefer to do metaphorically – their free time was running out.

"Later," he replied. "For now we must attend to a more important matter."

"The gym?" Templeton inquired.

"Indeed," Pravus agreed.

"Shall we race?" Templeton inquired.

"I daresay we shall," Pravus confirmed. And with that, the two men threw down their swords, then dashed out of the throne room. Pravus's royal guards rushed behind them, trying in vain to keep up. Through the hallways out of the castle the two men went, blasting through the silver doors of the kingdom's inner Gate. And made their way to the gymnasium Pravus had built in the center of Cumulus, the capitol of the kingdom that bore his name. A three-mile run, which served as a nice little warm-up for his already stiff

31

and aching muscles, still recovering from the two workouts he'd stimulated them with the day before.

His personal guards followed behind dutifully, most hopping on horses on account of not being able to keep up with him otherwise. For Pravus and Templeton's abilities were beyond those of most men, not out of a sense of competition, but because the cultivation of their bodies was the subject most magical to them.

So, in the spirit of joy rather than winning, he and Templeton decided to race the horses instead of the men. And as fate would have it, he and Templeton were the first to the gym.

Pravus slowed to a quick walk, admiring the ginormous statues of muscly men and women surrounding the magnificent structure. He burst through the double-doors at the entrance, holding the door for Templeton. Then he strode into the facility, his pride and joy: an absolutely *gorgeous* gym, complete with every type of free weight, machine…and everything in-between.

Pravus took a deep breath, taking in the scent of soap and steel. For the gymnasium was cleaned nightly, per royal decree. Soon it would reek of slick, salty sweat and manly musk, with a whiff of womanly musk for good measure. A medley of scents akin to a bouquet of flowers…and what would grow from them was not fruit, but big, beefy, bulging muscles.

"We're back darling," Pravus greeted, extending his arms as if to embrace the entire gym. "Did you miss us?"

"I'd wager she did," Templeton replied. And while Pravus thought of the gym as a masculine creature, otherwise he agreed. "Shall we?" Templeton inquired.

"We shall," Pravus confirmed. "What say you to a few deadlifts to start us off?"

"I say 'but of course,'" Templeton answered at once. And it warmed Pravus's heart to hear it. For Templeton – sweet, dearest Templeton! – was a singularly sunny chap, a ray of sunshine always. And he was a specimen of a man, tall and slender, with rather broad shoulders tapering down to a ridiculously narrow waist. And then flaring on in the back with a pair of spectacularly sculpted buttocks, all perky and oh-so-lovingly embraced by his deliciously tight golden shorts. And – to cap it all off – Templeton was possessed of the same short black hair and sky-blue eyes that Pravus had. Eyes that a man could get lost in…and that wasn't all. For there were several other areas Pravus would quite like to lose himself in, if only Templeton would consent to such explorations.

To Pravus, Templeton was a vision. One that Pravus had visualized in his mind's eye on a ridiculous number of occasions, for the purposes of achieving a rather specific sequence of muscular contractions.

Pravus was singularly grateful for having the man in his life, and what's more, to have him there daily. And what Pravus wouldn't give to *have* him daily, in a far different way!

But alas, it simply wasn't meant to be.

The two men went to the nearest squat rack, and Templeton gestured for Pravus to take the first set.

"After you, cousin," he prompted.

"A gentleman at the gym!" Pravus declared.

"All should aspire to be," Templeton replied.

"Quite so, dearest Templeton," Pravus concurred. It was a shame that so many gym-goers knew so little of proper lifting etiquette. This despite Pravus's insistence that the staff post signs all over the gymnasium on how to properly behave. It appeared that a distressingly large proportion of people only behaved when *he* was here. Why, it was enough to shake his faith in humanity.

With that, Pravus loaded the bar with a 45-pound plate on either end of the 45-pound bar. And, setting it on the floor, he assumed the perfect deadlift position: gripping the bar with his hands just outside his knees, with his butt down and his back neutral. And though it was weight that – to him – felt for all the world like a feather, Pravus lifted it as respectfully as if it weighed a thousand pounds.

The first half of the movement was a leg-press, pushing the floor with his feet until he'd lifted the bar to knee-level. Then came the second half: a vigorous pelvic thrust, shoving his groin forward until his buttocks were maximally clenched, his back straight. A movement he was quite adept at…or so he'd been told.

"Well done," Templeton congratulated, admiring Pravus's form. Pravus lowered the bar back in the reverse of the way he'd lifted it, setting it gently – not dropping it – on the floor. He executed this perfect pattern precisely twenty times, until his muscles were nice and warm.

"Your turn," he prompted, stepping back from the bar…and watching as Templeton took his place there. Naturally, Pravus had chosen to stand behind and to the side of his cousin, for maximum viewing pleasure. And to that effect, he'd chosen one of the few squat racks that didn't have a mirror in front of it, so that poor Templeton wouldn't be the wiser.

*Mmm mmm mmm*, Pravus thought, leering as Templeton finished the first repetition with an admirable pelvic-thrust. A movement accentuated by a pert buttock-clench at the end, to Pravus's delight. Templeton continued for twenty reps, offering a visual smorgasbord that Pravus planned on utilizing for the forearm-finishing workout he'd enjoy that night.

"Perfect," he breathed as Templeton lowered the bar one last time to the floor. With nary a *cling* or a *clang* of impact, so controlled was the movement.

"I had a perfect teacher," Templeton declared, beaming Pravus a smile. And oh! How it filled Pravus's heart with joy to hear it.

So went their workout, at least the beginning of it. Pravus added a few plates to the bar, then lifted it just as before. Set after set, more weight was added, until to lift it took everything Pravus and Templeton had. Until the thought of having to lift it was daunting indeed, given the temporary suffering that each trial would bring. But in facing these trials instead of fleeing them – and conquering them one-by-one – the two men earned something far more valuable than bragging rights, or even muscle: the lesson that trials were not to be feared, but to be faced head-on. And in doing so, one would discover that there was simply nothing to be afraid of.

By the time they were done with deadlifts, Pravus collapsed onto the floor, his buttocks, legs, and back trembling and twitching.

"Marvelous!" he gasped, wiping sweat from his eyes. Templeton lowered himself to the floor to a similar position beside Pravus.

"Fantastic!" he agreed. And then moaned, his quadriceps visibly spasming. "Oh!" he gasped.

"Go into the pain, Templeton!" Pravus advised. "Welcome it!"

"Indeed…I…shall!" Templeton grunted, issuing forth yet another moan. Pravus eyed his cousin's twitching legs.

"Shall I massage them?" he inquired, hoping beyond hope.

"Perhaps it will help," Templeton replied. Which wasn't quite consent, but good enough for Pravus. He slid on his buttocks over to Templeton, then got to work gently massaging Templeton's thighs.

"Oh!" Templeton blurted out, wincing terribly.

"Shall I stop?"

"No," Templeton answered. "Give me your worst old boy!"

"I'll give you my best," Pravus vowed. And with that, he massaged quite vigorously…and comprehensively, getting terribly close to the one area he most desired to massage. But he remained a perfect gentleman, resisting his baser impulses and focusing on the task quite literally at hand.

"Am I getting in deep enough?" Pravus inquired.

"Go as deep as you can," Templeton replied.

"I don't want to hurt you, dearest cousin."

"With pain comes the pleasure of its end," Templeton declared bravely. And this of course, was the lesson of the iron. Pain was not to be feared, for its end could be ecstasy, much as ravenous hunger before a feast.

"Just so, dearest Templeton," Pravus concurred. "I'll go as deep as you allow me."

"Ahem," a voice interjected. Pravus frowned, glancing up to see a man standing there. Some sixty-odd years old, he was short and frumpy, with a body rather like a candle that'd been half-melted. This the old man had attempted to conceal with a fine black-and-gold suit, with minimal success. He'd also attempted to conceal his baldness with a ridiculous combover, with similar results.

"Ah, hello Desmond," Pravus greeted. For it was none other than his personal man-servant…and on a part-time basis, one of his royal advisers. "Come to work out?"

Desmond eyed Pravus's hands, which were still milking Templeton's muscles, then returned his gaze to Pravus.

"No," he answered.

"Then to what do I suffer the displeasure of your company?" Pravus inquired irritably. For there was nothing more irritating to him than workout interruptus…except of course for not being able to work out in the first place. As he'd learned during The Dark One's siege on his kingdom.

"A guest requests an audience with you in the castle," Desmond replied.

"Denied," Pravus replied instantly.

"It's an important person," Desmond countered.

"Not as important as me," Pravus shot back.

"Debatable," the old man replied. Pravus glared at him, then sighed, releasing Templeton and standing up with some difficulty. For any pleasure he'd been getting from handling his cousin was now gone.

"Not important *to* me," he argued. "Have someone else meet with them."

"They want you, sire," Desmond replied.

"I don't blame them," Pravus retorted, striking a rather heroic pose. And glancing at himself in a mirror to his right while doing so. On reflection, he was most impressive. "But they can't always get what they want."

"They insisted."

"Tell them to de-sist," Pravus shot back.

"They're from the Order of Mundus," Desmond revealed. Pravus blinked, then frowned, putting his hands on his hips...while striking a lats pose, for the mirror's sake.

"Well why didn't you say so, Desmond?" he scolded. "Next time lead with that!" The Order of Mundus was, after all, a guild of powerful wizards. And seeing as how they rarely deigned to grant an audience with anyone – even kings – it would be foolish to deny them.

"I admit I enjoy torturing you sire," Desmond...well, admitted.

"If that were true," Pravus replied, "...you'd be the happiest man I know."

"You haven't met my wife," Desmond countered.

"Is she really that bad?"

"Worse," the old man replied at once.

"Well now I want to meet her," Pravus stated.

"As your advisor, I'd advise against it," Desmond warned.

"You know Desmond, sometimes I think you're just pulling my chain," Pravus mused.

"I've no interest in pulling your chain," Desmond replied.

"And I've no interest in you pulling it," Pravus stated, grimacing at the thought. "In any case, I'm sure your wife is a lovely woman."

"If she was, she wouldn't have married me," Desmond pointed out. Pravus considered this.

"A fair point," he conceded. "Now, back to our unexpected guest. Did they offer a reason for their visit?"

"No sire."

"Very well," Pravus decided. "Templeton, I'm afraid we'll have to defer the remainder of our workout until this afternoon."

"Afternoon it is!" Templeton confirmed, rising unsteadily to his feet. With that, Pravus and Templeton hobbled toward the exit, the deadlifts having deadened their legs.

"Desmond?" Pravus prompted.

"Yes sire?"

"Did you perchance bring a carriage?" he inquired hopefully.

Desmond said nothing, opening the door instead. But Pravus was not offended by his dour servant's silence. For there, parked on the street, was the old man's answer: a gilded carriage just for him.

"You know Desmond, sometimes you disappoint me far less than you usually do," Pravus confessed. "And this is one of those times."

"Heartwarming," Desmond droned.

With that, Pravus and Templeton made their way to the carriage. And to the castle, to meet their unexpected – and uninvited – guest.

"Does this wizard have a name?" Pravus inquired as he made the treacherous step down from the sidewalk's curb to the street. His legs shook and nearly gave out, and it was only by virtue of his heroic will that they did not.

"I believe her name is Zella," Desmond answered. "Zella Trek."

# Chapter 5

After naming little Chaos Little, Valtora and Chauncy went to bed. Or rather, Valtora went to bed. For after Chauncy helped her up the stairs and into their bedroom – and Valtora eased herself onto the bed, Chaos clutched to her bosom – she dismissed him with a wave of her hand.

"Okaybye," she told him. He blinked.

"Bye?"

"Baby's going to sleep," she explained. And indeed, the little tyke was drifting off. "Don't want to wake the little bastard up."

"You mean Chaos," he corrected.

"You should probably sleep on the couch," she told him. "You're a little bitch when you're woken up in the middle of the night." Which was true.

"Oh," he replied. "Right."

She stared at him unblinkingly, until he realized she meant for him to leave now. He leaned over to give her a kiss, and she offered her cheek, probably because she didn't want to jostle the baby.

"G'night my love," he murmured. Sexily.

"Night m'Lord," she replied. Sleepily.

And that, to Chauncy's disappointment, was that.

He made his way back downstairs, rounding the corner into the living room and plopping down on the couch there. As luck would have it, he and Valtora had recently enjoyed quite a bit of couch cuddle-time under a warm pink blanket, which was still bunched up on one end. He laid down, pulling the blanket over himself and staring up at the ceiling. It proved a perfectly blank canvas for his mind to ruminate on.

"Well," he told himself. "You're a father now, Chauncy."

He pictured his sweet son cradled in Valtora's arms, and felt a gush of lovey-dovey pride. He was a father, and honest-to-god *father*…of a healthy baby boy. A bastard, yes. Named Chaos, which was hardly conventional. But he supposed that, all things considered, it was conventional for the child of two wizards to be unconventional. After spending most of his life trying to fit in, outfitting his son with a name that could never be normal might end up being a service to him. For fitting in to a way of life that was no life at all would be a terrible mistake…one that Grandma Little had convinced him to make, rest her soul. She hadn't known any better, of course, having been born in Borrin, and having swallowed its lies whole. Her heart, however, had been in the right place, and she'd only wanted what she thought was best for him. A life safe from danger and secure from risk. A Borrin life indeed.

But despite what she'd done to him, Chauncy still loved her dearly, for she'd loved him in just the same way. And, since magic was one's relationship with the world, when Grandma Little had been in his, she'd been the one part of that world that'd been magical to him.

"I did it Grandma," he whispered, a tear coming to his eye. He wiped it away with the edge of the blanket, taking a deep breath in. Grandma Little's words came to him then, uttered the day she died.

*You're lonely,* she'd told him. *You need a wife and kids. Oh, but they bring such joy into a house!*

"We'll get married tomorrow," he decided on the spot. After all, there was no point in waiting any longer now that their sweet little bastard was born. Then they would be husband and wife, and Grandma Little's prescription for him would be complete. For she'd wanted nothing more than for him to meet a nice woman and settle down to have children. And while Valtora wasn't quite the woman that Grandma Little would've picked for her son, his happiness was all she'd really cared about…in her own way.

Armed with a plan for matrimony, Chauncy felt his worries fade away. For the male mind was mostly concerned with completing missions and releasing emissions, and with a mission in mind – if not an emission, on account of being quite spent – he found himself soon falling fast asleep.

* * *

Chauncy woke to the sound of screaming.

He bolted upright in bed, his heart pounding in his chest. It took him a moment to realize that it was neither morning nor was he in bed. For it was still dark, and he was in the living room on the couch. But the screaming was still…well, screaming. And it was coming from upstairs.

39

Chauncy recalled at once that he was a father, and was struck with the terrible realization that his baby was in danger.

"Coming dear!" he cried valiantly, leaping off the couch and rushing upstairs. He burst into the bedroom, spotting Valtora sitting upright on the bed. Chaos was lying on his back between Valtora's legs, in the process of getting his diaper changed. Which was rather striking, considering his screams had sounded for all the world like his limbs were being torn off and eaten.

"Go back to bed," Valtora muttered wearily, finishing the change. She laid back, cuddling Chaos to her chest.

"Right," Chauncy mumbled.

He went back downstairs to the couch, lying down and closing his eyes to go to sleep. And usually the combination of being exhausted, it being night-time, and having one's eyes closed would've done the trick. But instead, his mind began playing tricks on him…in that he could swear he heard the baby crying again.

He opened his eyes, staring up at the ceiling.

Still the phantom cries came. And while he knew they weren't real, he couldn't shake the feeling that they were. So he got up, trudged up the stairs nearly to the top, and listened.

No crying.

Chauncy frowned, listening for a bit longer. But there was only silence. So he went back to the couch, snuggling under his pink blanket and closing his eyes…only to hear the phantom cries again.

*Pull yourself together man,* he told himself, setting his jaw firmly. *It's all in your head.*

But these tough proclamations did nothing to stop the phantom cries, much to Chauncy's consternation. He rolled onto his side, telling himself to quit it already and go to sleep. If Chaos was crying, Valtora would take care of it, after all. There was no reason whatsoever for him to worry about it.

*Waaaa. Waaaaa.*

"For the love of…!" he hissed, gritting his teeth. With that, he leapt off the couch, going upstairs again to listen. And again, there was no crying. No sound whatsoever.

*I'm going crazy,* he realized, a chill running down his spine. *Nonsense,* he countered. For it was clear he was just a sweet father concerned about the welfare of his newborn child. *Or maybe not,* he thought. Then he realized that he was arguing with himself over whether or not he was going crazy, which itself was evidence supporting that conclusion.

"Go back to sleep," he hissed at himself.

Chauncy went back downstairs, lying down on the couch. And this time the phantom cries no longer plagued him. His eyes drifted closed, and he fell fast...

"Waaaa!"

Chauncy's eyes snapped open. This time, there could be no doubt that the cries were real. He sprung off the couch, racing upstairs to the rescue...and came through the bedroom door just as the crying stopped. It was followed by the sound – and shortly thereafter the sight – of Chaos sucking at Valtora's breast.

"Oh," he blurted out, standing at the doorway. Staring.

"He's just hungry," Valtora reassured.

"Oh," Chauncy repeated. Whilst still staring.

"Go back to bed," Valtora told him.

"Okay," he agreed. He tore his gaze away, going back downstairs and lying down on the couch. Under the blanket he went...and with a heavy sigh, he closed his eyes.

Only to be haunted by more phantom cries.

*For the love of...!*

Chauncy grit his teeth, putting his hands over his ears. And while this did make the cries softer, it only made him more paranoid that he was missing them. He sighed again, taking his pillow and covering his head with it. Still, he couldn't help but listen even more intently, knowing full-well that in doing so, he would hear exactly what he...

*Waaa.*

"Fuck!" he swore into the pillow. And felt immediately terribly guilty that he'd said it. What kind of father would get so angry on the first night of their precious child's birth?

*Maybe I'm not cut out to be a father,* he thought. *Maybe I'm just like my father,* he added, followed by a surge of self-loathing.

For his father, after having...deposited Chauncy in his mother, had skipped town, never to be seen or heard from again. After discovering that Valtora was pregnant, Chauncy had managed to convince himself that he was better than his father. That he'd rise above the sins of...well, of half of who he was. But now he wasn't so sure.

*You're just exhausted*, he reminded himself. Which was true. But it also meant that if he didn't get more sleep, he'd be even *more* exhausted in the morning...and that certainly wouldn't help him be a better father.

41

But as it turned out, getting more sleep wasn't in the cards, so to speak. For Chauncy was doomed to toss and turn to the sound of cries both real and fictional for the rest of the night. Such that, by the time the first hint of sunlight streamed through the windows and the chirping of birds heralded the start of a new day, Chauncy was *not* in a good way.

* * *

"Chauncy!" he heard Valtora shout from the bedroom.

"Urrmmmf," he groaned, rubbing his eyes wearily. He sighed then, sitting up on the couch. And staring blankly at his feet. He felt nauseous, and what's more, had a bit of a headache.

"Chauncy!" Valtora shouted again.

Chauncy felt a flash of irritation, and suppressed it as best he could. He got to his feet, stomping up the stairs and going into the bedroom, as he'd done all night long. But while previously his journeys upstairs had been with fatherly – and significant-otherly – heroics in mind, now he was rather put out by Valtora's summons. So when he poked his head through the bedroom doorway and saw Valtora all comfy-cozy in her bed – and snorting Chao's neck to boot – he found himself quite annoyed.

"What?" he snapped. Valtora turned to look at him in surprise. For Chauncy *never* snapped…especially not at her.

"Wow," she breathed. "You look like shit."

"I feel like shit," Chauncy agreed. "Freshly-shat shit," he added.

"I believe it," she told him. "I mean, at first I thought you were a zombie."

"I feel like a zombie."

"Well don't bite the baby," she told him, lifting the boy from her chest and handing him to Chauncy. Chauncy blinked, taking the baby and holding him awkwardly. Valtora got off the bed – with a series of groans – then fixed Chauncy's incompetent holding technique.

"What are you doing?" he asked.

"Bath," she answered. With that, she went to the bathroom, closing the door. Chauncy had made another Wetstone after destroying Nettie's in the lava atop Mount Thrall during their epic battle with The Dark One. This one, however, was for use in the bath instead of the battlefield.

Chauncy sighed, staring down at Chaos, who took one look at him…and starting shrieking.

"Um…" Chauncy said, following Valtora into the bathroom.

"What?" she asked.

"He's dying."

"He's upset," Valtora corrected. "Did you do the triple-check?"

"Triple-what?" Chauncy asked.

"Triple-check," she repeated. "Booty, booby, bedtime."

"Oh," he mumbled.

"In that order," she added.

"Right."

He went to the bed, putting Chaos down, even as the baby continued to shriek. And, after the night he'd had, each shriek cut into Chauncy's soul. He grit his teeth, taking off the diaper hurriedly…and saw that it was indeed wet. He looked around the room, but couldn't find the…

"Diapers are in the drawer!" Valtora yelled.

Chauncy frowned, looking around the room. There was a bureau, a nightstand with their "special" drawer, and another nightstand by Chauncy's side of the bed. Which was like, nine drawers.

"Which one?" he yelled back, even as Chaos continued to shriek like a banshee. Or rather, like the awful harpies they'd battled the better part of a year ago.

Valtora didn't answer.

Chauncy sighed, rushing to the bureau and checking each of the drawers. None had anything resembling a diaper.

"Which *one?*" Chauncy snapped.

"What?" Valtora yelled from the bathroom. Chauncy cursed under his breath, for the little bastard was still screaming…and what's more, the pitch was rising to the point where it made Chauncy want to claw his ears off. He rushed to Valtora's nightstand, yanking open each of the drawers…and found diapers stacked neatly within the bottom one. He grabbed one, rushing to Chao and fumbling to put it on. Eventually he succeeded, and picked the boy back up, triumphant at last.

But Chaos kept shrieking, his little face scrunched up like an ugly little…

"Shit!" Chauncy swore. "Why's he still crying?"

"Triple-check!" Valtora yelled from the bathroom.

"Right," Chauncy mumbled. Booty, booby, bedtime. Which meant booby was next. Unfortunately, he didn't have any. So he'd just have to try bedtime.

He set Chaos down on the bed, then waited. But the shrieking continued, Chaos's little face scrunching up and turning red. The baby clenched his fists, shaking them furiously. Chauncy scooped him up, trying to hold him to his chest like he'd seen Valtora do. But this did nothing at all to pacify him. Chauncy tried to bounce him up and down a bit, but this only made things worse. Chaos's shrieks hit an all-time peak pitch, one that drove Chauncy mad.

"Fuck," Chauncy swore under his breath, right after another ear-piercing scream from the baby. He had the sudden urge to pick the boy up, shake him vigorously, then throw him across the room into a wall. Or preferably, through a window.

It was only the timely entrance of Valtora back into the bedroom that stopped him.

"I got him," she said, taking the baby from him. She positioned the baby so his mouth was at her nipple, and he moved his head side-to-side frantically, until he'd maneuvered it into his mouth.

Chauncy glanced at Valtora, then at Chaos, then lowered his head in shame. For within seconds of Chaos being put to her breast, the horrible, fiendish noise was silenced, replaced by the merciful sound of rhythmic suckling.

"Poor hungwy widdle baby boy," she cooed. "All you wanted was Mommy's big ol' boobies."

"Breasts," Chauncy protested half-heartedly. For he was struck with sudden, crippling guilt. His recent murderous urges ushered in an appropriate level of horror, and a revulsion for the violence he'd just fantasized about carrying out. And along with it, a heaping dose of soul-crushing shame.

And though little Chaos was just fine now, happily feeding on his mother's breast, as Chauncy stared down at his son, he felt as if he'd actually committed the acts he'd imagined. As if he were a baby-murderer, beyond any hope of redemption.

*I can't do this,* he realized. *I'm a terrible father!*

He'd nearly hurt poor Chaos, and all the little guy had been guilty of was a hungry belly. To think of what might've happened if Valtora hadn't come when she did…

He recoiled from the thought in horror, a chill running down his spine.

"Your turn," Valtora told him.

"Huh?"

"You stink," she explained, pinching her nose with her free hand. "Take a bath so I can love you all proper and shit."

Chauncy nodded, flashing her a weak smile, then beating a hasty retreat out of the bedroom and into the bathroom. He went to the tub, which was empty, and stripped his clothes off, getting in and grabbing the Wetstone from the side. He squeezed it gently, and warm water streamed out of it. Such that, in no time at all, the tub was filled.

Chauncy sighed, wrapping his arms around his shins and holding himself in a hunched position. He stared off into the abyss of nothing in particular, feeling like utter crap.

*How could I even* think *that?*

He shook his head, gritting his teeth against a fresh wave of guilt. It hadn't even been a full day since Chaos had been born, and already Chauncy had lost his temper with the poor, innocent little boy. His son had been suffering, and all he'd focused on was how inconvenient it'd been for *him*.

*You need to do better,* he told himself, setting his jaw firmly. *You* have *to do better!*

He set forth then in the grim task of scrubbing himself, not just to clean his skin, which was a mere surface. No, it was to clean his very soul. For with each vicious scrub of his soapy, rough washcloth, he imagined that he was cleansing himself of the stink of the awful thoughts he'd had…and the unspeakable act he'd nearly committed.

Only when he was thoroughly clean, his skin so red and raw it looked for all the world as if he'd been sunburned, did Chauncy drain the bathwater…with the vow of not throwing away the baby with it.

He got out of the bath, returning to the bedroom to see Valtora snuggling the baby in bed, perfectly content. Oblivious to the horrific homicide that she'd narrowly averted. Her eyes lit up when she saw him.

"Ooo, lookie my boyfwend with his coot widdle booty," she cooed. "C'mere and let me *touch* you."

"Um…" Chauncy said, hesitating. "Kinda not in the mood."

"A challenge?" Valtora inquired, arching an eyebrow. "I accept!"

"I think I'll go…I mean I'm…bye," he stammered. For he was hardly in the mood for affection, seeing as how he still felt sullied by his horrible near-act.

Valtora blinked.

Suffice it to say, she had never heard such a thing from a man, much less a man like Chauncy. Having spent thirty-four of his years as a virgin, he'd spent the last year or so fervently making up for lost time. He'd said no before, in a half-hearted kind of way, but had always eventually succumbed to her succubus-like charms.

Chauncy turned about before she could formulate a reply, dashing downstairs. No, it was more like fleeing, in that it wasn't dashing at all. But an unfortunately-placed sock made him slip on the stairs, and he tumbled all the way down on his buttocks with a symphony of swears.

*Frickin' cat!*

His buttocks thusly bruised, he collected himself, then stormed into the kitchen to make breakfast, turning on the oven and throwing a few sausage links on the pan. He set about cracking some eggs, pouring their innards out one-by-one, then finished off with some seasoning.

Then came that fateful knock on his door, the one he'd missed twice before. The third time's the charm, or so they say, and in this particular case they're right. For it was destiny knocking on Chauncy Little's door, and it was there that they would – at long last – unite.

# Chapter 6

So, having met his destiny at his front door – in the form of Imperius Fanning, of course – Chauncy fled right quick, blistered his prick, and listened to Imperius's discourse. Which, if you'll recall, consisted of the dire warning that a wizard named Zella Trek was bound and determined to murder him.

"Fuck," Chauncy swore. Which was quite unlike him, for he rarely uttered that word. But the last twenty-four hours had tested him sorely, and having had almost no sleep at all on account of his child, he found himself failing that test.

"So what do you want *us* to do?" Valtora inquired, putting her hands on her hips and glaring at Imperius. Without her patented jawline-ripple, Chauncy noted. Not yet, anyhow. Valtora had been using it a bit overzealously recently, and as with anything in life, the more one was exposed to something fearful, the less fearful it became.

"*You* should want to do something," Imperius corrected. "What I needed to do, I've done." With that, he turned away from them, striding toward the front door.

"So that's it?" Valtora pressed. "You're just going to leave?"

Imperius stopped, turning around to eye her critically.

"Yes," he answered.

And so he did, striding right out the door and slamming it shut behind him.

Valtora and Chauncy stared at the door, their mouths agape. Then they turned to stare at each other.

"Well," Chauncy stated, not knowing what else to say.

"Shit," Valtora replied, finishing his thought for him.

"What are we going to do?" he asked, more as a rhetorical question than anything else. A sudden screaming could be heard coming from upstairs, and Valtora sighed, lowering her hands to her sides.

"Feed the bastard, I guess," she replied. "You okay?" she added, eyeing his undercarriage. Which was covered by his wizard's robe.

"Nope."

Valtora left him on the kitchen floor, going upstairs to try the triple-check on Chaos Little. Chauncy took the opportunity to lift his robe and peek at his peter...and promptly passed out cold.

\* \* \*

Upon awakening from his impromptu nap – and having his wounds gently bandaged by Valtora – Chauncy dressed himself in his wizard's robe, sans underwear of course. For his special underwear were terribly constraining, despite there being almost nothing to them at all. Much like obligations, which despite having no mass at all, were often possessed of nearly overwhelming weight.

So it was that Chauncy found himself seated gingerly at the kitchen table across from Valtora as she ate breakfast, and at the same time, as Chaos enjoyed his. And as their son sucked, Chauncy reflected on how quickly his life had joined the boy. For in less than twenty-four hours, he'd gone from blissful to miserable...a startling transition indeed.

"This sucks," he declared.

"It's okay," Valtora replied cheerfully.

"Okay?" he blurted out incredulously. "How is it okay?"

"So we gotta kill an asshole wizard," she replied with a shrug. "Big whoopie."

"I can barely walk!" he protested.

"Me neither," she reminded him. "We both got gimpy groins. So what? We'll just go get Rooter and heal 'em."

"Oh," Chauncy mumbled. He'd forgotten all about the little stone golem. Rooter had a magical plant atop his head...one that could suck the life out of anything, and even more importantly, give that life to whatever needed it. Particularly his particulars. In fact, they'd used Rooter's power to heal the crotchety wizard Skibbard's peepee nearly a year ago, after Marie Merrick had had it...pruned.

"See?" Valtora said, continuing to smile. "Everything's gonna be just fine."

"I guess," he conceded, smiling reluctantly.

With that, Valtora finished her breakfast, as did Chaos, and she stood up, carrying the little guy back upstairs.

"Where are you going?" Chauncy asked, standing up with considerable difficulty. His burn throbbed something fierce, and each step he took...well, not to get too graphic, but it *rubbed*.

48

"Packing," she called out from halfway up the stairs. "Duh," she added, unproductively.

"Now?" he protested.

"You're the one crying about his peepee," she reminded him. Chauncy grimaced at the term, and at the pain in his groin as he followed slowly behind her.

"It's not a peepee," he protested. "That's what a baby's is called."

"Penis?" she called out, from the bedroom now.

"Eh," Chauncy replied, wincing as he took each step upstairs one at a time.

"Cock?" she queried.

"I mean that's better," he conceded.

"Big ol' deeeeick?" she proposed.

"Well it's more accurate, right?" he replied.

"Eh," she countered, adding insult to a considerable injury. "Are you coming upstairs?" she asked.

"Well yes," he answered, already halfway there. He gazed at the summit of the second story, taking a break and screwing up his courage for the second half of his journey.

"Well don't," she told him. "I'll pack us."

Chauncy sighed, turning around and gazing down the steps. A journey of equal distance, it was equally daunting. He thought about leaping down and getting it all over with, but decided against it.

"You've suffered worse," he told himself. After all, he'd had a job. One he'd hated at the time, when there'd been no magic in it. In comparison, that was a far worse fate than a scalded scrotum.

At length he reached the bottom of the stairs, and went back into the kitchen to sit down. It wasn't long before Valtora came downstairs with two backpacks bulging with stuff, and a bag bulging with baby stuff. She set them by the door, then hobbled back upstairs.

"You're sure you don't need help?" Chauncy pressed, hoping beyond she said no. It was in his nature to be chivalrous to a fault, so if she said 'yes,' it would most certainly be *his* fault.

"Why, because I'm a woman?" she shot back.

"Not touching that one," he yelled, well-aware that it was an attempt at an argument.

"Not until Rooter heals me," she shouted back.

At length, Valtora returned with little Chaos, held to her bosom with a very pink wrap.

"Ready?" she asked. Chauncy stood.

"Ready," he agreed.

And with that, their newest journey began. For their destiny was waiting for them, somewhere out there in the world. Although where precisely, or even generally, Chauncy hadn't a clue. Imperius had been awfully vague on the details, in that he'd given almost none at all. Still, neither Chauncy nor Valtora would be able to defeat Zella Trek in their current state of health. So off to the Kingdom of Pravus they'd have to go, to meet up with Rooter…and Chauncy's newest destiny.

* * *

"I still think we should take a carriage," Chauncy complained as he and Valtora hobbled down the sidewalk toward the center of the city of Southwick.

"Don't want anyone to see us go through the Gate," she reminded him. Which was why they'd ended up waiting to go at night. The sun had just set a half-hour ago, the stars beginning to peek out from under the inky-black veil of the heavens. And far ahead, the faintest sliver of the crescent moon shone down on them, as if it were an eye nearly closed.

Valtora had insisted on carrying Chaos in her wrap, snuggled face-first in her considerable bosom. A position that he'd feared would suffocate the poor child, but to his surprise, Chaos seemed to like it just fine. It appeared that one was never too young to enjoy the finer things in life. For, nestled against his mother, Chaos needed nothing else to be perfectly happy.

There was a lesson there, Chauncy supposed. In that life's intended pleasures were simple and straightforward, and had nothing to do with money or power or fame or the acquisition and possession of things. Rather, they could be found in one's connections with people – and the world in general – such that a loving touch could be worth more than a fortune in gold.

Something Gavin Merrick, former owner of the Evermore Trading Company, had learned too late. For by the time he'd discovered what had really been the source of magic in his life, his wife Marie Merrick had died…of Valtora punching the woman in the head with her diamond fist.

In any case, without a carriage to ride, the journey to the city center, across the courtyard, past the statue of Archibald Merrick, and beyond A Little Magic to a wide street leading to the Gate, took a terribly long time. And what's more, it chafed Chauncy something awful, to the point where he was worried his disturbingly large blister might pop. Luckily, it didn't, and they made it to the two-hundred foot tall structure dividing the Republic of Borrin from the Kingdom of Pravus. It was known quite accurately as the Wall, within which the massive silver double-doors of the Gate had been built. Doors that, until a bit over a year ago, hadn't opened in thousands of years…or so Chauncy had been told.

They neared the doors, and spotted a lone guard nearby.

"Well shoot," Valtora whispered.

"I've got just the thing," Chauncy whispered back, reaching into the pocket of his wizard's robe. The right pocket, where he kept two of his inventions: the new Wetstone, and the Sunstone. He drew out the Sunstone, flashing her an impish smile. "I am the night, remember?"

"I remember you saying that right before Harry hit you in the balls with that boulder," she replied with a grin of her own. Chauncy grimaced, recalling the event all-too-well. In fact, almost certainly more poignantly than she did.

"Yes, well," he grumbled. He focused, willing the Sunstone to absorb light powerfully. In doing so, it created utter darkness all around them, making them impossible to see. "Come on," he whispered.

They hobbled up to the gate, Chauncy's eye on the guard as they went. To his dismay, the guard turned to look right at them.

*Crap.*

But then the guard rubbed his eyes, blinked, and then stared again. Then rubbed his eyes *again*, and looked suddenly rather afraid. It occurred to Chauncy that to the guard, they'd look like a black splotch in his vision, moving slowly toward the gate. Chauncy cursed silently, realizing that the Sunstone would only make them invisible if they were flying, and if the guard was looking up at them on the background of a starless night sky.

But as luck would have it, the plan worked, just not the way Chauncy had expected. Which was kind of how magic seemed to work.

They stopped at the Gate, and Chauncy gestured for Valtora to open it…and promptly realized she couldn't see him. So he reached out instead, touching the Gate.

There was a *thunk*.

Chauncy couldn't help but smile, remembering the first time he'd come here, on that fateful night when he'd first visited the Gate. He'd touched the doors just like this, and heard the same sound. Back then, he hadn't realized he'd been a wizard, and that only wizards could unlock the Gate, with the merest touch.

That was the day Grandma Little had died...a recollection that stole the smile from Chauncy's lips...and the magic from the moment.

"After you," he whispered.

The door opened ever-so-slightly, and Chauncy felt Valtora slip by him. He went next, then closed the door quietly behind him. Only then did he inactivate the Sunstone...and before them lay the magnificent, magical Kingdom of Pravus.

Which looked like any other place, really. For magic was everywhere and nowhere, in that it was one's relationship with the world, not the world itself.

A wide road led off into the distance ahead, and Chauncy sighed, suddenly acutely aware of the vast distance they had to walk. For Rooter was miles and miles away, living with his big stone-giant friend Rocky at their favorite bridge. A very nice bridge, according to the old wizard Harry, in that it was gneiss.

"I can't do this," he realized with dismay.

"Do what?" Valtora asked.

"It's too far," he explained. "I can't make it with my..." he added, gesturing at his...

"Big ol' deeeeick?" she asked.

"Right."

"That's okay," Valtora replied cheerily. "I've got a plan."

"You do?"

"Yep," she confirmed. Chauncy paused, waiting for her to elaborate. Which she didn't, maddeningly enough. Given his piss-poor sleep the night before, he found himself rather irritated at her.

"And that is?" he snapped.

"Well, the way I see it, if my peter comes, we won't have to worry about your big ol' deeeeick anymore."

"Your...peter?"

"My Peter," she corrected. Chauncy frowned, then recalled that Peter was the white horse that she'd transformed into a rainbow unicorn. Her magic power was to bedazzle things, after all...and to everyone's surprise, this didn't just mean making things beautiful.

No, her power had actually transformed Peter into a *real* unicorn, one with powers of his own.

"But there's no rainbow," Chauncy pointed out. For that's how Peter could travel vast distances, by appearing wherever a rainbow was.

"Peter only comes when it's wet," Valtora agreed, reaching into Chauncy's pocket.

"Yeep!" he yeeped, jerking away. For she'd gotten awfully close to jostling his bubbly bits. She grabbed his Wetstone, pulling it out and lifting it up.

"Blast it with your staff, Chauncy!" she commanded, throwing it up in the air.

Chauncy obeyed, swinging his Staff of Wind at the stone as it flew up overhead. The subsequent blast of wind struck the stone, sending it flying higher…and triggering it to release a blast of water outward. The wind scattered this, making it rain – quite literally – all around them. Valtora caught the Wetstone as gently as she could, but the impact with her hand still caused it to spray them both.

"Ptthhh," Chauncy spat, wiping water from his face. Poor little Chaos began to cry, having been drenched quite thoroughly.

"Oops," Valtora said, patting Chaos gently. "Totally forgot about the baby."

"And the sun," Chauncy pointed out. For rainbows didn't have a habit of showing up at night-time.

"Oh," she mumbled. "Right." Then her expression brightened. "The Sunstone!" She reached into Chauncy's pocket again, drawing out the Sunstone and handing it to Chauncy. "Let's try it again," she prompted.

With that, they repeated the whole shebang, but this time Chauncy used the sunstone to provide some light…and Valtora turned away from the water-blast so Chaos wouldn't get drenched. To Chauncy's surprise, the process worked, the very faintest hint of a rainbow appearing before them.

"Come, Peter!" Valtora cried.

And to Chauncy's further surprise, the rainbow changed shape, converging into the shape of none other than Peter himself…and Peter himself appeared as if leaping through an invisible portal, landing proudly before them. He was just as Chauncy remembered him, a tall, handsome creature indeed. With a perfectly-muscled body as white as snow, a long, flowing rainbow-colored mane, and an equally rainbow-colored horn, he was a sight to behold. As was one other rainbow-colored part of his showy body. One that, to make a long story short, made what Chauncy had assumed was long seem very short indeed.

Comparison was the thief of joy, or so they said. And whoever they were, they were absolutely right.

"Oh yay, he's back," Chauncy muttered. But Valtora was predictably overjoyed.

"Peter-poo!" she cried, rushing forward and practically leaping at Peter's barrel chest, embracing him tightly. Chaos shrieked, crushed by the impact…and Valtora jerked backward, gasping in horror. "Oh baby!" she cried, clutching Chaos tightly. "I'm so sorry!"

"Ooo," Chauncy said, flinching in empathy. For she'd really done a number on poor Chaos. Who continued to shriek, utterly beside himself.

"Oh baby, I'm sorry," Valtora apologized, taking poor Chaos out of the wrap and rocking him frantically. "Mama didn't *mean* to."

Peter eyed the baby, then Chauncy, the snorted dismissively.

"He'll be okay," Chauncy reassured, having absolutely no idea if that was true.

"How do you know?" Valtora asked, calling his bluff.

"Um…we're going to Rooter," he answered, saving himself in the nick of time. Valtora gave a relieved smile.

"Oh, right," she realized. Then she turned to Peter. "Can you take us to Rocky's bridge, Peter-poo?"

Peter neighed, then posed heroically. And despite the fact that the unicorn wasn't remotely human, Chauncy found himself powerfully jealous of the creature.

"Good," Valtora replied, smiling radiantly. "Can Chauncy and I ride you at the same time?"

Peter eyed Chauncy with a withering look, then nodded reluctantly.

"Yay!" Valtora exclaimed. And very nearly rushed to hug the stallion again. Only the fact that Chaos was still shrieking stopped her, and instead, she climbed with some difficulty up onto his back. It was far from the former vaulting she'd…well, formally done. "Come on, Chauncy," she prompted, patting the spot behind her.

"Um…" Chauncy replied, eyeing Peter's back, then considering the state of his scrotum. "I think I'll walk."

"Suit yourself," Valtora replied.

Peter trotted forward on the road, Valtora bouncing up and down on his back. Or rather, bouncing once up and once down, before yelping in pain.

"Stop!" she blurted out. Which, with a fair bit of surprise, Peter did. "Sorry Peter," she added, patting his back. "I tore my coochie."

Peter turned to eye Chauncy, then gave Valtora a doubting look.

"Pushing out the baby," Valtora clarified.

Peter relaxed, clearly accepting this far more likely scenario.

Chauncy grimaced, not at all liking the unicorn's insinuations. But he kept his protestations to himself, knowing that any comparison with the stallion would leave him coming up...short. Peter walked quite slowly then, making sure that Valtora's ride was as smooth as possible. Such that she didn't bounce up and down on Peter like she usually did.

"That's better," she told him, rewarding Peter with a vigorous rubbing. Peter tossed his gorgeous mane, snorting happily at this reward.

"Bet you like a good rubbing," Chauncy grumbled, recalling how Valtora had bedazzled the stallion. Or rather, how he *assumed* she'd bedazzled him. For she needed to touch what she bedazzled, and in addition to giving him a rainbow horn, she'd handed him a rainbow...

"...Peter?" Valtora asked. Chauncy blinked, torn from his morbid reverie.

"Huh?"

"Would you like to ride Peter?" Valtora repeated.

"Um..." he began, fully prepared to say no. But each step he took sent agony through his loins, and he decided to relent. "Fine," he decided.

"Peter, go down for Chauncy," Valtora instructed. Peter stopped, then complied, clearly irritated at this imposition. Apparently the unicorn wanted her all to himself. Chauncy got on top of the stallion, riding behind Valtora and carrying his backpack in front of him. And to his surprise, as Peter continued forward, he felt not a trace of bouncing or any other cause for genital discomfort.

"Huh," he mumbled.

"Is this your first time riding Peter?" she asked.

"It is," Chauncy confirmed.

"Not bad, right?"

"Actually, no," he agreed. "It doesn't hurt nearly as bad as I thought it would."

"He's very gentle," Valtora said, giving Peter another good rubbing. "He knows how to take it slow, so he won't hurt my coochie."

"Um…"

"Isn't that right, Peter?" she cooed.

Peter snorted in the affirmative.

Chauncy decided to ignore them both, slouching on Peter's back as they continued forward on the road. Having barely slept the night before – and barely napped that afternoon, on account of Chao's cries – Chauncy wasn't in the mood for talking. Or for being here, for that matter. If they'd taken a carriage, he could've rested his eyes. But on Peter's back, he had to stay awake, or risk falling off the glorified horse and killing himself. A prospect that, to be fair, was not as terrible now as it might've been a day ago.

*This sucks*, he told himself. As if on cue, Chaos burst out into a squealing cry.

"It's okay," Valtora reassured. But whether she was talking to the baby or Chauncy, Chauncy wasn't sure. Either way, he knew beyond a shadow of a doubt that she was wrong.

So it was that Chauncy Little began his newest adventure on the metaphorical wrong foot, having gotten up on the wrong side of the bed due in part to not having slept on it. The only silver lining was that Valtora had intervened before Chauncy had done something terrible to Chaos that morning.

For if she hadn't, their poor little baby boy would've been dead.

# Chapter 7

King Pravus sat on his ridiculously large throne, gazing across his ridiculously large – and ornate – throne room at the double-doors at the end. He'd placed himself in a posture of practiced boredom, leaning his left elbow on the armrest and propping his broad chin in one hand. Desmond stood beside the throne, waiting patiently. As were the assorted royal guards and such. Pravus sat as motionlessly as a statue, though his hamstrings and buttocks were on fire on account of the deadlifts he'd so recently performed.

Over a minute passed.

"How about now, sire?" Desmond inquired.

"Feeling fidgety?" Pravus inquired.

"Bored, sire."

"Then so is our guest," Pravus declared. "Which means it's about time we let her in." After all, it wouldn't do to seem overly excited about a visit, even from a powerful wizard from the Order of Mundus. Forcing them to wait would also irritate them, and if there's one thing Pravus knew, it was that irritation interfered nicely with one's decision-making abilities. "Go on," he told the guards by the doors.

They opened said doors, and moments later, a most curious character came in.

It was a woman of startling beauty, tall and composed. She had long, straight raven-black hair, skin as pale as fine ivory, and large eyes with deep purple irises. She wore a long black cloak that completely hid her body…and trailed on the floor behind her for quite a distance, ending in twin forks like a snake's tongue. Black tattoos crawled all the way up the sides of her neck and in front of her ears, continuing up to just beyond her scalp-line.

In short, she was not at all what Pravus had been expecting.

"And you are?" he inquired with the bored-est tone he could muster. The woman stopped at the appropriate place, a good seven yards from the throne.

Then she threw her arms out to the sides...and her cloak flew off of her, in the most intriguing of ways.

It rose into the air, rippling majestically. The arms then arched to touch each other, forming a kind of mouth...and the fork at its tail-end went forward through that mouth, looking for all the world like the tongue of a huge serpent.

This hung in the air for a moment, then descended, shrinking as it did so. It closed its jaws on the woman's head from behind...and then melted into her skin, becoming a tattoo there. Such that twin snake fangs protruded down her forehead, and a snake's tongue came down from her lower lip and down her chin, ending halfway down her neck.

And beneath her cloak, the woman wore a skin-tight black uniform, one so shiny it shimmered with her every move. A sleeveless suit, displaying heavily and intricately tattooed arms, all the way down to the backs of her hands. A very *very* tight uniform. So tight it showed things.

Pravus found himself quite impressed.

"Well *well*," he murmured, sitting up a bit straighter. And if he'd been straighter, he would've found her enormously attractive. For she was everything men seemed to find magical; tall, slender but oh-so-curvy, and mildly frightening.

"King Pravus," she greeted, inclining her head.

"Wizard," he replied. He turned to Desmond. "Desmond old boy, don't you think it's terribly *rude* when people don't bow before royalty?"

Desmond paused, clearly sensing a trap. For if he answered in the affirmative, then he would be accusing a powerful wizard of being rude. But if he disagreed, he'd be insulting his king.

"I leave the thinking to you, sire," Desmond answered at last. Clever bastard that he was.

"Not much of an advisor then, are you?" Pravus mused.

"Only half," Desmond replied coolly. Which was quite correct, seeing as he was half-advisor, half-servant. Pravus pursed his lips, miffed at being temporarily outwitted by the crafty codger.

"In any case," he stated, returning his attention to their guest. "Welcome to Pravus and so forth. What do you want?"

The woman smirked.

"I am Zella Trek," she introduced.

"That's who you are, not what you want."

"You didn't let me finish," she shot back. "Typical man."

It was Pravus's turn to smirk.

"You'll find I'm far from typical," he retorted. "But do go on," he added, gesturing for her to continue. "What does the Order of Mundus want with me?"

"Nothing," she replied.

Pravus arched an interested eyebrow.

"The why did they send you?" he inquired.

"They didn't."

"I'm afraid I don't understand," he confessed. It was her turn to smirk. Again.

"They didn't send me because I'm not with them," she revealed. Pravus frowned, eyeing Desmond.

"You said she *was* from the Order," he accused.

"She said she was," Desmond replied, rather defensively.

"I was," Zella confirmed. "But they kicked me out."

"She didn't mention that," Desmond argued.

"Perhaps you should have vetted her," Pravus pointed out.

"Vetting isn't my job," Desmond pointed out. "Your vetters vetted her."

"Well then my vetters should've done a better job," Pravus grumbled. He sighed then, returning his attention to Zella. "In any case," Pravus stated, "…you're here, as was your intention. I'll ask you one last time: what do you want?"

"Justice," Zella answered.

"For?" Pravus prompted.

"The universe," she replied.

"I suppose you'd like world peace as well?" he inquired.

"Hardly," Zella retorted. "Just a piece of Chauncy Little."

Pravus frowned, leaning back in his throne and eyeing the woman shrewdly.

"Chauncy the Chosen One?" he inquired.

"Correct."

"But why?" he pressed.

"My husband cheated on me," she revealed.

"With Chauncy?" Pravus asked. It was plausible enough, given Chauncy's *spectacular* purple robe.

"With the whore who gave birth to him," Zella corrected.

"Ah," he replied. "So what precisely do you want with Chauncy Little?"

"I want to erase him," she answered. Pravus blinked.

"Pardon?"

"My husband cheated on me and sired a son," Zella explained. "Chauncy Little shouldn't exist…and I'm going to make it so that he doesn't."

Pravus arched an eyebrow, rubbing his chin with one hand.

"And why should I help you?" he inquired. "The Chosen Ones saved the Great Wood…and my kingdom."

"After The Dark One nearly destroyed it," she pointed out.

"I'll grant you they were late," he replied. "But better late than never. The point is, why should I aid a rogue wizard in murdering the man who helped save my country?"

"Because," she replied. "If you don't, it'll be as if he never did."

He frowned.

"Pardon?"

"Tell me where Chauncy Little is right now," she commanded, raising her slender, tattooed arms to either side. "Or I'll finish what The Dark One started…and destroy your pathetic little kingdom."

Pravus gripped his armrests firmly, glaring down at her with every ounce monarchal menace he could muster.

"Consider your request denied" he declared. She lowered her hands to her sides.

"Very well," she replied. "I think I'll start with this itty-bitty castle."

# Chapter 8

By the time Chauncy and Valtora reached the first tiny village the road from Southwick passed through, Chauncy was practically delirious. If it hadn't been for Valtora, he surely would've fallen off of Peter more than once. The sun had just started to rise above the horizon, making the few buildings in the center of the town cast long shadows over the road. It was the same little place they'd passed through on their last two adventures, population fifty-one now, perhaps on account of a baby being born, for it'd been fifty before.

"Ugh," Chauncy mumbled, feeling absolutely dreadful. His head ached and his eyes burned, and he felt as nauseous as if he had a hangover.

"To the inn, Peter!" Valtora cried, somehow as bubbly as ever. Which for some reason irritated the hell out of Chauncy. Chaos, to his credit, had slept for much of the trip. And to his discredit, that meant that the little bastard was now wide awake, and probably would be for quite some time. Right as they were reaching the one place Chauncy had any chance of getting some sleep.

Peter stopped by the inn, which was a large rectangular two-story building with all the style and charm of a casket. Chauncy got off, then helped Valtora and the baby down, taking her backpack first, then the baby, then allowing her to slip off Peter herself.

"Are you gonna be okay out here, Peter?" Valtora asked, taking her backpack and the baby from Chauncy. Peter nodded, then snorted, and Valtora beamed him a gorgeous smile, running in to give him a hug.

"Baby!" Chauncy cried out. Valtora froze right before crashing into Peter's chest and crushing poor Chaos again.

"Shit," Valtora swore. "Sorry baby," she added, petting his head. She lifted her gaze to Peter. "I'll come for you," she promised.

"Bet you will," Chauncy muttered under his breath. Either Peter ignored him or didn't hear him. The unicorn tossed his rainbow mane quite handsomely, so as to catch the sunrise perfectly. And while it wasn't nearly as impressive as Valtora's signature hair-tosses, it was still a sight to behold.

"Damn," she breathed, much as everyone else did when *she* did it.

"Let's go," Chauncy grumbled, stomping off to the entrance to the inn. Valtora blew Peter a kiss, then followed behind Chauncy, Chaos still strapped to her chest. Chauncy yanked the door open, going in first.

"Oh," Valtora mumbled, clearly expecting him to have held it open for her in his usual manner. And while Chauncy felt guilty for being a bit rude, rude was in keeping with his mood. To the innkeeper they went, a tall, robust bearded man who looked every bit the part, standing behind a wooden counter.

"Mornin'," the innkeeper greeted, sounding precisely the way he looked. "I'm Gerald and this is my inn. What can I do for you?"

"Sleep," Chauncy replied instantly.

"I can get you a place to do that," Gerald replied without skipping a beat. "Looks like you need it." He paused. "Fresh baby?"

"Born yesterday," Valtora confirmed. The day before, actually, but Chauncy was too tired to argue the point.

"You *definitely* need it," the innkeeper replied. "Breakfast first?"

"No," Chauncy answered at once…and heard Valtora's mouth *click* shut. Again, he felt guilty, for she was probably starving. "You go eat," he told her. "I'll sleep."

"No, we can sleep first," she offered. "That way you don't miss breakfast."

Chauncy stared at her, then at the baby. The thought of Chaos going to their room, and of Chauncy snuggling in bed, falling asleep…and then having that needy little *bastard* cry again…

"F…ine," he replied. For what he'd been about to say would have quite literally fed up their day.

"Come with me," Gerald prompted.

The innkeeper stepped around the counter, gesturing for them to follow him rightward. They went past a bartop, continuing to a door to their left. This led to a staircase to the second floor…and to a hallway with doors on either side. Gerald brought them to their door.

"Here it is," he told them. "One silver."

"Right," Chauncy grumbled, patting his pockets. But of course he had no money in them.

"Here," Valtora said, reaching into her pants pocket and pulling out a silver coin. The innkeeper took it, then inclined his head.

"Enjoy," he told them. Then he eyed Chauncy. "And get some sleep."

Chauncy nodded numbly. For while he wanted desperately to fulfill the innkeeper's command, he knew damn well that it wasn't up to him.

Valtora opened the door, and Chauncy followed her into the room beyond. It was small, with two narrow beds and a window, and a separate room for a chamber pot.

"Guess we'll have the baby sleep on the floor," Valtora decided.

"Oh," Chauncy mumbled. For he hadn't even thought of the baby's accommodations. But as it turned out, Valtora had. She set her backpack on the floor, pulling out a small, thick blanket. This she set on the floor. Then she got *another* blanket, this one much thinner, and set it atop the first, using it to swaddle the child. This done, she stood up, putting her hands on her hips and giving a rather proud smile.

"There," she declared.

"Huh," Chauncy mumbled, feeling more than a little guilty. He hadn't really been thinking about little Chaos while they'd prepared for this trip; he'd been so absorbed in himself that he hadn't considered anyone else.

*Some father I am,* he thought darkly. And not for the first time, he scolded himself, telling himself that he *had* to do better.

"Go to sleep," Valtora urged, shoving him toward one of the beds. He caught his balance, and nearly shot her a glare when he realized she was smiling playfully. He gave a rueful smile back.

"Nighty night," he told her.

"Day-y day," she corrected.

And with that, Chauncy rolled onto his side in bed, pulled the covers over himself, snuggled his head into his plush pillow, and fell fast…

"Waaaa!"

Chauncy's eyes snapped open, a very specific thought coming to him. One that was not a fatherly thought. Or a husbandly thought. It was, on reflection, a very dark thought. Or rather, The Dark One's type of thought. And as soon as he had it, he recoiled from it in horror.

"Aww," Valtora cooed. "Widdle Chaos wants some *titty*."

"Breast," he complained automatically. For it was inappropriate – and rather dehumanizing – to refer to a woman's anatomy that way.

"C'mere baby-kins," she said, picking Chaos up and bringing him to her bosom. So began the sound of rhythmic suckling, followed by a shuddering sigh of contentment. "There," Valtora said when it was done. "Now it's time for sweepy-teeps, my widdle snuggle-poo."

And so it was, for Chaos…and for Chauncy. For at long last, he went to sleep.

\* \* \*

A new parent's sleep was, Chauncy discovered, like so many other things in a new parent's life. Desperately desired, but disappointingly short-lived. Unsatisfying. And in the end, the subject of endless internal struggle and resentment. So it was that he woke no less than fives times during the short period between sunrise and noon, to the point where going back to sleep was impossible. For even though he no longer heard phantom cries – being in the same room as Chaos seemed to banish them – he spent much of his time waiting for Chaos to cry again. Just lying there, waiting for the inevitable.

It was torture, this morbid anticipation. And Chauncy found himself not only anticipating the crying itself, but his reaction to it. And thus his irritation grew, even when Chaos did nothing. So by the time he decided to get out of bed, he was not in a good way.

Valtora was already up, feeding little Chaos once again. Chauncy watched this numbly, and when Chaos finished, then promptly fell asleep – with the most peacefully content look on his face – Chauncy was struck with the sudden urge to cry.

"Baby's fed," Valtora declared triumphantly. "Our turn, Chauncy!"

Chauncy followed her back down to the first floor of the inn, and they sat down at a table there. Valtora chose her usual morning helping of sausage and eggs, while Chauncy had tea.

"Your sausage tastes *so* much better," Valtora told him.

"Thank Addie," he replied. For he got his meat fresh from his former crush Addie, who'd married the late city grocer. After being given a magical staff that gave her confidence – by sucking it out of others – Addie had blossomed, expanding her business to numerous stores. In thanks, she gave Chauncy her best meat for free every day he wanted it.

"Bet she still wants it," Valtora mused. Chauncy frowned. "Huh?"

"Your sausage," she explained with an eyebrow-waggle.

"Eh," he replied.

"You sure you don't want to eat something?" she pressed, giving him a funny look.

"Not hungry."

"Ooookay," she replied. She finished, then got up. "Let's go find Peter."

She paid for lunch, then led them outside.

"Come, Peter!" she cried.

And come Peter did. For the unicorn was grazing in a grassy field by the road, and upon hearing Valtora's siren call, galloped gallantly up to them. He struck a pose in front of Valtora then, making sure to show his showiest parts to maximum effect.

"My *hero*," Valtora gushed, rushing to leap at Peter and throw her arms around his neck. She stopped herself, remembering poor little Chaos, and got on his back instead. Chauncy joined them, his backpack in his lap, but not touching it. For his groin was practically pulsating with pain.

With that, they bid the little town of fifty-one residents goodbye, and continued their journey to Rocky and Rooter.

At length Chauncy spotted the telltale stone bridge ahead, crossing over a river not a mile away. The prospect of having his blighted bits healed put him in a better mood, and by the time they reached the foot of the bridge and dismounted, Chauncy found himself in a more typical Chauncy Little mood.

"Rocky!" he called out.

"Shmookie tookums!" Valtora cried, far louder than he had.

To both of their reliefs, none other than Rocky himself appeared at the other end of the bridge, bounding across it toward them. A giant twenty feet tall, with skin covered with patches of rock, Rocky was a formidable friend. And Rooter, the little stone golem they'd come to see, sat on his perennial perch on Rocky's shoulder, the plant sprouting from his little head bouncing cutely.

"*So* adorbs," Valtora groaned, clutching her hands to her bosom as they approached. Rocky stopped before them, and both the stone giant's and Rooter's eyes locked on the baby strapped to Valtora's chest.

"Huuuy," Rocky greeted, waving with a goofy grin. "Bayyybeee," he added, pointing to the baby.

"Hi tookums!" Valtora gushed, once again struck with the obvious urge to leap at Rocky and hug him. But to her credit, she didn't, as the impact surely would've killed Chaos. The sheer effort required to inhibit her usual impulses was clearly monumental. Particularly considering that inhibitions were something that, until recently, Valtora hadn't possessed. "This is Chaos," she introduced.

"Huyyy," Rocky said, waving at Chaos. Rooter smiled happily, jumping up and down on Rocky's shoulder.

"Awww," Valtora replied. "Chaos tore my coochie, and Chauncy burned his dick. Can you heal us Rooter?"

Rocky set Rooter down, and within moments, the deed was done. Chauncy ran away at once, then lifted his robe, peering at matters below. And to his profound relief – experienced with a sob bursting from his lips – his peepee was perfect again.

He ran back – over the moon that he could do so – and found Valtora hopping up and down and doing various other calisthenics, with a huge smile on her face.

"Muh coochie's *back*, bitches!" she declared, engaging in a few vigorous hip-thrusts. Then she lifted her shirt, exposing her belly...and gasping. "My stretch marks!" she exclaimed. "They're gone!"

"Thanks Rooter," Chauncy said, smiling down at the little golem. Valtora whirled on him.

"I thought you said you liked them," she accused.

"Huh?"

"My stretch marks," she clarified. "You said you liked them. That they meant I was a mommy, and it was hot."

"Um, I meant thanks for healing us," Chauncy told her.

"Uh huh," she grumbled, putting a hand on her hip and glaring at him. "What else did you lie to me about?"

"I didn't...I wasn't..."

"You thought they were ugly, didn't you?" she accused.

"No!"

"Yes you did," she insisted. "I can't believe you, Chauncy," she added. "I bet you were all disgusted and shit when you looked at me, but were too much of a pussy to say so. All while pining after hot, young girls *without* stretch marks, wishing I looked like *them*."

"I…no!" he protested. With her power of bedazzling, that hadn't been an issue, for no woman had yet matched her beauty. "That's not true!"

"Uh huh."

"It isn't," he insisted, glaring back at her.

"Bet you were all fantasizing about Addie and shit," Valtora mused, shaking her head. "Did you imagine I was her while we…"

"Stop it!" he yelled, making her jump. He realized he was scowling ferociously at her, his hands balled into fists. Rocky stared down at him stonily, and Rooter's smile had vanished.

Then Chaos began to cry.

"FUCK!" Chauncy screamed, grabbing his hair and tugging on it. He stormed away from them, stomping up to the side of the bridge and kicking the side-wall. Then he flung his backpack over the side of the bridge…and right into the water below.

He stared at it, his shoulders heaving. Then he realized his Staff of Wind had been tied to it.

"Figgity fraggity fuckity fuck fuck *fuck!*" he shouted, jumping up and down and stomping his feet. He stood there then, staring first at the ripples spreading outward from his now-sunken backpack, then at the blue sky at the horizon.

Then he sat down, curled his knees up to his chest, and sobbed.

Minutes passed, and eventually Chauncy stopped weeping, and just sat there, feeling like utter shit. For he realized that he'd acted quite badly…and what's worse, in public. There was no coming back from what he'd done. Everyone had seen him at his absolute worst.

So he stood, then walked toward the side of the bridge to jump.

"Chauncy," he heard Valtora call out. He resisted the urge to turn around, not wanting to face her or the others. Footsteps approached from behind, and he felt a warm hand on his shoulder. "Chauncy," Valtora repeated.

He pulled away, facing the edge of the bridge with grim determination.

That is, until a very *hard* hand grabbed his other shoulder. One with a grip so powerful it couldn't be escaped.

"Ow!" he blurted out, just as Valtora used her diamond hand to spin him around. But to his surprise, she looked not angry, or disappointed. Rather, she looked concerned.

"Chauncy, are you okay?" she asked.

His lower lip trembled, and he shook his head mutely. And promptly burst out crying again.

Valtora leaned in to hug him, crushing poor Chaos between them. This caused Chaos to cry, which only made Chauncy cry harder. Rocky and Rooter came up to them, as did Peter. All watching him bawl his eyes out like a little baby.

At length, both he and Chaos stopped crying, and Chauncy took a deep breath in, then sighed.

"I was just arguing for fun you know," Valtora told him. "I didn't mean any of it," she added reassuringly.

"Oh," he mumbled.

"You took it like a lil' bitch," she said, less reassuringly.

"Not helping," he grumbled.

"What's wrong?" she asked. "I've never seen you like this."

Chauncy hesitated. He had the urge to confess everything, right then and there, but with everyone watching, he couldn't.

"Go away," Valtora told everyone. She even took Chaos out of his wrap and handed him to Rocky. When they'd gone far enough to be well out of earshot, Valtora smiled at Chauncy. "Okay baby," she prompted. "Get it all out."

And that's precisely what Chauncy did.

At first he was cautious, picking and choosing what to say. But as each confession came out of him – and Valtora merely smiled encouragingly – he ended up telling her every last little sordid detail, starting with Chaos's first night with them. Even the ugliest of thoughts, like when he'd been driven to harm the poor child. An admission that send a chill down his spine, for as he told her, he realized that he was confessing to something forbidden. To having crossed a line that would change her perception of him forever.

That he was a monster.

He hung his head in shame afterward, feeling absolutely miserable.

"I'm sorry," he told her.

"For what?" she asked.

"For not being the man you deserve," he replied. "Or the father Chaos deserves."

"Bullshit," she retorted. He blinked.

"What?"

"Please," she replied, giving him a look. "You know how many times I wanted to throw that little bastard down the stairs?"

Chauncy blinked.

"Oh *hell* yeah," Valtora said. "Every time I'm about to fall asleep and I hear that goddamn cry. And don't get me started on the phantom cries."

Chauncy's eyes widened.

"You hear them too?" he gasped.

"Drives me *insane*," she confirmed. "Honestly, half the time I go to feed him, I think about smooshing his ugly little gremlin face in my boob and smothering him to death."

"Oh."

"Like, 'til he turns frickin' blue," she continued. Rather cheerfully, he noted, in stark contrast to the subject matter.

"Well then," he mumbled.

"You wouldn't *believe* some of the thoughts I've had," she reassured him. And the way she said it, he believed it.

"I guess that makes me feel better," he replied. She beamed him a gorgeous smile.

"We're *not* good people, remember?" she said. The same thing she'd told King Pravus after their last adventure. Chauncy smiled ruefully.

"I guess not."

"I mean, we named our kid Chaos," she pointed out. "And remember, you're engaged to The Dark One's ex-wife," she added. "Nothing bad surprises me anymore."

"Thanks," he told her. "I needed to hear that."

"Honestly, if we don't kill this kid by accident, we'll probably do it on purpose," Valtora assured him. Which wasn't reassuring at all. "Might have to keep Rooter in the house for the first year or two."

"Actually, that's not a bad thought," Chauncy admitted.

"It's a good thought to balance out the bad thoughts," she agreed, flashing him another gorgeous smile. He chuckled, then leaned in, giving her a big hug.

"Thanks poopy-dooz," he told her.

"You're welcome," she replied. They separated from each other. "So we need a plan."

"Agreed," he...well, agreed. "I'm a terrible person when I don't get sleep."

"Hell yeah you are," she agreed. "I can at least fake it."

"What's that supposed to mean?"

"Fake being a good person," she clarified.

"Kidding."

"Go get some sleep," she told him. "I've got sleeping bags and stuff in our backpacks."

"Um…about that," he stated, his cheeks flushing. For his backpack was underwater now, along with his Staff of Wind. "Kind of screwed that up too."

"And?" she said, giving him a funny look. "You're a wizard, remember?"

Chauncy blinked, realizing she was right.

"I *am* a wizard," he declared.

He thrust his hand outward, and his Staff of Wind shot out of the river – quite a distance away – and flew right back into his hand. Along with his backpack, which it was still tied to. Which would have been quite impressive, if that backpack hadn't slammed into Chauncy, knocking him off of his feet and onto his back…and soaking him to the bone.

"Pffthhh!" he spat, blinking rapidly.

"Need Rooter again?" she asked.

"Sure…do," he gasped.

Valtora helped him up, and they walked back to the others. Valtora snaked her hand into his, and Chauncy smiled, feeling better than he had in days. For while he still hated how he felt physically, he no longer hated himself.

# Chapter 9

King Pravus the Eighth stared imperiously at the womanly wizard who'd just threatened to destroy his kingdom – starting with his castle – rising from his throne with considerable difficulty, then putting his hands on his ridiculously narrow waist. Whilst flexing his ludicrously wide lats, naturally. A heroic pose, which was quite appropriate, considering that everyone he asked told him he was a hero.

"Firstly," he began his rebuttal, "…my kingdom is neither little nor pathetic." The former was undeniably true; Pravus was actually rather large compared to its neighbors. The latter, of course, was in the eye of the beholder. But his eye beheld a rather admirable kingdom indeed.

"And secondly?" Zella Trek inquired, arching an already impressively arched eyebrow.

"Secondly," he replied, "…I resent you threatening to destroy my castle. Especially after my generous hospitality."

"You merely let me in," she pointed out.

"Letting people in is as hospitable as I can get," Pravus replied. Which was true in all manner of metaphors. Zella smirked, clearly of a similarly metaphorical mindset.

"If Chauncy Little's mother hadn't let my husband in, we wouldn't be in this predicament," she retorted.

"I hardly see why I should be punished for the crime of his conception."

"Because you're being difficult," she replied.

"A bit disproportionate a punishment, to destroy my castle and my kingdom on account of difficulty," he pointed out.

"I enjoy blowing things out of proportion."

"As do I," he confessed. Blowing things that were out of proportion was, in fact, one of his favorite activities. "But this is disproportionately disproportionate."

"Even so," she replied, crossing her arms over her chest. "I'll give you one last chance," she warned. "Tell me where Chauncy Little is and I'll spare you my wrath."

"No," he replied. Firmly.

71

"Oh *goody*," she replied. "In that case, I'd like you to meet one of my Inklings."

She thrust her arms out to the sides dramatically…and something dramatic happened. The tattoo of the snake that had melded with her skin came to life, detaching and rising above her as an ever-growing snake-head. It grew to simply massive proportions, its head nearly reaching the ridiculously high ceiling of the throne room, and its long body extending right out of the throne room's entrance. Its great big maw opened, a long, forked black tongue flicking out. Then it hissed, a sound that would've sent creepy-crawlies down Pravus's spine, had he been at all concerned.

Instead, he found himself quite delighted.

"A serpent, eh?" he exclaimed, making a motion as if drawing a sword from a non-existent scabbard on his back. This summoned a very real weapon…his trusty golden greatsword. He struck a spectacularly heroic pose, facing this creature valiantly.

"Be careful, my liege," Desmond warned.

"Nonsense old man," Pravus shot back, giving Desmond a look. "Felling sizable serpents is my specialty!"

With that, he strode forward, holding his sword before him. Or rather, he hobbled, for his legs felt like wobbly jelly.

"Oh Fang," Zella stated in a singsong tone, clearly addressing her serpent. "Wreck this little king's castle, would you?"

Fang hissed again, then reared its head back…and lunged forward to strike!

"Have at you, fiendish Fang!" Pravus cried with gusto, not even bothering to dodge. Instead, he swung his massive sword down at the serpent's huge head as it zoomed right at him, horrible black fangs bared horribly. His golden blade slashed through the middle of the beast's nose, even as that very nose rammed into him, sending him flying backward into his throne. Which, being quite sturdy, didn't budge.

And, seeing as how he was wearing a magical crown and the magical uniform of a damn king, he barely felt the blow. What's more, he'd quite conveniently fallen to sit on the seat.

"Ha!" he cried out, watching as Fang jerked back. Its upper jaw was split in two, and oozed black blood. Or perhaps it was ink. Pravus stood with great difficulty from his throne, waving his sword menacingly at the creature. "You've split," he declared valiantly. "Now it's time for you to run."

But Fang did not split and run. Instead, the serpent lunged at him again. And this time, the damn beast was a bit too quick for Pravus, smashing into him before he could wind up for a proper slashing. He flew backward, slamming into the wall beside the throne with a *whump*.

Which again, he didn't feel. But a bit of the snake's inky blood had spattered the front of his uniform. Which was *irritating*.

"Very well," he decided, limping forward fearlessly. "No more mister nice monarch. Die, villain!"

He charged at the serpent, winding up for a powerful horizontal slash. But his legs defied his commands, nearly giving out underneath him, and the serpent swung its tail across the floor in a sweeping motion to trip him up. Pravus leapt over it...or at least he tried to. For while it would have normally been an easy feat, today was leg day. And leg day had a way of transforming ease into impossibility.

As such, Pravus's leap was more of a wobbly hop, and Fang's tail struck him on the ankles, sending him falling onto his left shoulder with another *whump*.

Pravus grunted, scrambling rather unheroically to his feet.

"I could watch this *all* day," Zella mused, flashing an irritating smirk. Which had its effect, irritating Pravus. He glared at her. Irritably. Then he realized that his royal guards were still standing there, staring wide-eyed at the creature instead of doing their jobs.

"Are you my guards or am I yours?" he snapped at them. Which snapped them out of their collective inaction. They unsheathed their swords, inching toward the serpent. All whilst glancing at Pravus, clearly waiting for him to take the initiative.

Which, being a kingly sort, he did.

"Attack!" he cried, hobbling toward the serpent again. Fang performed another tail-sweep, but this time Pravus swung his sword at the creature's tail instead. The blade sliced right through, cutting it in two. "Ha!" he exclaimed triumphantly, even as Fang's stump spurted black blood. And then immediately stumbled backward as those spurts spurted all over him. The blood was surprisingly cool, room temperature even. And awfully sticky.

And it smelled like...ink.

"Bravo little king," Zella congratulated, clapping her hands with disrespectful slowness. And then she lifted her arms up into the air...and Fang levitated upward above her, then descended and shrank to merge with her skin again as a tattoo.

"You're next," Pravus warned, wiping ink off his face.

"Oh *really*," Zella replied.

Then the snake-tattoo rose from her flesh again...and from it grew Fang. But to Pravus's surprise, the serpent was utterly whole, its wounds magically healed. Fang loomed over Zella, hissing menacingly at Pravus...and causing Pravus's guards to backpedal slowly away from it.

"Ignore the serpent," Pravus commanded. "Kill the wizard!"

The guards hesitated, clearly waiting for him to charge. He rolled his eyes, then did just that, charging as best he could at Zella Trek. Fang coiled himself around her, protecting her with his thick serpentine body, then rammed his forehead into Pravus, even as Pravus thrust his sword deep into the creature's skull.

The blow made Pravus stumble backward, and tore his sword from his hands. Fang retracted his impaled head, Pravus's sword still sticking out of it. Then he swung his tail in a circular sweep, knocking down every last one of Pravus's pointless guards.

Fang retracted back into his tattoo-form then, depositing Pravus's sword into Zella's hands. She strolled forward then, not toward Pravus...but toward Desmond, who backed away...until he'd been backed into a wall. She stopped before him, pressing the tip of the sword rather ungently against his chest. The tip cut through the poor man's clothes easily, shoving an inch or so into his flesh.

"Ow," Desmond complained.

"Aww," Zella pouted. "Does it hurt?"

"A bit," Desmond confirmed.

"Leave him alone!" Pravus commanded, getting to his feet rather clumsily. For his deadlifts had deadened his legs.

"Why should I?" Zella inquired, shoving the tip in a bit further. Desmond grimaced.

"You...remind me of...my wife," he told her, gasping in pain.

"Unhand him at once," Pravus warned, struck with a sudden surge of rage. "Or I'll make it my life's mission to destroy you!"

"Tell me where Chauncy Little is," Zella countered, twisting the blade a bit. Desmond groaned, sinking to his butt on the floor. "Or I'll kill this little old man."

"Do it and I'll..." Pravus began.

"Chauncy's location," Zella snapped, her tone suddenly ice-cold. She twisted the blade further, blood pouring from around the tip of the blade. Desmond howled in agony.

"Desmond!" Pravus gasped in horror, hobbling toward his advisor. Zella put up a hand to stop him.

"Come any closer and I'll shove it all the way in," she warned. Pravus froze on the spot. "Chauncy's location," she repeated.

"I cannot betray the Chosen Ones," he protested.

"Then you'll be betraying him," Zella replied, gesturing at Desmond.

"Chauncy..." Desmond gasped.

"Desmond, I..." Pravus began.

"...lives in Southwick, a city beyond the Gate," Desmond revealed. "In Borrin."

"Desmond!" Pravus gasped in horror. Zella smirked, pulling out of Desmond...and leaving a bloody mess behind. She tossed the sword onto the floor before Pravus with a clatter.

"Well, at least *someone* here has good sense," she declared. She turned to Pravus. "A shame it wasn't you," she added. "Your father was a *far* better king, by the way."

With that, she turned about, and Fang un-merged from her skin, growing to full size before her. She got on him, riding on his back...right out of the throne room. Pravus's royal guards just watched her go, wide-eyed and utterly useless. Which Pravus knew was probably good sense. For if he couldn't defeat her, they wouldn't stand a chance.

He turned back to Desmond.

"Are you all right?" Pravus asked. Desmond clutched at his bleeding chest, giving him a pained look.

"I've been penetrated, sire."

"I see that," Pravus replied.

"Against my will," Desmond added.

"Yes."

"So no," Desmond concluded. "I'm not alright."

"Fetch the doctor!" Pravus commanded, addressing no one in particular. And everyone present, being appropriately guilty about their collective cowardice, hurried to make it up to him. "Will you live, Desmond?"

"I'm afraid so," Desmond answered.

"Why did you do that?" Pravus pressed, his irritation with his part-time advisor returning. "Why did you betray Chauncy?"

Desmond gave a rare, sad smile.

"So you wouldn't have to, my liege," he replied.

"But now that...*witch* knows where he is!" Pravus complained.

"Indeed sir," Desmond agreed, seeming inappropriately fine with this.

"That's bad," Pravus pointed out.

"If you think so."

"I do," Pravus replied. Which meant a lot, because he was king. He paused. "You don't?"

"I don't, sire."

"Well why not?" Pravus demanded.

"For one, Chauncy is a Chosen One," Desmond explained. "One who defeated The Dark One and Gavin Merrick."

"True," Pravus conceded.

"Who better to defeat Zella Trek?" Desmond inquired. Pravus furrowed his brow, considering this.

"Indeed," he conceded. Reluctantly, because he was still miffed that Zella had gotten what she wanted. Without consent, which was rude.

"And seeing as how we know where she'll be going," Desmond continued, "...we can organize sufficient aid to defeat her."

Pravus's eyebrows went up, and he stood up as abruptly as he could.

"Which means *I* can come to Chauncy's aid!" he realized, his heart filling with heroic joy. "By the gods Desmond, you're right!"

"Again," Desmond agreed.

"I'll ready my dragon at once," he declared valiantly. "With my help...and my sword," he added, limping to retrieve it, "...Zella Trek will be brought to justice!"

# Chapter 10

It was late afternoon by the time Chauncy woke from his slumber, all snuggled up in his sleeping bag. And, with Chaos safely out of earshot – and having deferred responsibility for the baby's care to others – it'd been a gloriously uninterrupted slumber. Such that, when Chauncy got to his feet, stretching his arms up overhead whilst gazing at the sun hanging over the horizon, he felt quite wonderfully fine.

"Hello day," he greeted, smiling happily. He even waved to the sun, not caring if it made him look like an idiot. For the trials of life were far easier to bear when one was well-rested, including the trial of public humiliation.

Chauncy gathered his sleeping bag, then walked back over the bridge to where the others had set up a kind of camp. They'd built a little campfire at the foot of the bridge near the road, with Rocky, Rooter, Valtora, and Peter circled around it. Sweet little Chaos Little was lying swaddled in a gloriously pink blanket – atop an equally pink blanket – and was awake, but content to just be. As was Chauncy, who sat down beside Valtora, flashing her a loving smile.

"Hey there, poopy-dooz," he greeted.

"Hey there, Chauncy," she replied, leaning in for a kiss. A kiss that he relished, for it was warm and soft and quickly became terribly inappropriate, what with the addition of tongue. Chauncy melted into it, giving as good as he got until she pulled away.

"Hot damn," he murmured, gazing at her in adoration.

"Damn right," she agreed, tossing her hair. Which provided every last bit of data to prove her right.

"Daaaaaammm," Rocky breathed, clearly impressed.

"Feel better?" Valtora asked.

"*Oh* yeah," Chauncy replied. "I guess I just needed some sleep."

"Well duh," Valtora said. "Next time, tell me."

"I felt guilty."

"Pffft," she shot back. "I want you to tell me you're going to f'ing go to sleep, or you'll murder me and little Chaos, and set fire to the house, and take a dump on our charred bodies before you bury them in shallow graves."

"Um…okay," he agreed. "I'll tell you when I'm tired." Which was a reasonable compromise, in his view.

"Pussy."

"You can't say that," he protested.

"Why not?"

"It's inappropriate," he explained.

She rolled her eyes, in clear disrespect of his respectful opinion. "Let's go," she prompted.

And with that, Valtora mounted Peter. In a remarkably agile maneuver, now that her groin was back in working order. Rocky got on all fours, and Chauncy climbed up onto his back, sitting cross-legged on it and riding him, with Rooter at his side. In this way, they continued forward in their journey, following the road as it meandered through the land. To where, Chauncy hadn't a clue. But he knew well enough that Imperius Fanning's gut was inevitably right, and that whatever he was doing, it was probably what he *should* be doing.

So Chauncy trusted that whatever he was doing was precisely what he was supposed to be doing, and that in the end, everything was going to be alright.

Thus they continued on their journey, following the road as it wound through the kingdom of Pravus. Rocky's broad back swayed as the giant carried them forward, and Chauncy found himself eyeing the plant on Rooter's head as it bobbed and swayed.

"Skibbard!" he blurted out suddenly, making Rooter jump.

"Huh?" Valtora replied from ahead, bouncing up and down on Peter. Rocky sped up so that he was right beside Peter, so Chauncy and Valtora could talk.

"We should find Skibbard," he explained. "Maybe he can help with…well, whatever it is we're doing."

"Nah," she replied.

"Why not?" he asked.

"Don't you remember what he did the last time we needed his help?" she inquired. He frowned.

"I mean, not specifically."

"Right," she agreed. "Because he didn't do anything."

"Yes he did," Chauncy protested.

"Nope."

"Sure he did," he insisted. "He saved me from those goblins."

"I mean other than that," she said. Chauncy paused, thinking it over.

"I guess you're right," he admitted, though he felt a little bad saying it. "How about Harry and Nettie?" he proposed. "We could definitely use their help."

"Oh right," Valtora replied. "They're probably at the Isle of Mundus." Which apparently was an island where the Order of Mundus, a super-powerful group of super-powerful magicians, was located. Including Imperius Fanning.

"Right," Chauncy agreed. Then he frowned. "Where's that?"

"Shrug," she replied. With a shrug.

"Well shoot," he said. "Well…how do we find out?"

"Pretty sure King Pravus would know," Valtora reasoned. "We could go to Cumulus."

"Cumulus?"

"The capitol of the kingdom," she clarified.

"Ah," he replied. Then he paused. "Where's that?"

"I know the way," she reassured him. "The Dark One was always making plans to annihilate Cumulus."

"Makes sense," he replied. "Well then," he added, gesturing at her. "Lead the way, m'Lady."

"Yes m'Lord," she replied, batting her eyes at him.

And with that, they began their journey to Cumulus, Valtora leading the way. Chauncy gazed at her as they rode side-by-side, Peter matching pace with Rocky. Just seeing her made him smile with happiness and pride, for despite all odds, she'd agreed to be his bride.

"Poopy-dooz," he prompted.

"Yes?"

"I was thinking, since we've done the whole bastard thing," he began. "Um…when would you like to get married?"

"Eh."

"You don't care?" he pressed, feeling rather disappointed in her lack of excitement.

"Nope."

"But…why not?" he asked.

"I was married to The Dark One," she explained. "And I hated the last three years of it. Marriage doesn't mean anything if you've already been married," she added. "It's just legal bullshit. A business contract."

"Um…oh," he mumbled. For he held an entirely different view.

"It's the relationship that matters," she continued, beaming him a smile. "I want to be with you for as long as I want to."

"For the rest of our lives?" he asked hopefully.

"How should I know?" she answered with a shrug. He frowned, feeling increasingly ill-at-ease. But Valtora turned forward, smiling happily as she rode Peter, her diamond hand glittering in the afternoon sun. It was clear that she was done with this particular conversation, even if Chauncy wasn't.

So, rather too soon after he'd recovered from assuming he was a terrible father, Chauncy found himself wondering if Valtora truly wanted to be his wife. He didn't have long to ruminate over this monumentally depressing thought, however. For on the road ahead was a large black carriage pulled by a large black horse, stopped sideways on the road. Such that it blocked said road.

"Uh oh," Chauncy warned, gripping his staff tightly. For black was the color of bad, at least according to every book he'd ever read. "Hold up Rocky," he ordered. "We've got company."

The stone giant stopped, as did Peter and Valtora. They all stared at the beastly carriage. It was impossible to see inside, as the windows were mirrored, showing only their reflections.

Chauncy jumped off Rocky's side, stabbing the butt of his staff down in mid-air. The resulting downward blast of air slowed his fall – whilst rippling his robe – such that he landed quite bad-assedly on the street. At the same time, Valtora vaulted valiantly from Peter's back, then began striding toward the carriage, her diamond fist clenched into…well, a fist. Rocky rose from all fours to a standing position, towering twenty feet tall, and even Peter posed, the perfect picture of a powerful stallion.

"Ready?" Chauncy asked them, striking a wizardly pose.

"Ready," Valtora confirmed.

"Yaaaah," Rocky agreed. Peter neighed, and even Chaos cooed.

And with that, the door to the oversized carriage opened, and their enemy emerged to face them:

A rather robust elderly woman with short, curly white hair, dressed in a blue shirt and white pants, with two big jugs of water at her hips…and behind her, a tall and bent slender old man dressed in a brown shirt and pants, wearing his signature vest of stones and such. The woman crossed her arms over her considerable bosom, glaring at them…while the old man peered at them from over slightly crooked silver glasses.

"Ready for what?" the woman demanded. "Gettin' yer asses kicked?"

Chauncy dropped his pose, breaking out into a huge smile.

"Nettie!" he cried, rushing up to her and giving her a hug. "Harry!" he added, giving the old wizard a hug too. "What are you doing here?"

"Hold on kid," Nettie told him, pushing him aside and making her way up to Valtora. "This yours?" she asked, eyeing Chaos.

"Yep," Valtora confirmed. "We made him," she added.

"Don't I know it," Nettie grumbled. For it was likely she'd been nearby when they had, almost certainly back on Mount Thrall. "Give 'er here," she prompted, holding out her hands and wiggling her fingers. Valtora took the baby out of her wrap, handing him to Nettie. Who looked down at him and made a face. "Well aren't you an ugly little shit," she mused, rocking him gently.

"He's my ugly-ass baby," Valtora agreed proudly.

"What's his name?" Nettie asked.

"Chaos," Valtora replied.

Nettie blinked, staring at Valtora blankly.

"What?" she blurted out.

"Chaos," Valtora repeated.

"Chaos Little," Chauncy added. Nettie stared at Valtora for a bit longer, then whirled on Chauncy.

"Chauncy!" she complained. "Why'n the hell did you let her name your kid that?"

"Um…I sort of came up with it," Chauncy confessed, blushing a bit.

"Oh did ya now?"

"It just came to me," he insisted. "Like…magic."

"Bet Chaos felt like magic coming outta ya too," Harry piped in, with a devilish grin.

"Shut up Harry," Nettie grumbled. "I'm tryin' to tell these idiots that they're idiots." She eyed Chauncy and Valtora. "You're idiots!"

With that, Chaos began to cry.

"Now ya done it," Harry said. Nettie shot him a look, then handed the baby back to Valtora.

"So anyway, what're you guys doing here?" Chauncy asked.

"Heard you were in deep shit," Nettie replied. "Came to help dig you out of it."

"I mean, not in *deep* shit," Chauncy countered. Nettie's eyebrows rose.

"You got Zella Trek after you?" she inquired.

"Well yeah."

"Then you're definitely in deep shit," Nettie concluded. "The deepest pile of shit that's ever been shat," she added non-reassuringly.

"Why?" Chauncy asked.

"If you thought The Dark One was bad, you ain't see nothin' yet," Nettie answered. "Zella Trek is a crazy, psycho, murderous little bitch," she added.

"Got that in common, don'tcha?" Harry quipped, grinning down at Nettie.

"We both do," Valtora agreed.

"...and she's also one of the most powerful wizards in the world," Nettie continued, ignoring them both. "And she just so happens to really *really* want you dead."

"But why?" Chauncy asked. "I didn't do anything to her."

"Your daddy did," Nettie retorted. "Hell hath no fury like a woman scorned, kid. And Zella Trek? She's your daddy's wife."

# Chapter 11

Chauncy stood in the middle of the road, staring at Nettie.

"Huh?" he asked.

"The wizard that wants you dead is your daddy's crazy, psycho wife," Nettie told him.

"My dad had a wife?"

"*Has* a wife," Nettie corrected. "Didn't Imperius tell you anything?"

Chauncy hesitated, then shrugged.

"Zella Trek is your father's wife," Nettie repeated. "She's a wizard, like your father was. And she *hated* your father after he left her. For your mother, in fact."

Chauncy just stared at her. Blankly.

"Your dad left Zella after he met your mother," Nettie explained. "Fell in love with your mum, or so they say. Zella was pissed, but your dad…disappeared. So she wants her damn revenge."

"Against me?" Chauncy asked.

"Right," Nettie replied. "She knows it'll get your daddy's undies in a twist if she kills you."

"Wait," Valtora interjected. "Chauncy's dad is alive?"

"Ish," Nettie replied.

"Ish?" Chauncy asked.

"Ish," Nettie confirmed.

"What does 'ish' mean?" Chauncy pressed.

"More alive than dead," she answered. Chauncy blinked.

"Huh?" he asked.

"Point is, you're in deep trouble," Nettie told him. "And you'll need all the help you can get if you want to beat that crazy bitch. Otherwise she's gonna beat you."

"Doesn't sound so bad," Harry mused. "Maybe she'll beat me first."

"Go beat yourself," Nettie retorted.

"Guess I had that comin'," he replied with a mischievous grin.

"*Any*way," Nettie continued. "Zella's a damn powerful wizard."

83

"Better than my Chauncy?" Valtora countered.

"Yep," Nettie confirmed.

"Oh," Valtora mumbled. Then she frowned. "Better than you?"

"Afraid so," Nettie answered. Which clearly made Valtora happy to hear.

"Better than Harry?" Chauncy piped in. Nettie glanced at Harry, who just shrugged.

"Beats me," he replied. With another grin. Nettie elbowed him in the side, then yelped, rubbing her elbow.

"Why ya gotta be so hard all the time?" she accused.

"Haven't been beaten yet," Harry replied.

"Shut up Harry!"

And, ever the agreeable sort, Harry did just that.

"So what's the plan?" Chauncy asked.

"How the hell should I know?" Nettie retorted, putting her hands on her hips. "Imperius told us you were in trouble, so we came to help."

"Thanks," Chauncy replied with a smile. He was filled with a sudden affection for the two geriatric wizards. They'd been through thick and thin together, after all. And together, they'd managed to save the world not once, but twice. The first time by saving magic, and the last time by defeating The Dark One.

"What was *your* plan?" Nettie inquired.

"We were going to Cumulus," Valtora answered. Nettie frowned.

"Now why'n the hell would you go there?" she asked.

"To get help finding the Order of Mundus," Valtora replied.

"Why?"

"To find you two," Valtora answered.

"Well you found us," Nettie stated, putting her hands on her hips.

"*We* found *you*," Valtora argued.

"We found each other," Harry reasoned. Which unfortunately was correct. Unfortunate because it nipped Valtora's line of argumentation in the bud, so to speak. To her clear disappointment.

"Anyway, if we're gonna beat Zella Trek, we'd better get going," Nettie prompted. Chauncy frowned.

"Get going where?" he asked.

"Where else?" Nettie shot back. He paused, then shrugged. "The Great Wood," she told him. "And then the Cave of Wonder."

"What? Why?" Chauncy pressed.

"Why else?" Nettie retorted. "It's prophecy and shit."

"Stealing my lines," Valtora grumbled. For it was clear she'd been about to say it.

"No it isn't," Chauncy argued. "Imperius didn't say we needed to go to the Great Wood *or* the Cave of Wonder this time."

"Then what did he say?" Nettie asked.

"Um…nothing," he answered. "Just that she was coming for me and that she was going to try to kill me."

"Well that's what he told us," Nettie said.

"He's very consistent," Harry noted.

"Shut up Harry."

"Okie dokie," Harry agreed. Which wasn't technically shutting up, but ensured that he would in the near future.

"Well I don't care if he didn't tell you to do it," Nettie declared, crossing her arms over her chest. "When you don't know what to do, go to the Cave of Wonder. Which is in the Great Wood. So we're going there…unless any of you got a better idea."

Chauncy glanced at Valtora, who shrugged.

"That's what I thought," Nettie declared. "Come on you two," she added, hobbling back to the carriage. "Let's go."

* * *

So it was that Chauncy found himself riding atop Rocky's back with Rooter, Valtora riding Peter, and Nettie in the carriage with little Chaos Little. For Nettie had insisted on holding the baby for a bit. Chauncy had caught her snorting Chaos's little neck before going inside the carriage, much as Valtora had. Although as to why, he hadn't a clue.

Being thusly separated, they traveled in silence, which was just fine by Chauncy. It'd been a good nine months since he'd gone on his last adventure, and he found it rather nice to get away from the shop for a while. Onward they went, passing through another village, then continuing onward. The sun drifted toward the horizon, eventually dipping below it…which meant that it was time to make camp.

They did so in the usual fashion, Chauncy helping Harry pitch two tents, then setting up a crackling campfire. One that was soon blazing merrily. Everyone sat 'round it, and even Peter laid down on his side to enjoy its warmth. For a campfire was a wondrous thing, its magic the power to bring people together, so warm was its…well,

85

warmth, and so hypnotic were its flickering flames. In this way, humans weren't that different than moths in being drawn to fire. Except that humans, thankfully, didn't throw themselves blindly into it.

"Remember when we roasted that harpy?" Valtora asked with a grin, clearly thinking along the same lines. But while Chauncy had naturally approached the campfire in a philosophically pleasant way, Valtora had not...as per the usual.

"See, a hero wouldn't smile at that," he protested.

"But one did," she pointed out, her eyes brightening.

"A typical hero wouldn't," he corrected.

"Well I'm hardly typical," she said, executing a perfect slow-motion hair-toss. One that immediately halted the conversation. For her patented hair-flings were more hypnotic than even campfires.

"Sure missed that," Harry breathed. Nettie blinked, the spell broken by his interruption. She glared at him.

"Keep your eyes to yourself, ya lousy creep," she grumbled.

"I can't do that," Harry replied.

"Why the hell not?"

"'Cause then I wouldn't be able to see you," he explained, wrapping a long arm around her shoulders. She smiled despite herself, snuggling up against him.

"You're just trying to get in my pants," she accused.

"Is it working?" he asked hopefully.

"You'll find out soon enough," she assured him.

"Oh boy," he said, rubbing his hands together eagerly. While waggling his eyebrows at Chauncy, a twinkle in his eye. Thankfully Chauncy's brain was too tired to conjure visions of what the old couple was referring to. In fact, while his afternoon nap had recharged him for a short while, its effects had suddenly vanished.

"I'm going to bed," he declared, standing up. Nettie's brow furrowed.

"Aren't you gonna eat first?" she asked. The question immediately brought Chauncy to a bad place in his brain. To a darkness he'd only recently learned existed...one where he was capable of harming a sweet, lovable baby. Valtora must've spotted this sudden psychosis in his eyes, for she immediately stood, pushing Chauncy toward the tent.

"Go on babe," she urged. "I'll save you some food for later."

Chauncy stormed off to his tent, throwing open the door flap and stomping up to his sleeping bag. Then he stomped back to the flap, making sure it was good and closed. That done – the world safely separated from his evil mood – Chauncy went to sleep.

* * *

When Chauncy woke, it was morning. To his surprise, for he'd expected to be woken by Chaos's cries. But it was awfully bright in his tent – and what's more, neither Valtora or Chaos were in it. He got up, stretched, and emerged from his tent. To his further surprise, the sun was shining in a bright blue sky, quite a bit farther above the horizon than he would've expected.

And to his delight, he felt absolutely, gosh-darn *marvelous.*

"Hello day," he greeted, beaming a smile at it all.

Rocky was sitting by the campfire, throwing a rock straight up, then catching it, while Rooter and Peter were nowhere to be found. Harry was by the carriage at the side of the road some fifty feet away, cleaning the windshield while whistling a warbly tune. But Valtora and Nettie were missing. Chauncy immediately suspected they were in Nettie's tent, and strolled up to it.

"Valtora?" he called out. After which a baby began to scream.

The flap to the tent flung open, and Valtora stormed out of it, a screaming Chaos in her hands. Her hair was uncharacteristically frazzled, her eyes crazy. Like, psychotic. She shoved Chaos into Chauncy's arms, being not at all gentle about it, then whirled about, vanishing right back into the tent.

Chauncy stood there, staring at the tent, then lowered his gaze to Chaos. The baby's little face was all scrunched up and awfully red, his little hands curled into fists.

"Aww," Chauncy cooed, bouncing up and down a little. "It's okay little guy."

A moment later, Valtora re-emerged from the tent, pointing one shaky diamond finger at him. Or rather, at the baby.

"Get the *fuck* away from here!" she screamed.

Chauncy froze. Which was precisely the opposite of what he'd been told to do. But unfortunately, he was the type of person that choked in an emergency, while braver souls sprung into action.

"FUCKING GO!" she shrieked, balling her hand into a glittering fist.

"All right all right," Nettie soothed, emerging from the tent and gently dragging Valtora back into it. "Get some sleep," she urged. Then she emerged from the tent, closing the flap-door behind her.

"Wha…" Chauncy began, but Nettie shot him a warning look, gesturing for him to skedaddle. Which he did. She followed behind him, until they were by the carriage with Harry. Who was still cleaning it.

"Y'know that dark cesspool your mind was in yesterday?" Nettie asked Chauncy.

"Yeah."

"Well your girlfriend's there right now," she warned. "She stayed up all night with Chaos, so you could get some sleep."

"Oh."

"Oh is right," she grumbled. "She broke around midnight."

"Broke what?" Chauncy asked.

"Chaos's arm," Nettie answered.

Chauncy blinked.

"Huh?"

"She broke his arm," she repeated. "With her diamond hand. Squeezed too tight when she got frustrated and couldn't calm him down."

"You can't be serious," Chauncy protested, looking down at poor Chaos with concern. But the baby was asleep, perhaps lulled by their escape to the carriage. "His arm doesn't *look* broken."

"That's 'cause I got Rooter to fix it," Nettie told him. "I spent the whole rest of the night in that tent with her making sure she didn't do somethin' worse."

"Why didn't she just have you take care of him?"

"Do I look like I make milk?" she retorted. "My tits dried up decades ago."

"Breasts," he protested automatically.

"Whatever."

He gazed down at his son, swallowing past a lump in his throat…and hardly believing his ears. To think that Valtora – his sweet, adorable girlfriend! – could've done something so terrible to a poor, sweet baby…

Well, he couldn't exactly blame her, considering the awful things *he'd* had nearly done.

"I should've stayed up with her," he muttered, kicking himself.

"Then you both would've been useless today," Nettie retorted. "We need a plan to let you two get your rest, or that poor baby ain't gonna make it past the age of…well, today."

"I can't believe it," he mumbled, shaking his head. Tears welled up in his eyes. "I thought I'd be a good dad. And that Valtora would make such a good mom. But…"

"You're useless when you're tired and Valtora's got a temper…and a diamond hand that crushes stones," Nettie interjected. "And bones, unfortunately. Problem is, you're regular parents with irregular powers."

"That's not an excuse," he protested.

"Don't need an excuse," Nettie retorted. "You got a choice, kid. You either focus on the problem or you focus on solving it. The first one means giving up and the second one means giving it another go…and most people go with option one."

Chauncy grit his teeth, then nodded.

"Alright," he agreed. "What do I do?"

"You're the kid's father," she replied. "You figure it out."

"But…how?" he asked. She turned about and hobbled away, back toward Chauncy's tent.

"Quit acting like you're helpless," she shot back. "You're a wizard, remember?"

Chauncy stared at her retreating back, then gazed down at Chaos.

"I *am* a wizard," he realized. And also realized that he'd consistently forgotten that fact. A lifetime of living an ordinary life had blinded him to the extraordinary, such that he needed to rediscover it from time to time. "What I need is magic," he told himself.

And whenever Chauncy needed magic, why, he went for a walk.

"I'll be back," he told Harry, who was polishing a wheel.

"Okie dokie," the old man replied good-naturedly. As if he hadn't just heard that Valtora had broken a baby's bones.

So, with Chaos in his arms, that's precisely what Chauncy did.

# Chapter 12

A walk was a strange thing, in that it involved merely putting one foot in front of the other. As a way of getting from point "A" to point "B," it was rather slow and inefficient, at least compared to a carriage. But when there was no "B" to get to, a walk had the curious power of allowing Chauncy to just...well, *be*.

And that, he supposed, was where the magic was. In being where he was, doing what he was doing. Where and what that was...was beside the point. Magic wasn't found over the next hill, or sometime in the future. It wasn't something found at the end of a search, or a power that completing some trial would allow.

It was, according to The Magic of Magic, Here and Now.

Chauncy smiled, shifting to holding little Chaos with his right arm while reaching into his robe pocket with his left. He drew out the book he'd taken from the Cave of Wonder, gazing at its glittering, purple, rather ridiculous cover. For its title was so large the words fell partly off the page. Perhaps because the magic of magic could not be contained in a mere book. Or maybe because it was a subject too large to cover. With a cover.

He had half a mind to stop to read the book, but with Chaos in his arm, he found it too cumbersome. So back in the pocket it went.

They'd traveled quite far off the beaten path, so to speak, to a small forest. Chauncy enjoyed the sun warming his skin and the breeze affectionately ruffling his hair. His arms, however, were getting quite tired, burning after carrying Chaos for so long. For though the little tyke weighed next to nothing, next to nothing got heavier the longer it was held. Thus, what had once been a joy became a burden...not only for Chauncy's body, but for his peace of mind.

"Well this is irritating," he grumbled, stopping his walk to switch arms yet again. Then he sighed. "Guess we'd both better sit down," he decided. So he did, putting Chaos in his lap. "Much better," he stated.

He sighed, looking down at the little tyke…and was surprised to find that the little tyke was looking right back at him. With a very skeptical look. Still, it was awfully cute, even though Chaos was awfully ugly.

"Hi there," he greeted, waving a little. Chaos just stared at him. Not even blinking, for a rather disturbingly long time. "I'm your daddy," he added.

Chaos's face scrunched up in a furious frown.

"I know," Chauncy said. "I'd be nervous too."

Then Chaos's face turned bright red…and he farted. With a little pop from his bum that Chauncy felt in his lap.

"Oh," he mumbled.

Then he smelled it.

"Oh!" he blurted out, squeezing his eyes shut and turning his head away. "Wo*wee!*" He held his breath for a bit, then took an exploratory sniff. To his relief, the worst was over…and Chaos seemed perfectly content.

Then they just sat there, doing a whole lot of nothing.

At first Chauncy felt a bit antsy, and had to resist the urge to get up and keep walking. Instead, he studied the trees around him. They were tall but with relatively thin trunks, and last year's leaves had broken into a blanket of brown bits that covered the forest floor. Partially buried roots squiggled through the earth like veins bulging out of the back of a thin man's hand. Spots of sunlight struck the ground, swaying with the leaves.

It was all very peaceful and quite ordinary, the landscape of the wild. Which was not so much wild as it was uncontrolled by man. For the wild was in fact orderly and complex in a way that was beyond human comprehension. Any attempt to control it and shape it merely simplified it, by destroying most of its marvelous complexity…and as a result, losing what made it special. The most humans could do was try to emulate nature, jealous as they were of its accomplishments; perhaps in a thousand years, they might get close. But nature was here and now, and the fact that humans hadn't created it did not lessen its splendor.

It was in this philosophical frame of mind that Chauncy found himself when he lowered his gaze to nature's newest accomplishment: little Chaos. The boy was staring up at him with light brown eyes, his little hands resting on his belly. And in that moment, Chauncy saw him as he'd seen the trees and their roots, and the carpet of leafy bits on the ground. As something quite utterly extraordinary, beyond his comprehension. Something he'd had a part in making, but without a clue as to the how. Chaos had grown out of Valtora but *of* her and him. In a way, he *was* them, a continuation of their lives in one being. A way to go on living after they'd died.

"Why, I'll live forever," he realized, a chill running down his spine. "Not as me, but as something new."

He smiled, picking Chaos up and holding the boy against his chest, facing outward.

"This is the world," he told Chaos. "There's so much to do. And if you open your heart to it, one day it'll bring out the magic in you."

With that, he felt a sudden, inexplicable connection with this moment, with his son in his arms. As if his heart was pouring into the boy, even as Chaos poured into him. And as a wizard, he knew beyond a doubt that what he'd just felt was magic. To what end, he hadn't a clue, but nevertheless, it was true.

He stood then, cradling Chaos with one arm. And while it was awkward at first, that didn't bother Chauncy one bit. For he was enjoying simply *being* with his son.

"Let's go for a bit longer," he told Chaos, continuing their walk. After all, Valtora needed all the sleep she could get. He sighed then. "We're not good people when we're tired," he confessed. "I didn't realize that 'til now. I guess we have to learn how to take care of ourselves so we can take care of you."

And that meant that Chauncy had to start taking care of Valtora the way she'd been trying to take care of him.

He took a deep breath in, realizing that he had a lot of work to do, at least if he wanted to be a good father. And that required being a better boyfriend, so Valtora could be the best version of herself.

"I can do this," he told himself. "I *have* to do this."

* * *

By the time Chauncy spotted the camp in the distance, it was a bit after noon, and Chaos was furious. With a full night's sleep, Chauncy found himself remarkably patient with the boy. While each scream still grated on his nerves, they didn't provoke the blind rage he'd felt before. So it was that he found himself reciting the triple-check Valtora had taught him.

"Booty, booby, bedtime," he stated, stopping at the road by the carriage. He almost put Chaos down on the dirt, then thought better of it, continuing to the camp before setting him down on the grass. Nettie and Harry were busy putting away Chauncy's tent, while their tent was still standing. He fumbled with the diaper, finding it clean and dry. "Booby," he reminded himself, lifting his gaze to Nettie and Harry's tent, where Valtora was sure to be. "Hoo boy," he said, picking Chaos back up. For he and Valtora hadn't exactly parted on the best of terms, what with her telling him to leave in no uncertain terms. Using rather inappropriate terms, he recalled with dismay. But before he could start a bit of cowardly fingernail-biting and lip-picking, the tent flap opened and none other than Valtora herself emerged. She spotted Chauncy and Chaos, and gasped.

"Baby!" she cried, rushing up to him. Chauncy beamed at her, puckering his lips for a kiss – while unpuckering quite another part – but Valtora ignored him, grabbing Chaos and practically tearing the baby from his arms. "Oh I *missed* you my widdle pop-pop!"

"Pop-pop?" Chauncy inquired.

"He pops when he farts," she explained, putting the still-screaming baby right on her right breast. Which made the boy quite happy, naturally.

"He does," Chauncy agreed, recalling his experience back in the woods. "Death farts," he added.

"He gets it from big Mama, doesn't he?" Valtora cooed, rubbing noses with the boy. "My widdle stinky pop-pop."

"I…um, heard about Chaos's arm," Chauncy confessed. Valtora's face immediately fell.

"Sorry," she apologized. "It was my strong hand," she added, showing her glittering diamond hand. The same hand that'd murdered Marie Merrick with a single punch, and had reduced – over a period of time – the statue of Archibald Merrick to partial ruins. And that'd punched countless holes in Grandma Little's walls for Chauncy to patch up.

"It's okay," Chauncy interjected. "I get it."

"You do?" Valtora asked, biting her lip fetchingly.

"Yeah," he confirmed. "We both need to make sure we get enough sleep. We're not great parents when we're tired."

"You're not even good," Nettie corrected.

"Some would say that's a snap judgement," Harry quipped. Nettie rolled her eyes at him.

"I didn't *mean* to," Valtora argued, clutching onto Chaos protectively. As if someone else had broken his arm.

"Better keep Rooter near you," Nettie warned. "Just in case."

"Good idea," Valtora agreed.

"Considerin' Chaos's mother's a homicidal hussy," Nettie added unproductively.

"Here we go," Harry said, stuffing his hands in his pockets and settling into the moment.

"I am *not* homicidal," Valtora argued. "I didn't *kill* him."

"You killed Marie Merrick," Nettie pointed out. Valtora's eyes lit up at the memory.

"Hell *yeah* I did," she agreed happily. Then she frowned. "But I'm not a hussy."

"You probably don't even know what a hussy is," Nettie retorted.

"Sure I do," Valtora countered. "Hussy. Noun. A mischievous, impudent, or ill-behaved girl," she recited. Having memorized the dictionary long ago, for the purposes of flavoring her arguments with fancy phrases.

Nettie just arched an eyebrow.

"Well what do you know," Valtora exclaimed, her eyes brightening. "I *am* a hussy!"

"Who likes to ride Peter," Harry piped in. Peter – who had trotted up to them during their conversation – neighed a bit in agreement, tossing his gorgeous rainbow mane.

"The point is," Chauncy interjected, desperate to get back to the point, "…we need to let each other know when we're in a bad place, and take over when that happens."

"Good idea babe," Valtora agreed, beaming a smile at him. She leaned in for a kiss, and Chauncy happily obliged her. The kiss quickly turned into one more suited to the bedroom, as it usually did with Valtora.

"Break it up," Nettie grumbled. Valtora broke away, but gave Chauncy a very naughty look.

"My coochie's all better," she reminded him.

"Mine too," he replied with a smile. "I mean my…uh…peter."

Peter gazed down at Chauncy's…peter, giving a dismissive snort. One that made it clear that the unicorn didn't think Chauncy's peter was better at all.

"It's time to take down your tent, not pitch it," Nettie argued. "Let's pack up and go."

And that's precisely what they did. Chauncy helped Harry take down his tent, and they packed everything back in the carriage. That done, Chauncy decided to ride Rocky again, while Valtora rode

Peter, carrying Chaos in her wrap. Chauncy figured she was still guilty about breaking his arm, and wanted a little snuggling to make up for it. He was glad to see her in her usual cheerfully inappropriate spirits, and was himself feeling quite a bit better. For, after a good night's sleep – and a few hours taking care of Chaos without incident – he felt like he might just be able to handle being a father.

"You can do this," he told himself.

Assuming Zella Trek didn't kill him first, that was.

# Chapter 13

After the royal physician treated poor Desmond's wound – using a magical gel that mended his flesh before King Pravus's royal eyes – Pravus summoned Templeton and Desmond to his royal office for planning purposes. He found himself unable to sit behind his ridiculously large desk, however. Not only because it was leg day, and he'd likely have a devil of a time getting out of his chair after their business was concluded, but also because he felt himself filled to the brim with vim and vigor. And also the desire for revenge.

So, thusly spurred, Pravus pace-limped before Desmond and Templeton, his chin in his hand.

"Where's that damn fire dragon," he asked for the third time in as many minutes.

"Coming," Desmond assured. Pravus continued to pace, irritated that it hadn't arrived yet.

"It's been nearly twenty minutes since she left," he complained. And by "she" he meant Zella. "She's going to be halfway to Borrin by the time our ride gets here."

"Your ride *is* a dragon, sire," Desmond reminded him. Which was unnecessary, considering Pravus had just mentioned that fact. He shot a glare at the man.

"It is?" he replied, feigning surprise. "My god Desmond, whatever would I *do* without you?"

"You nearly found out," Desmond reminded him.

"Until you betrayed Chauncy Little in defiance of your king," Pravus snipped. "I could hang you from the rafters, you know."

"But you won't," Desmond replied, seeming disappointed by that fact.

"Fear not my liege," Templeton reassured. "The fire dragon will be here any moment now, and then we'll ride him all the way to Borrin to roast that villain!"

"Indeed Templeton," Pravus agreed, even smiling a bit. Templeton's indomitable cheer never failed to soften his heart…while hardening matters further south. "With you at my side, I have no fear of failure!"

"I'll be right behind you," Templeton vowed.

"Where you can serve me best," Pravus agreed.

"In any case," Desmond interrupted, "…our emissary to the Order of Mundus has already departed, and should arrive at the Order in a few weeks."

"They'll be late for the execution," Pravus grumbled.

"A backup plan, sire," Desmond replied. "In case the unthinkable happens."

"The unthinkable?" Pravus inquired.

"Failure," Desmond clarified.

"The thought hadn't crossed my mind," Pravus retorted.

"That's why it's the unthinkable, sire," Desmond replied evenly. "It's something you wouldn't think of."

"I'm offended *you* would," Pravus argued, still feeling snippy. He probably needed to eat, he realized. After a workout, if he *didn't* eat, he turned into an utter monster. Rageful and all that. Why, he positively *picked* fights while in such a state, unlike his usual self.

"I'm your advisor," Desmond countered calmly. "It's my job to think of things you wouldn't think of."

"Quite," Templeton agreed cheerily. "And we're grateful for it, old boy!"

"Hrmph," Pravus harrumphed. Desmond eyed him critically.

"Would a sandwich help your temper?" he inquired knowingly.

"In a bit," Pravus answered. "I'm enjoying my *exceedingly* evil thoughts toward you at the moment."

"I exist to serve," Desmond droned.

"Violent thoughts," he added unnecessarily.

"I understand, my liege."

"Do you?" Pravus inquired, itching for a fight.

"I do," Desmond declared.

"Do tell," Pravus pressed.

"I have them toward my wife," the old man explained. Pravus arched an eyebrow.

"How often?"

"Whenever I think of her," Desmond answered.

"Ah."

This admission subdued Pravus's ire. And while he hated to see it go – there was something terribly pleasurable about entertaining one's rage, particularly when hungry – go it did. He sighed, stopping his pacing and crossing his ridiculously developed forearms over his perfectly proportioned pecs. He was about to complain once again about the fire dragon's absence when the floor rumbled under his feet, a muffled *boom* following soon after.

"And there's our ride!" Templeton exclaimed.

"To the fire dragon!" Pravus commanded. And promptly strode out of the office. Or rather, limp-strode out. Templeton joined him with a similar post-leg day waddle…one that Desmond could keep up with, for once. "On this day, we'll strike back against that villain Zella Trek," Pravus vowed. "And save the man who saved the world!"

# Chapter 14

It took the usual amount of time for Chauncy and the others to reach the Great Wood, this being their fifth time visiting it. Chauncy happened to be holding Chaos at the time, whilst perched upon Rocky's back, so as to let Valtora take a nap in the carriage with Nettie. He spotted the telltale tree line of the Great Wood a quarter-mile ahead…a sight that simply could not be missed. For not only was it the greatest source of magic in Pravus, but it was magical to behold.

The Great Wood hosted the tallest trees Chauncy had ever seen, massive beech trees with trunks easily forty feet in diameter. Their bark was like an elephant's skin, spectacularly silver. Their massive branches extended not only vertically, but also horizontally, traveling over a hundred feet from their trunks. How these branches didn't just break off under their own incredible weight was beyond Chauncy…but they didn't.

And high, high above, the trees' copper leaves danced in the breeze, forming a brilliant canopy against the bright blue of the sunny sky.

As they drew closer, more details became apparent. For each tree in the Great Wood was home to moss and lichen, to mushrooms that clung to their trunk and birds that nested in their branches. To vines and other plants whose roots plunged deep into each tree's bark. And, Chauncy knew, to a bewildering array of insects that made their home within the soil and the trees.

Life upon life upon life, all living together without anyone telling them what to do. Without a plan or an authority of any kind. It was an impromptu dance to an invisible song, done without any other purpose than to keep the music playing.

There was no other purpose for the Great Wood than the forest itself. And that, Chauncy – and every other wizard worth their salt – knew, was more than enough. It was in fact the very point that *made* a wizard…to know that, in the end, there wasn't one. And that there never needed to be.

They made it into the forest, and Harry and Nettie and Valtora abandoned the carriage. Valtora rode Peter while everyone else rode Rocky, for the road ahead was too rocky for wheels. Eventually they made it to a familiar place: a great big lake within the forest. A ways away from its shore was a familiar lean-to...the one Harry had made over a year ago, and had repaired on their last adventure.

"Still erect," Harry noted, eyeing his handiwork with a proud smile.

"Been what, nine months?" Chauncy asked.

"Gotta be some kinda record," Harry mused, flashing Nettie an impish grin. She rolled her eyes.

"Knock it off before I knock it down," she quipped.

"Not the worst thing to happen to an erection," Harry noted, rubbing his chin.

"He's got a point," Chauncy admitted reluctantly. Considering this was his third adventure with the raunchy couple, their antics didn't bother him quite as much as they used to. As long as his mind's eye didn't inexplicably join in, that was. Nettie eyed the two men.

"Now see what ya did, you old fart?" she told Harry. "You got poor Chauncy thinkin' like you."

"Like a genius?" Harry asked.

"Like an idiot," she corrected.

"An idiot savant," Harry compromised.

"No, just a plain old idiot," she insisted.

"Well I am plain," he agreed. "And old. But that's why you like me."

"It is?" Nettie asked.

"Sure," he replied with a grin. "Means we got somethin' in common."

"You little shit," she swore, punching him in the flank. Then she yelped, shaking out her hand and shooting him a vicious glare. She fingered her Wetstone necklace, for Chauncy had given the Wetstone to her. Seeing as how her magic involved water, it was far more useful in her hands than in his. "I ought to drown you."

Harry only chuckled, and Nettie joined him.

"Soooo anyway," Chauncy interjected. "What now?"

"Now you go in the Cave of Wonder," Nettie answered.

"Me?" Chauncy asked.

"Who else?" Nettie replied. "You're the one gettin' murdered, right?"

"Um…I hope not?"

"If ya don't go in the Cave of Wonder," Nettie said, "…you will be."

Chauncy sighed, then nodded, turning to Valtora and Chaos.

"Wish me luck, I guess," he told them, kissing little Chaos, then Valtora. She gave him quite the kiss, as usual, with a generous helping of tongue. Then she pulled away, giving him sexy eyes…much like the ones ZoMonsterz gave him, disturbingly. "Uh oh," he blurted out.

"What?" she asked.

"ZoMonsterz," he replied. "We forgot to leave food out for her!"

"She's a hellcat," Valtora told him. "She'll be fine. Now go," she prompted, leaning in for one last kiss. "Enjoy that cave, lover boy," she purred. "But when you're good and finished, come back to me so I can *reclaim* you."

"Uh…" he replied, not knowing quite what to say. She'd told him the same thing the last time he'd plunged into the Cave of Wonder.

"I'm practicing," she told him. "For Addie."

"Addie?"

"Mmhmm," she replied with a naughty gleam in her eye. It was only then that he recalled their conversation back at the shop.

"Not happening," he told her.

"Totally happening," she retorted.

"No it isn't," he insisted.

"Yes it is."

"I'm not arguing with you," he grumbled.

"Yes you are," she argued. Which was true.

"Well, not anymore," he replied. And with that, he turned away, striding rather irritably toward the lake. He followed its shore to the right, circling around its perimeter until he reached the rocky cliff wall at the opposite end of it. There, he found the entrance to the Cave of Wonder, a narrow slit in the wall, barely big enough to allow him to squeeze into. But squeeze he did, entering into a slightly less narrow tunnel beyond. A very dark tunnel. One that required a source of light to navigate.

Luckily, Chauncy had the Sunstone.

He reached into his robe pocket to draw it out…and realized it wasn't there. He searched about blindly for it, then felt inside of his other pocket, where The Magic of Magic book was. Still no Sunstone.

"Well crap," he blurted out.

Right as something slammed into his head.

Chauncy cried out, stumbling backward and falling out of the cave opening. It was so tight that his shoulders got wedged in it, leaving him pinned there, his arms at his sides. Utterly exposed...and helpless to defend himself.

"Crap!" he shouted. "Help!" he added.

To his horror, a figure stepped out of the shadows of the tunnel toward him.

"Help!" he cried, trying in vain to free himself from the narrow cave entrance.

The figure drew closer, looming over him menacingly...and then came fully into the light!

Chauncy *shrieked.*

It was a man, he discovered. One nearly a foot taller than Chauncy, and formidably muscular, clad in a dark gray cloak. He had long golden hair framing a strong jaw and piercing green eyes...and was rubbing his forehead vigorously.

"Ow," he complained. Then he blinked, stopping in his tracks. "Chauncy? Is that you?"

It was Chauncy's turn to blink then. And to do a very surprised double-take. He drew in a sharp gasp as realization dawned on him.

"Gavin!" he blurted out.

For it was none other than Gavin Merrick himself, the president of the Evermore Trading Company. The man who'd tried to destroy magic itself...and Chauncy's former mortal enemy.

\* \* \*

"Oh hey Chauncy," Gavin greeted, breaking out into a smile. "Sorry for bumping heads with you. Lost my torch in the cave."

Chauncy just stared at the man, his shoulders still wedged in the entrance.

"Here, let me help you," Gavin offered. "Going in or out?"

"Um...out," Chauncy decided.

Gavin grabbed Chauncy's shoulders then, easily prying him free. They both stepped into the sunlight. Chauncy stared at the man, hardly believing his eyes.

"What are you doing here?" he asked. Gavin frowned.

"You're the one who told me to come here," he reminded Chauncy.

"That was nine months ago," Chauncy retort-reminded Gavin.

"Really?"

"Really," Chauncy confirmed.

"Are you sure?" Gavin pressed, giving him a funny look.

"Quite sure," Chauncy replied. "I made a baby and delivered it since we last met."

Gavin processed this.

"Huh," he murmured. "Guess I was in there for longer than I thought. For me it's only been a couple of weeks or so."

"Really?"

"Really," Gavin confirmed. "Congratulations, by the way."

"Thanks," Chauncy replied. He eyed Gavin then, studying the man. For in the light, it was clear that Gavin was no longer wearing his green suit and golden tie, not even under his gray cloak. Instead, he seemed to be wearing a very tight knitted orange jumpsuit under a knitted gray cloak. A very *bright* knitted jumpsuit with knitted booties and knitted gloves. With a big, gray, marvelously fancy knitted "G" on in the center of his chest on his equally knitted jumpsuit.

And, within knitted scabbards on a knitted gray belt at his waist, were twin golden knitting needles.

In that moment, Chauncy did the only thing a man could do when faced with such a sight.

He stared. Hard. With his mouth agape.

"What's wrong?" Gavin asked. Chauncy paused, then pointed at him. "You'll have to be more specific," Gavin added.

"What's with the…that?" Chauncy asked, gesturing at him.

Just then, Chauncy heard splashing from behind him, and turned to see Nettie riding a large wave across the lake toward them, Harry at her side. They reached the shore, stopping a few yards from Chauncy and Gavin.

"Are you alright?" Nettie asked.

"We heard a woman screaming," Harry added.

"That was um…that was me," Chauncy replied, his cheeks burning furiously. "Gavin surprised me, that's all."

"Hell of a surprise," Nettie agreed, eyeing Gavin. She blinked…and then her mouth fell open. "What in the hell kind of getup is that?" she blurted out.

Gavin looked down at himself.

"You mean my wizard's uniform?" he asked.

"Is that what that is?" Nettie inquired.

"Looks comfortable," Harry noted.

"It is," Gavin confirmed. "I made it myself."

"Did ya now," Nettie muttered. She shook her head. "The hell happened to you in there?" she asked, gesturing at the entrance to the cave. Gavin turned to gaze at it, smiling contentedly.

"I found myself," he answered. He turned back to her. "My magic."

"If your magic's fashion," she replied, "…you might wanna take up destroying the world again."

"Catches the eye though," Harry said, eyeing Gavin's bright orange jumpsuit. "Doesn't let go, neither."

"Takes 'em hostage," Nettie agreed.

"That's right," Gavin agreed. If he was offended by their offensive comments, he didn't show it. "All my life I've done things because they were profitable," he added. "Always doing to profit from the doing. Never for the doing itself."

"So…you knit that thing because no one would buy it?" Nettie pressed.

"I knit it for the knitting," he corrected.

"I think I get it," Chauncy said, smiling at Gavin. After all, he'd felt the same way about his life before becoming a wizard. Back when he'd been selling lies instead of magic. When he'd gone to the shop day after day doing something he didn't believe in – or want to do – just so that he could profit enough to not have to do it anymore by the time he was elderly. Now he did what he did for the joy of doing it…and the profit was a pleasant bonus.

"Uh huh," Nettie grumbled, clearly not convinced. "So what now, you think you're a wizard?"

Gavin shrugged.

"I'm me," he replied. "Unreservedly."

"He rhymed," Harry pointed out. Nettie sighed.

"Guess you are," she decided. For she herself had been the one to tell Chauncy that wizards rhymed. It was the first sign of a wizard, in fact. For they played with words…just like they played with everything else.

"What are you up to?" Gavin inquired.

"Tryin' to save Chauncy's ass," Nettie answered. "Turns out Chauncy's a bastard."

"I've found him honorable," Gavin countered, in Chauncy's defense.

"They mean literally," Chauncy explained. "I'm actually a bastard."

"Ah," Gavin replied.

"His daddy cheated and knocked up his mommy, and his wife ain't happy about it," Nettie continued. "She wants her husband dead, but she can't kill him, so she's after the next best thing: Chauncy's head."

"Now *you* rhymed," Harry noted.

"Shut up, Harry," Nettie grumbled. "That's 'cause I'm a real wizard," she added. "Unlike Mr. Mittens here."

"Now now," Harry countered. "No need fer knit-picking."

"Didn't I say to shut up?"

"Must be losin' my hearing," Harry said with a grin, pointing at his ear. "Stone deaf."

"Right," Chauncy interjected. "Speaking of stones, I need to get my Sunstone," he told them. "I'll be back."

With that, he turned away from them, making his way back toward the lean-to.

"Wait," Gavin prompted. Chauncy stopped, turning around. "Do you need help defeating this…what's her name?"

"Zella Trek," Chauncy answered.

"I can be of assistance," Gavin stated. "It's the least I can do, after everything I've done."

Nettie gave him a doubtful look.

"Seeing as how knitting's yer magic," she replied, "…the least you can do is the most you can do."

Harry frowned, scratching his head at that.

"Shut up Harry," Nettie grumbled, depriving everyone of whatever reply the old man might've come up with.

"Quit needling him," he countered, choosing not to deprive everyone. She elbowed him, then yelped, rubbing her elbow.

"I don't know," Chauncy said, eyeing Gavin warily. "We're with…you know."

"Valtora?" Gavin guessed.

"Right."

Which was rather awkward, considering Valtora had murdered Gavin's wife. A bit unnecessarily, and what's more, rather gratuitously.

"My adventure within the Cave of Wonder has given me…perspective," Gavin replied. "While I cannot imagine that I would ever be friends with Valtora, I would like to think I could be friends with you, Chauncy."

"With me?" Chauncy asked. "Why?"

"You gave me a second chance at life," Gavin explained. He gestured at the entrance to the Cave of Wonder. "And you showed me magic. When I had no reason to live but revenge, you offered another way. A way that brought me peace…and happiness."

"Oh," Chauncy mumbled, not knowing what else to say. It was heady stuff, after all, and he had the feeling he didn't deserve to be honored this way. After all, he'd only done what he felt was right at the time, letting Gavin live.

"The Cave of Wonder taught me why you saved me," Gavin revealed. Chauncy blinked.

"It did?"

"That's right," Gavin confirmed with a smile. "Because you saw yourself in me. A man lost to the Borrin way of life. Empty." He paused. "A man craving magic, and not even realizing that's what he needed."

Chauncy inclined his head, not knowing what to say. It was true enough.

"As thanks, I will help you," Gavin proclaimed. "Not because it's the right thing to do, but because I truly want to."

"Rhymed again," Harry observed, eyeing Nettie significantly. She rolled her eyes.

"I appreciate it," Chauncy replied with a smile. "Guess we could use all the help we can get."

"Against Zella Trek?" Nettie said. "That's for sure."

"I'm surprised I've never heard of her, considering my former information network," Gavin stated. "Can you tell me more about her?"

"She's a wizard," Nettie explained. "Formerly of the Order of Mundus. She was accepted into the Order along with Chauncy's father, at least for a bit."

"Until my father left her?" Chauncy asked.

"Not quite," Nettie answered. "Turns out Imperius's gut told him to kick her out after your daddy knocked up your mom. She…didn't take it so well."

"What do you mean?" Chauncy pressed.

"She went full-on psycho bitch," Nettie replied. "Lost her damn marbles. Demanded that your daddy quit the Order with her. He refused, and she got pissed."

"Then what?" Chauncy asked.

"Yer daddy...well, let's just say he skedaddled. And Zella disappeared."

"I see," Gavin murmured. "What are her capabilities?"

"Tattoos," Nettie answered. Chauncy frowned.

"Well, that doesn't seem too bad," he said.

"That come to life when she wants them to," Nettie added.

"Still not that bad," Chauncy opined.

"Of dragons and serpents and a whole lot of other bad shit," she added to her addition. "Monsters that'll make Magmara look like a pet iguana."

Chauncy frowned.

"Oh," he mumbled.

"Right," Nettie quipped.

"I heard she's quite the looker," Harry piped in. Nettie shot him a glare.

"Who the hell cares?" she shot back.

"Well I do," Harry answered.

"Well I don't."

"Do we have a catalogue of what tattoos she has, and their capabilities?" Gavin asked. Which was a really good question. The kind of question a leader would ask. And also a question that it hadn't even occurred to Chauncy to ask, depressingly.

"Some," Nettie answered. "The Order had a dossier on her. But that was a while ago, and I'm sure she got a whole mess of new tattoos since then."

"Oh boy," Harry replied, his eyes lighting up.

"He likes tattoos," Nettie informed Chauncy.

"They're naughty," Harry said with a gleam in his eye. The kind of gleam he normally reserved for Nettie, and occasionally Valtora. "Makes for naughty thoughts."

"Naughty my ass," Nettie retorted.

"Sure is," Harry agreed.

"So *any*way," Chauncy interjected. "We should make a list of all of her tattoos so we at least know some of her abilities. And we need to figure out where she is, so we can, you know, find her."

"Unless we let her find you," Gavin proposed. "She's looking for you...which means you don't need to worry about looking for her."

"He's got a point," Harry noted. "She *is* a looker."

"Shut up Harry!" Nettie snapped. And Harry, being ever the agreeable sort, was happy to oblige.

"So what, we just sit around waiting for her to find us?" Chauncy asked.

"No," Nettie answered. "We spend time training you to suck less at fighting so you might have a chance at beating her."

"Ah," Chauncy mumbled. And while he felt a bit offended at this, he also knew it was true. For while he'd managed to defeat The Dark One –by virtue of his magical power of being able to put things inside things – both Harry and Nettie could still beat him easily when sparring. "So more sparring," he guessed.

"More gettin' yer ass kicked," Nettie corrected.

"Yay," Chauncy muttered.

"Better get Rooter," Nettie advised. "Harry here's a real ball-buster."

Chauncy grimaced, his groin twinging a bit with the memory of his last sparring match with the old man. For the balls that'd been busted had been his own.

"What about the Cave of Wonder?" he asked, glancing at the opening to the fabled place.

"I'll bring ya back to camp to get your Sunstone," Nettie offered. "Come on you," she added, eyeing Gavin. "You can come too."

With that, Nettie hobbled to the edge of the lake, then stepped into it. And with her touch, it shaped itself into a great big wave, one that carried everyone all the way across to the other end of the lake…and back to the lean-to. Chauncy retrieved his Sunstone, then walked his way back around the lake, returning to the entrance to the Cave of Wonder. He paused there, taking a deep breath in.

"Here goes," he mumbled…and squeezed his way inside.

# Chapter 15

The Cave of Wonder wasn't at all the way Chauncy remembered it. In fact, as he recalled, it'd been different each time he'd ventured inside. This particular time, the narrow entrance gave way to an irregular tunnel that sloped steeply downward, each step threatening to roll his ankles and send him tumbling to his death. Or at least, to a painful variety of broken bones. The perilous journey forced him to take his time. To pay attention to what he was doing instead of his destination. So pay attention he did, and in doing so, he felt his anxieties fade away. For while each step represented a potential danger, it was an immediate danger he could do something about.

Unlike Zella Trek, who was a threat in the future.

The thought caused him to lose his concentration, and he slipped on a rock underfoot, barely catching himself from taking a tumble. He cursed, refocusing on the slope.

*One step at a time*, he told himself. *Don't get distracted.*

In this way – one step at a time – Chauncy eventually found himself at the bottom of the slope, the tunnel leveling out ahead. And straightening out, the floor perfectly flat stone now, as were the walls and ceiling. He followed it for a little while, seeing nothing but darkness some twenty feet ahead and behind him. Then he followed it for a long while…and then a *longer* while, until he wondered if it would ever end.

But after what seemed like an hour, it didn't.

Chauncy paused then, glancing back the way he'd come. Again, all he saw was darkness. And ahead…darkness. There was only light where he was standing, and nowhere else.

He chewed his lip, eyeing the Sunstone nervously. For if it ran out of light, it would plunge him into darkness…and he'd be utterly helpless.

"It won't run out anytime soon," he reassured himself. After all, he'd kept it by the window at home almost all the time, soaking up sunlight day after day for the better part of a year. Still, the mere idea that it *could* run out of power was terribly anxiety-provoking…and prompted him to continue forward without further delay. He walked faster, hurrying toward his destination.

But even after what seemed like *another* hour, his destination was nowhere to be seen. There was only darkness behind him and darkness ahead, as if the tunnel vanished into nothingness in both directions. He stopped again, gritting his teeth.

"Is this *stupid* frickin' tunnel ever going to end?" he asked out loud. His voice echoed through the tunnel…but only behind him, not ahead. Which he thought was rather strange. For what was ahead was equivalent to what lay behind. Which was to say…nothing.

He frowned, becoming aware of a familiar presence at his left hip. The Magic of Magic, he realized, with its peculiar power of always falling to the right. He withdrew it from his pocket, finding it glowing a deep purple, and glittering spectacularly. But to his surprise, it felt rather too light. And what's more, it was terribly thin.

"Huh," he murmured, tucking the Sunstone under his chin, then opening the book up. To his further surprise, whereas before it'd had innumerable pages, now there was a single page in it. Page nine, in fact. It was instantly familiar, in that it was a poem written in the floweriest calligraphy he'd ever seen, so fancy with its twirls and whirls and hoops and swirls that it was nearly illegible. But having penetrated its mystery once before, he penetrated it again with ease:

*To Before and After it*
*Will never bow,*
*For The Magic of Magic is*
*Here and Now.*

He read this, then flipped the page, seeing the inside of the back cover…which was black. In fact, so was the inside of the front cover.

It occurred to Chauncy then that the Cave of Wonder was trying to tell him something. Or rather, to teach him something.

"Oh," he blurted out.

He looked ahead, seeing the tunnel vanishing into darkness beyond the edges of his light. And behind, where it did the same.

"Duh," he said, slapping himself on the forehead. "I don't need to get there. I'm already here."

And with that, the Sunstone shone blindingly bright…and when its light faded, he found that he was.

Chauncy stood within a large, domed chamber, the floor, walls, and ceiling composed of the deepest, purplest amethyst crystals he'd ever seen. Before him were magnificent wooden bookshelves at least seven feet tall, arranged in a broken spiral toward the center of the chamber. A great library within the Cave of Wonder; great not because of its size, but its splendor. For each of the books it held had been lovingly crafted, as evidenced by their intricately decorated spines.

At the outer edges of the chamber, near its walls where Chauncy found himself, were numerous wooden doors placed at regular intervals. Each was labeled with a symbol; the leftmost ones were painted on, from copper to silver to gold. Beyond these, the symbols were made of gemstones of increasing value, arranged in various shapes. In fact, they were precisely the same shapes he recalled from his first visit here: a tornado, an ocean wave, a flame, a lightning bolt, a man, and the last door, a woman made of pure diamond. He'd chosen the last door during his first visit, stupidly enough. But starting at the end had turned out all right in…well, in the end.

However, Chauncy found his gaze drawn not to the diamond woman, but to the door next to it. It featured the symbol of a man, wrought of what looked to be pure onyx.

"Huh," he mumbled. He glanced at the other doors, then at the bookshelves behind him. But to be honest, he didn't feel much like reading. So he turned back to the door with the onyx man-symbol. "Might as well," he decided, opening it up. Beyond, he saw a crystalline tunnel sloping upward.

He hesitated then, recalling how…unpleasant his last two trials within the Cave of Wonder had been.

"You're not going to get it over with by not getting it over with," he reasoned with himself. And his self found that quite reasonable. Still, it didn't stop his guts from squirming, and the rest of his body from following suit. "Come on old boy," he prompted, rolling his shoulders a bit and bouncing on the balls of his feet. "You're a frickin' wizard, remember?"

And, if bravery was defined as forging onward despite a secret, shameful cowardice in one's heart, Chauncy met his newest trial bravely indeed.

\* \* \*

The crystalline tunnel led upward for a short while, eventually leading Chauncy to a second wooden door at the top. He opened this, stepping through…and found himself standing in a field. The moon loomed large overhead, bright and full amidst a sea of stars. Blades of grass at his feet were cast in dull silver, spreading out around Chauncy as far as he could see in an endless, flat field.

He turned around…and saw no doorway back to where he'd been. It was gone…and with it gone, there was nowhere to go. For everywhere he looked was the same. And no matter where he looked, there was nothing but grass. No destination to settle upon. Nothing to differentiate one direction from another.

He waited. And waited…and waited. But nothing happened. So he did the only thing he could think to do, and starting walking.

Chauncy chose a direction at random, trudging along dutifully. After about a mile or so, there was *still* nothing in the horizon that stood out. He stopped, then glanced back. More grassy field, without any evidence of his passing.

"Huh," he mumbled.

He turned forward, continuing onward for a while. How long, he wasn't sure. But no matter how far he went, it was as if he'd ended up at the same place. It wasn't true, of course – that would be impossible – but it might as well have been. For when everything was the same, to know one part was to know it all.

At length, Chauncy stopped again, feeling a growing frustration. It occurred to him that he had to be missing something. For the Cave of Wonder never taught him its lessons directly. That way of learning never led to revelation, merely information. And revelation – knowledge that was *felt* – had a far more profound effect.

And that feeling…why, it was wonder.

"The Cave of Wonder," Chauncy murmured, smiling despite himself. He slapped himself on the forehead. "Duh," he added. "Can't believe I missed that."

For it was true of all of his adventures. The journey to the Great Wood – then the Cave of Wonder – had always seemed like a waste of time, particularly after the first time. After all, it was never done to get any particular thing. But each time, it'd shown him *wonder* itself, and thus revealed the secrets of the universe. Or rather, his relationship with it. Not in a book – not even in The Magic of Magic – but in having a different point of view.

With this particular revelation in mind, he decided to change the point of his view. So he looked up.

The moon greeted him in its full, globular glory, shining down at him from high above and ahead. Which gave Chauncy something the fields didn't; a sense of direction. It provided a kind of mental anchor, in that it assured him that there *were* directions in this odd place. And also a spiritual anchor, in that it placed him squarely where he was, rather than the anywhere he'd feared he'd been.

He smiled up at the heavens, having the sudden, unmistakable feeling that its thousands of twinkling stars were the eyes of a loving universe peering down at him from the heavens. And – with a feeling precisely like the one he'd first felt when gazing across the lake in the Great Wood the very first time he'd been there, and on the night that Grandma little had died, when he'd stared up at the moon in wonder – Chauncy marveled at the moon. At the fact that such a massive thing could be suspended in nothing, and be so very far away…but at the same time, inextricably connected to the world. And to him.

"Hello," he greeted, waving at the moon.

It smiled back.

Or rather, a shadow descended over the top of it, until it was a crescent moon shaped like a smiling "U."

Chauncy blinked.

The shadow lifted, making it a full moon once again. Chauncy paused, staring at it.

"Huh," he mumbled, not knowing what to think.

The moon didn't reply. Which made sense because the moon was the moon, and shouldn't have been able to. He realized that he'd almost certainly imagined it…or that this was some trick of the Cave of Wonder.

"Imagine if the universe had feelings," Chauncy mused, feeling rather amused at the thought.

"We do," a voice behind him replied.

Chauncy *shrieked.*

He jumped, then ran away a few paces, then whirled around, seeing himself standing there. Quite literally; it was his *self* standing there. A mirror-image, it appeared. For it appeared exactly like him, save for a bit of gray at the temples.

"Who are you?" Chauncy blurted out.

"You," his doppelganger answered. In his voice.

"No, *I'm* me," Chauncy argued. "You're you."

"We're both you," the guy argued.

"How can that be?" Chauncy asked. His twin smiled.

"Where there's one, there's always two," he answered. Chauncy's eyes narrowed, and he crossed his arms over his chest.

"You rhymed," he accused. "You're a wizard!"

"As are you, which makes two," the guy pointed out. Rhyming again, of course.

"What's going on?" Chauncy asked.

"I'm the universe speaking to you."

"You're not the universe," Chauncy argued. "You're me!"

"Well they don't call it the me-niverse," the guy pointed out. "So you-niverse will do."

Chauncy stared at him blankly.

"You're confusing me," he admitted.

"You're confusing yourself," his mirror-image declared. "Don't worry," he added. "That's perfectly human."

Chauncy frowned.

"Where am I?" he demanded.

"Here," his mirror-image replied. "Where else is there?"

"What do you want?" he demanded.

"What you want," the guy replied.

"What do *I* want?" Chauncy pressed, feeling rather irritated at the man's obscure way of speaking.

"To not be me," he answered. "To not be you."

"That doesn't make any sense," Chauncy retorted. "Why wouldn't I want to be me?"

"Because you're afraid of your destiny," the man replied.

"And what's that?" Chauncy pressed.

"To be me."

With that, the man dissolved into countless tiny specks of light…which melded with the stars in the heavens, becoming indistinguishable from them. Chauncy stared at where the man had been, lowering his arms to his sides. Then he lifted his gaze to the cosmos. Specifically, the moon.

"What am I supposed to *do*?" he shouted at it.

"PLAY WITH ME," the cosmos answered.

"But who *are* you?" Chauncy yelled.

"YOU," the cosmos replied.

Chauncy blinked, processing this.

"So you want me to play with myself?" he asked out loud.

To his surprise, the moon nodded at him.

Then a shadow came over the moon like a curtain falling over it, and the moon was gone. The stars winked out…and without their light, there was no light at all.

He closed his eyes, rubbing them for a bit, then opened them. And found himself back in his library, standing before the door with the onyx man-symbol on it.

"Oookaaaay," he mumbled, scratching his head.

He shrugged then, turning away from the door to face the spiraling bookshelves. He considered perusing them, but he was still a bit too irritated and tired. As such, he decided to leave the Cave of Wonder.

So, for the first time, Chauncy left the mystical cave not with a sense of wonder, but wondering what the hell he'd missed whilst within it.

# Chapter 16

Chauncy emerged from the darkness of the Cave of Wonder, finding himself assaulted by the blazing light of the afternoon sun. He was forced to squint, his eyeballs aching with the sudden overstimulation. At length he recovered, and what had once been painfully bright became painlessly normal. For a constant stimulus stimulated not at all.

He sighed then, making his way sullenly back 'round the shore of the lake toward the lean-to at the opposite end. It was a long journey, made longer by the fact that he was unhappy at the moment. For it was the peculiar property of the human experience that happiness was momentary, but misery seemed to last practically forever.

At length, he completed his trek, trudging up to the lean-to. Harry and Nettie were sitting there, as usual, with Gavin having joined them. Looking ludicrous in his ridiculous knitted uniform, Chauncy noted with catty irritation.

"Oh, hey kid," Nettie greeted, eyeing Chauncy. "How'd ya make out?"

"Eh," Chauncy replied, stopping before them.

"That good, eh?" Nettie mused. "Didja learn anything or what?"

"I have no idea," he confessed.

"What'd'ya mean?" she asked, standing up with some difficulty. Gavin helped her up, surprisingly.

"It was confusing," Chauncy replied rather defensively.

"Maybe to you," Nettie stated, putting her hands on her hips. "Well go on now, tell us what happened."

"Well..." Chauncy began, feeling his cheeks flush. "I think...the universe spoke to me."

Nettie's eyebrows went up.

"And?" she pressed. "What'd it say?"

"It...um..." he stammered. "Well, it kind of told me to..."

"Spit it out kid!"

"...play with myself," he answered. With another cheek-flush.

116

Nettie blinked.

"It *what* now?"

"That's what it told me to do," Chauncy insisted, rather defensively. Harry grinned.

"Well shucks," he replied. "Sounds like good advice to me."

"It would," Nettie grumbled. "But how in the hell does that help us with Zella Trek?"

"There's the rub," Harry agreed.

"Shut up Harry!"

Chauncy shrugged.

"Maybe it will help to have some context," Gavin piped in. "Chauncy, tell us exactly what happened during your trial."

Chauncy did so, recalling the events of his latest stay within the cave. After he was done, everyone frowned at him.

"What do you think it means?" he asked.

"How in the hell am I supposed to know?" Nettie shot back.

"It was confusing," Harry added. Nettie ignored him.

"Maybe you weren't supposed to leave 'til you figured something out," she argued.

"I thought about that," Chauncy admitted. "But I didn't feel like staying."

"Oh, so you felt like dyin' instead?" Nettie pressed.

"Perhaps you experienced what you needed to experience," Gavin interjected. "But it'll only make sense in time."

"Says the wizened wizard," Nettie grumbled.

"He might be right," Chauncy countered. "Sometimes it takes time."

"Has to take time if it's some time," Harry noted.

"Shut up Harry!" Nettie snapped.

"Sometimes it takes a while to play with yourself," he added, ignoring her demand. "Don't wanna rush it."

"Right," Chauncy muttered. "Well, anyway…where's Valtora?"

"Hell if I know," Nettie answered. "She went off into the woods with Peter 'bout an hour ago."

"With Chaos?" he asked. Nettie gave him a funny look, then pointed to a bundle of blankets in the lean-to. Which, upon very little further investigation, clearly contained a sleeping baby. "Oh," he blurted out, blushing a bit."

"Men," she grumbled. "Can't see a damn thing."

"Male-pattern blindness," Harry piped in professorially, adjusting his glasses. "Can't see anything directly in front of 'em."

"Maybe I need to take a walk," Chauncy proposed, feeling quite done with their conversation. After his failure in the Cave of Wonder, he needed a little time to himself.

"Good idea," Nettie replied. And promptly sat back down, as did Harry and Gavin.

Chauncy waved goodbye, then turned toward the woods ahead, trudging toward them. He was soon surrounded by massive trees, dodging his way around their big silver trunks and hopping over fallen logs and big stones and such. The use of his body offered a respite from his mind, as exercise so often did. Such that, by the time a good fifteen minutes had passed, he felt quite a bit better. He'd actually begun to smile when he spotted something out of place ahead: a bit of glittery rainbow-colored stuff on the ground.

"Peter," he realized. It was the unicorn's rainbow-colored dandruff. Valtora must have rode the stallion through here.

He decided to follow the rainbow trail, which wound its way through the woods in a kind of drip-drop pattern. It wasn't long before the drip-drops got closer together…and Chauncy spotted something a good hundred feet ahead, partially obscured by the trees. A bit of whiteness, which he realized was Peter's well-muscled flank. He was about to speed up, excited at the prospect of seeing his poopy-dooz, but something told him to slow down and be sneaky instead.

So Chauncy snuck, weaving through the trees without a sound, until he drew closer. It *was* Peter, he soon discovered as he hid behind a tree. And Valtora.

That was, quite unfortunately, not the only thing he discovered.

For it appeared that he'd caught the two engaged in an act. One that, even *more* unfortunately, he'd caught the tail end of, so to speak. Chauncy's eyebrows went up, his eyes widening. And at the same time, his jaw traveled in the opposite direction. He just stood there, hardly believing his eyes…and shortly thereafter, his ears. For a great shudder went through Peter…followed by a sharp, ear-splitting *neigh*.

There were rainbows then, which was all Chauncy would ever say about what happened next. And they changed his relationship with rainbows forevermore.

He stepped out from behind the tree, feeling numb.

"What the…!" he blurted out.

118

Peter flinched, and Valtora froze, and they both stared at Chauncy rather guiltily. Valtora recovered rapidly, beaming a smile at Chauncy, even as the rainbows petered out.

"Oh hey Chauncy!" she greeted cheerily, even giving a little wave.

"What the hell?" he exclaimed. Valtora blinked, then glanced at Peter, who turned away from them, sweeping his tail dismissively. She turned back to Chauncy, her expression blank.

"Huh?" she asked.

"What the *fuck* just happened?" he snapped. Which wasn't precisely what had happened, but was close enough.

"Huh?"

"Don't play dumb with me," he continued angrily. "I saw everything!"

"Then why are you asking what happened?" she retorted, unhanding Peter and crossing her arms over her chest. "Duh."

"I want an explanation!"

"Peter was feeling stressed out, so I gave him a rub-down. You know, so he could take a load off."

"That wasn't just a rub-down," Chauncy retorted. She blushed, for it was quite obviously true. She shrugged.

"So?"

"So?" he blurted out incredulously. "So?!"

"I thought Peter would like it."

Peter turned to face them, nodding to indicate that he had very much enjoyed it. Which was also obvious, on account of his colorful…commentary.

"You can't do that!" Chauncy protested.

"Why not?" she asked.

"Because you're married?!"

"No I'm not," she shot back. He grimaced, for she was right.

"Fine," he grumbled. "Engaged."

"So?"

"So that's wrong!" he pressed, beyond angry that she didn't get that.

"Why?" she argued. "He's a unicorn, not a person."

"That's the point!"

"He's got needs, you know," she told him, putting her hands on her hips. "He doesn't have hands like you do."

"Really?" he blurted out incredulously, throwing up his hands. "That's your excuse?"

"I was curious," she added. "Don't you ever get curious?"

119

"Maybe," Chauncy hedged. "But you don't see me going off with a horse!"

"You totally could," she offered, her eyes brightening. Peter snorted, clearly not volunteering himself for this particular adventure. "Ooo, we could find a mare for you!" she exclaimed excitedly. "I could bedazzle her, too! A beautiful rainbow-unicorn mare for Chauncy, that you could ride whenever you want!"

This clearly caught Peter's attention.

"N…no!" Chauncy replied, grabbing his hair and pulling quite viciously. Enough that his eyes watered. He stomped with one foot, not knowing quite else what to do. And Valtora watched all this, her hands still on her hips.

"Peter was just letting out some steam," Valtora reassured him. Which wasn't reassuring at all. "Don't worry, you'll get your chance with Addie. Then we'll be even."

"I don't *want* to."

"Sure you do," she reasoned. "You've wanted to since you were a kid."

"Yes, but then I met you."

"So?"

"So I don't want to anymore!" he explained. Which he really shouldn't have had to do.

"Pfft," she replied dismissively. "You're really gonna just never have fun with anyone else ever again? For the rest of your life?"

"That's right," Chauncy confirmed. "It's called marriage!"

"Well that's stupid," she opined.

"No it's not."

"Yes it is," she argued.

"It really isn't."

"Well that's not gonna be *our* marriage," she retorted, crossing her arms over her chest again. "We're wizards, Chauncy."

"What does that have to do with anything?"

"We think differently," she answered. "We don't just do things because other people do them." She reached out to grab his hand, and he resisted the urge to pull away. "Anyway, wanna go back to camp? I'm like, frickin' *starving*."

He blinked.

"You mean just like that?" he asked. "Like none of this ever happened?"

"Well yeah," she replied. "What else are we gonna do?"

"This is a big deal," he pointed out. Which, to be fair, he really shouldn't have had to do.

"Only if you *make* it a big deal," she counter-pointed.

"Shouldn't I?"

"Nothing good ever came from 'should,'" Valtora recited. Which had been Nettie's advice to him during their last adventure. He'd been so stuck on "should" that it'd made him absolutely miserable…and had threatened their very relationship.

But no matter what Valtora might say, this *was* a big deal. And at the moment, it was more than he could handle. He needed time to think…and he couldn't do that around Valtora.

"I need to be alone," he declared. And with that, he pulled away, turning around and striding away from her – and Peter – in a hurry. She protested, but he ignored her, fleeing the scene of the crime. For after failing as a father, floundering in the Cave of Wonder – and being betrayed by his betrothed – Chauncy was done. His world was falling apart, his once-happy life in tatters.

And if he didn't focus on finding a way to defeat Zella Trek – and soon – his life wouldn't just be in tatters.

It would be over.

# Chapter 17

There was nothing quite as exhilarating to King Pravus the Eighth as riding a dragon. Flying high above his own kingdom, the wind in his hair, every powerful muscular contraction of the dragon's body pulsing between his legs…why, it was a simply splendid experience. And with Templeton behind him, muscular arms wrapped oh-so-firmly around his waist!

"Nothing quite like it, is there?" Templeton mused, clearly having similar sentiments, if not for the same reasons.

"You read my mind cousin," Pravus agreed. Which he fervently hoped wasn't true. For if Templeton only knew the ghastly, deliciously depraved fantasies Pravus had entertained in Templeton's honor…

"Almost there," Templeton declared, pointing ahead. And it was true; for there in the distance, Pravus spotted the great Wall, a two-hundred-foot-tall stone monstrosity…and the silver double-doors of the Gate. Beyond this was a city unlike any he'd ever seen. For it seemed to be composed of row after row of tall, rectangular buildings arranged in a grid…each so similar they were practically identical. And each building had been made of dull gray stone, so drab and boring that they had no character whatsoever.

"Egads cousin," Pravus blurted out in horror. "What *is* that?"

"Southwick, my liege," Templeton answered. "The southernmost city in Borrin."

"It's so…*ugly*," Pravus protested. "Are those all factories?"

"Apartment buildings, sire."

"Wait…people *live* in these things?" Pravus pressed as they flew closer.

"Hundreds of them per building, so I'm told," Templeton confirmed.

"How awful," Pravus declared. For in *his* kingdom, people lived in quaint houses bursting with character. As was only right. This city, in contrast, seemed to have been designed with the express purpose of conveniently packing as many people as possible in the available space, no doubt so that they could serve as underpaid labor for their wealthy masters. Like the Evermore Trading Company.

"I knew it was bad in Borrin," Pravus stated, shaking his head. "But I had no idea it was *this* bad."

"Oh, it gets plenty worse," Templeton warned. "You should see how they work."

"Do tell," Pravus requested.

"Most of Borrin's citizens must sign contracts to enter under service to authoritarian entities they call 'corporations'...lords under a different name."

"Ah."

"In exchange for renting out their labor, each citizen earns a wage many times lower than the value of their work, and the corporation keeps the difference for themselves."

"I see."

"Then the Republic of Borrin taxes these wages at the very highest rate of any kind of income," Templeton continued. "So that those who work under the lords – the corporations, rather – are the most disadvantaged."

"While the corporations are taxed at a much lower rate, I suppose?"

"Indeed," Templeton confirmed. "But it gets worse."

"Worse?"

"Laborers are taxed based on everything they earn, while the lords – corporations, rather – are taxed only on their profits. So the workers are taxed on money they spend for the necessities of living, while corporations are not taxed on money they spend for the necessities of existing."

"Diabolical," Pravus breathed. "Why don't the people revolt?"

"They don't know," Templeton answered. Pravus frowned.

"They don't know?"

"The government controls the educational system," Templeton explained. "They explicitly exclude any mention of how this all works."

"So the only people that learn are the heirs of the lords," Pravus realized.

"The corporations, yes," Templeton corrected. "As a result, most citizens are indentured servants, spending most of their lives trying desperately to earn their freedom...a process that takes about forty years."

"By the gods," Pravus blurted out. "That's practically their entire lives!"

"Indeed," Templeton agreed. "While the heirs to the wealthy are born free."

"And don't have to spend most of their lives under authoritarian rule to earn it," Pravus concluded. He shook his head sadly. "How do these wily overlords justify it?"

"By allowing citizens to choose which overlord to labor under," Templeton answered.

"Ah, the illusion of freedom," Pravus stated. "Devious!"

"It is an elegant system," Templeton admitted. "But you can see why they don't have much in the way of magic."

"Or wizards," Pravus agreed. "Magic can't thrive under conditions of compulsory productivity."

"Indeed," Templeton agreed.

They fell silent then, and Pravus studied the rectangular rows of rectangular buildings, all squished up next to each other with nary a hint of greenery or cheer. No flowers or meadows, no lakes or streams. Just never-ending drudgery as far as the eye could see.

"I think I'm depressed," Pravus confessed. "Let's not tarry here long."

"In and out, cousin," Templeton agreed.

Pravus smiled at that, for in-and-out was one of his favorite games. A bit of the old anatomical hide and seek, so to speak…a game he'd love to play with his sweet, dear cousin. Alas, he would have to be content with their non-metaphorical swordplay. Which, to be honest, he was.

They flew close to the wall, but not over it, for flying a dragon over the Republic of Borrin could be misconstrued as a threat of invasion or some such. Indeed, it was likely the backwards country would take it that way. The endless and desperate pursuit of *more* tended to make people paranoid that they might suffer the horrifying fate of having *less*.

Of course, Pravus knew it was more or less true that having more rarely made a person happy after their basic needs were met. And that sometimes having less allowed one to enjoy what they *did* have quite a bit more.

"See any sign of the sorceress?" Pravus inquired.

"None whatsoever," Templeton answered.

"Any hint of villainy?" Pravus pressed. "Screaming crowds or some such?"

124

"Nothing but peace and quiet, I'm afraid."

"Well confound it," Pravus complained. "Zella should've gone after Chauncy already!" Indeed, he'd been surprised that they hadn't caught up with the wizard while flying here.

"Perhaps she's come and gone," Templeton proposed. "Or perhaps she faked coming." A popular tactic, or so Pravus had heard.

"Hard to believe she could beat my dragon," Pravus retorted. Indeed, no woman ever had, so to speak. Or ever would, for that matter. "She must not have come."

"A ploy?"

"I suspect so," Pravus stated. "But to what end?"

"Getting you away from Cumulus, I'd wager," Templeton replied. This sent a proper chill down Pravus's spine.

"You suspect foul play, dearest cousin?" he pressed.

"It is the only kind of play foul people engage in," Templeton answered. "Shall we get back to the castle?"

"Indeed," Pravus agreed.

And with that, they turned Pravus's gigantic dragon around, pointing its head south. Toward Cumulus…and if Templeton was correct, one very *very* naughty wizard indeed.

# Chapter 18

"This sucks," Chauncy muttered to himself as he stomped through the Great Wood, making his way back to Nettie and Harry. Or at least he thought he was; he hadn't really paid attention to where he was going when he'd left the camp, and had refused to let Valtora help him. As a result, he was pretty sure he was completely lost. Which was fitting, because he was also feeling lost emotionally.

"Focus," he told himself. For he realized that his stomach was grumbling. Which had resulted in some pretty awful moods in the past, and was almost certainly contributing now. "You need to get home."

He *could* fly upward on blasts of wind, clearing the treetops and getting an aerial view of the Great Wood. The lake would be readily visible then. Of course, such a feat would require his Staff of Wind…which was far too many feet away, back at the camp.

But not, Chauncy realized, for a wizard.

"I'm a frickin' wizard," he recalled, stopping to slap himself on the forehead. A lifetime of being ordinary had given him the unfortunate habit of forgetting that he was *extra*ordinary.

With that, he thrust out his right hand…and within moments, his Staff of Wind flew right at him, weaving between the trees at incredible speed, then landing in his palm with an enormously satisfying *thwap!*

He was about to thrust the butt of his staff downward when he glanced up, seeing a bunch of tree branches directly above him. Very large tree branches…ones that brought back the painful memory of having attempted a similar act in the past, and hitting his head in the process. All while an army of goblins had been after him. If it hadn't been for Skibbard, he'd have been a goner.

Chauncy stepped to the side a bit, looked up, and was satisfied regarding his safety.

"Vertical Flight!" he cried.

Then he thrust downward with all his might, slamming the butt of his staff on the ground. This created a blast of air

126

downward…one that shot him upward at gut-sinking speed. He flew high into the air – halfway to the canopy far above – and repeated the maneuver again and again, thrusting his staff with abandon. This brought him to heights he'd never experienced before…far above the treetops hundreds of feet above the forest floor. The sight of the Great Wood below him – and spreading out as far as he could see – filled him with glee.

"Wee!" he shouted.

He spotted the lake over a mile to the southwest, and turned to it, thrusting his staff backward to shoot himself forward. Over and over again he thrust, flying in successive arcs with the power of the staff's stored wind. It wasn't long before he'd reached the lake, and he allowed himself to descend, thrusting down a few times to slow his fall. In this way, he landed quite gently a few yards from the lean-to, feeling downright wizardly…and a bit bad-ass, as Valtora liked to say.

The thought of his betrothed immediately spoiled his mood. Such that instead of finding the day magical, he found it sucky once more.

"Hey Chauncy," Harry greeted, still sitting under the lean-to with Gavin and Nettie. "You find yer girl?"

"Um…yes," he confessed.

"Where is she?" Nettie asked. "Gonna need to get going soon."

"After lunch," Harry countered.

"Oh, right," Nettie replied.

She stood, then gripped the Wetstone hanging between her…parts, squeezing it. Water formed a sphere around it, and she sent this water in a big, airborne stream to the lake many yards away. When the stream connected to the lake, Nettie was able to reverse the stream, sucking the lake water back to her. For Nettie's power over water was the curious power *of* water…that of a powerful bond to itself. Within moments, a generous quantity of fish surged out of the lake through that arcing stream, collecting in a watery sphere beside Nettie, like a fishbowl.

Then Nettie sucked all the water back into the Wetstone, and the fish plopped onto the ground beside her, flopping precisely like fish out of water.

"There," she told Harry. "Get cookin'."

"You got it good lookin'," he replied with a smile.

Harry got to work building a fire, and Chauncy helped the old man. Because it was the right thing to do, even if he didn't particularly feel like doing it. Visions of Valtora playing with Peter came to his mind as he gathered sticks, and while the visions were certainly colorful, it wasn't in the pleasant kind of way. He realized he was muttering under his breath as he worked, and forced himself to stop.

Harry grabbed a stick, sticking it point-down on a piece of wood and rotating it between his palm quickly. Nettie eyed both of them with her hands on her hips.

"Now why'n the hell are you rubbing that stick when you could just use that flint on your jacket?" she inquired.

"More fun to rub," Harry replied. "Sticks like it."

Which, Chauncy knew from recent experience, was distressingly true.

"They sure do," Nettie confirmed. "Bet ya want me to make a fire with yours."

"Then I'll put it out," Harry replied with a grin. Nettie chuckled, then glared at him for making her laugh.

"Shut up Harry," she grumbled. And then chuckled again.

Harry chuckled too, then turned back to finish what he was doing. It wasn't long before a wisp of smoke floated up from where the stick touched the wood; Harry put this on the tinder, and a fire was born. To this he added the fish, after prepping them.

"What crawled up your sorry ass?" Nettie inquired. Chauncy blinked, then realized she was talking to him.

"Peter," he grumbled.

"Peter went up yer ass?" she asked, arching an eyebrow.

"No," he replied. A bit more defensively than he would've liked. "It's just…" he sighed, his shoulders slumping. "I don't wanna talk about it."

"About what?"

"It," he answered.

"Did Valtora finish with Peter?" Nettie asked, attempting to change the subject and failing miserably.

"She sure did," Chauncy muttered. A bit too loudly, for Nettie overheard it.

"Lemme guess…you caught her in the act?" she said. He blinked, then blushed, then stammered.

"Uh…"

"Is that was this is about?" Nettie pressed. Chauncy hesitated, then did the only thing he could think of.

"Huh?" he asked, his face going blank.

128

Nettie burst out laughing.

Chauncy frowned, feeling quite taken aback. For it appeared that she was laughing at him. His suspicions were proven correct when she stopped laughing, pointed right at him…and then burst out laughing again.

"What?" he asked irritably.

"Never owned a stallion, have ya," Nettie guessed. "City boys," she added dismissively, shaking her head.

"What?" he repeated, even more irritably.

"Bet you think all horses are alike," she mused. "Don't even know the difference between a gelding and a stallion, do ya?"

"Um…"

"Geldings are boy stallions that got their parts chopped off," she explained, pantomiming that particular act of separation. Chauncy grimaced, feeling a familiar twinge in his own parts at the thought of it.

"And?"

"Stallions still got their parts," Nettie continued. "Like Peter."

"How could I not notice," he grumbled. For Peter's parts were particularly noteworthy.

"Well, if you wanna keep a stallion around, you gotta get 'em a mare," she warned. "Or handle 'em yourself. And if you hadn't noticed, we're fresh outta mares."

"So…what are you saying?" Chauncy asked.

"Well, Peter was gettin' antsy and ready to run off," Nettie explained. "So I told Valtora to take him and get him off instead."

Chauncy's jaw dropped.

"You *what?*" he blurted out.

"Can't let a stallion's evil build up," she lectured. "They go long enough without releasing the pressure, they end up doing bad things."

"Really bad things," Harry agreed, still cooking the fish. "Humans 'n stallions got that in common."

"Oh *do* they now," Nettie retorted, eyeing the old man.

"That's why I'm so nice all the time," Harry replied. "You never let the evil build up."

"Well that's true," Nettie conceded.

"So you're saying that you *told* Valtora to…help Peter?" Chauncy pressed. Nettie nodded.

"Sure did," she confirmed. "Just like the last time we were here."

Chauncy just stood there, gaping at her.

129

"Didn't tell her to bedazzle it though," Nettie added.

"Oh," Chauncy mumbled, feeling his depression fade. He smiled with relief. "Well that makes me feel better."

"Thought yer girl was cheatin' on ya with a horse, eh?" Harry guessed.

"Horsing around with a horse," Nettie quipped, shaking her head and chuckling to herself.

"Used to own stallions," Harry mused. "Me 'n the guys used to have races."

"Races?" Nettie asked.

"To see who could get the evil out quickest," he explained. "Won first place four years 'n a row."

"You don't say," Nettie grumbled.

"I was real popular in the army," he added, smiling wistfully across the lake.

Before Chauncy or Nettie could process that particular revelation, Peter came. More specifically, he galloped out of the woods toward them, Valtora riding on his back. With their gorgeous hair blowing in the wind, they were a remarkable sight…and seemed to come toward Chauncy in slow-motion.

"Damn," Nettie breathed.

"Hot damn," Harry added.

The two skid to a stop before them, and Peter rose up onto his hindquarters, neighing triumphantly. Then he landed, standing there looking as if he were glowing. Valtora did too…that was, until she met Chauncy's gaze.

"Oh," she blurted out, giving a little wave with her diamond hand. "Hey Chauncy."

"Hey Valtora," Chauncy replied, waving back. "Sorry I was…"

"Such a little butt-hurt *bitch*?" she finished for him, dismounting Peter in one practiced motion. Chauncy smiled reluctantly.

"I was, wasn't I?" he agreed. "It's okay, Nettie told me she's the one who asked you to…you know."

"Get Peter off?" Valtora replied. Peter snorted, tossing his head happily at the memory.

"Right."

"You were right Nettie," Valtora said. "Peter's *so* much happier now. Like, he was ready to *explode*."

"Bet he did," Harry quipped, making himself chuckle.

"Well, I'm glad that's behind us," Chauncy said, doing his best not to recall that particular image. He walked up to Valtora, giving

130

her a hug, then a kiss. She kissed him back with her usual exuberance…until they heard heavy footsteps approaching from behind. Everyone turned to see Rocky, Rooter, and Gavin coming toward them. Rooter was on Rocky's shoulder, as usual, while Gavin was cradling Chaos. Against his ridiculous, knitted chest.

"Hey guys," Gavin greeted. "How'd it go, Chauncy?"

"Huh?" Chauncy replied.

"In the Cave of Wonder," Gavin clarified.

"Um…I don't know," he confessed. "What were you guys up to?" he asked, eager to end the argument with Nettie and Valtora.

"Just taking little Chaos for a walk," Gavin answered. "He was fussy."

As if on cue, Chaos began to cry.

"My *baby*," Valtora gushed, rushing up to Gavin and taking Chaos from him. "Aww," she cooed. "Who wants mama's big ol' *titties?*"

"Breasts," Chauncy corrected, blushing at the term. Valtora straight-up pulled up her shirt, exposing one of her…um…dairy conveyance systems to them all. "Oh!" Chauncy gasped, rushing to hide the view.

"Oh," Harry murmured.

Chaos suckled, and Chauncy used his body to cover the view. When at length the boy was good and finished, it was Valtora who got to business.

"Ok," she proclaimed. "How'd the Cave of Wonder go, Chauncy?"

"Eh," Chauncy replied. He gave a quick run-down of what'd happened, and Valtora furrowed her brow throughout, rubbing her chin as if pondering the mystical nature of his experience. When he was done, Valtora nodded to herself.

"Right," she declared.

"What?" Chauncy asked. "You understand it?"

"Nope," she answered cheerily. "But you went, so we're done here." She turned to Nettie and Harry. "What's next?"

"How in the hell should we know?" Nettie replied.

"Gavin?" Valtora pressed, turning to the former villain. "Any ideas?"

Gavin knitted his brow, eyeing Chauncy.

"I suspect we'll know when the time comes," he replied. "But I think I understand what the Cave of Wonder was trying to tell me during my stay there."

131

"What's that?" Nettie asked.

"You'll see," he answered. Too cryptically for Nettie's tastes. But he wouldn't elaborate any further.

"Okay," Valtora stated, putting her hands on her hips. "Zella Trek is gonna try to kill Chauncy, but we don't know when or where. We have no idea what she's capable of, or what the Cave of Wonder was telling Chauncy. And Gavin might know, but he won't tell," she summarized. "Because he's an asshole," she added non-constructively. But Gavin only smirked.

"Sometimes," he admitted. "But I'm more than just that."

"Well sure ya are," Harry agreed, clapping the man on the shoulder with one big hand. So hard that Gavin stumbled. "You're an ass too."

"And a dick," Valtora added cheerfully, taking the other side. Rather literally, in this case.

"But'cha got balls, I'll give ya that," Harry concluded.

"We're gonna need 'em if we want to fight Zella," Nettie warned. "About time we had someone with balls around here, other than Harry."

"Hey," Chauncy protested.

"Face it kid," Nettie said. "You got potential, but you're not nearly the wizard you could be. And that's 'cause you don't got the guts to trust yourself."

Chauncy grimaced. It was true enough…and each adventure he'd gone on had proven it. Heck, most of the time, he forgot he was even a wizard. Like in the forest earlier. And even when he *did* remember, he usually screwed things up anyway.

He *didn't* trust himself. To be a wizard…or a good father. And certainly not to defeat an experienced wizard in mortal combat.

Chauncy glanced at Chaos, sleeping comfortably in Valtora's arms. He grit his teeth, knowing that there was more on the line now than just his own measly life. He had a family now…and they needed him.

If he didn't figure out how to start trusting himself soon, he wouldn't only let himself down. He'd let them down too.

# Chapter 19

It was too late to start traveling again after Chauncy's return from the Cave of Wonder, so they stayed at the camp instead. Harry helped Chauncy build another lean-to, one quite a distance from Harry and Nettie's…and facing away to boot. Gavin proved a quick study, building his own lean-to by watching them work and emulating them. It occurred to Chauncy that he'd forgotten just how accomplished and proficient Gavin was, on account of his newly knitted uniform. Had the man been wearing his impeccable green suit and golden tie, Chauncy would've thought quite differently about him.

Strange, that people were so easily swayed by what amounted to mere costumes. And that changing the exterior seemed to change the interior. He himself felt different when he donned his wizard's robe; just to wear it made him feel more powerful and wizard-ly. He wondered how Gavin felt, having changed from a high-powered executive's uniform to…well, to whatever the heck his new outfit was.

"Alright Chauncy," Valtora stated as they snuggled under their blanket, Chaos laying between them. The roof of their lean-to covered them nicely, but Chauncy could still see the starry night sky beyond it.

"Alright what?" he inquired. She rolled onto her side, staring at him with her gorgeous eyes.

"Do it."

"Do what?" he pressed.

"Play with yourself."

He blinked.

"Excuse me?" he asked.

"Go on," she pressed. "The universe told you to, remember?"

"I don't think it…"

"*Do* it," she insisted, her pupils growing disturbingly large. And then she waited. Chauncy squirmed, feeling not at all comfortable with this. Particularly not with Chaos between them.

133

"I can't," he protested.

"Why not?" she asked. "You did it all the time before you met me."

"Well yeah," he admitted. "But it's...a private thing."

"Why?"

"Because," he answered.

"Just do it," she ordered.

"But the baby's here," he pointed out.

"He's sleeping."

"I don't want to wake him up," Chauncy reasoned. Which was a pretty good defense, if he did say so himself.

"Fine," she grumbled, grabbing Chaos and standing up.

"Where are you going?" he asked.

"For a walk," she answered. "You've got ten minutes. Don't disappoint me Chauncy."

"But..."

"The universe told you to," she reminded him.

"I don't think that's what it meant..."

But she left without saying another word, leaving Chauncy alone under the lean-to. He sighed, realizing that it was better if he just buckled down and did what she wanted. He hardly wanted to keep arguing about it when she came back, after all. So it was that he obeyed Valtora's interpretation of the universe's demand. He'd gotten quite a ways into the performance – and was rather vigorously rounding the corner to the final act – when he heard a rustling sound from somewhere ahead of him.

He froze, pricking his ears.

There was another rustling sound, closer this time.

"Hello?" he whisper-yelled. But there was no response. He unhanded himself, the hairs on the back of his neck rising on-end. "Valtora?" he hissed.

More rustling, even closer now, from directly ahead.

He whisper-cursed, covering his...handiwork with his blanket. Then he saw a familiar feminine silhouette stepping toward the lean-to, slinking in the shadows and being all stealthy about it. Chauncy relaxed.

"Valtora," he whispered. "You scared the crap out of me."

She crouched down, then slinked under his blanket. And it wasn't long before Chauncy felt her continue what he'd started...but in a far more preferrable manner.

134

"Oh," he blurted out. He felt her put a hand on his chest and press him forcibly onto his back, and being an agreeable sort, he laid there. It wasn't long before she'd returned him right to where he'd left off, in the final act of this particular performance.

And then, as was typical for any good story, tensions rose, leading to a singularly explosive climax…followed by an incredibly satisfying resolution.

Chauncy laid there, his forehead sweating. And giggled. Uncontrollably. For quite a while.

He sat up a bit then, propping himself on his elbows, and saw Valtora stirring under the blanket.

"Wow*ee*," he breathed, shaking his head in wonder. "That was by *far* the best you've ever done, poopy-dooz," he exclaimed. And it was undeniably true. He put a hand where he supposed her head was, patting it affectionately.

Blackness spread from his hand on the blanket, wet and sticky.

"What the…!" he blurted out, jerking his hand back. It was covered in wet blackness. Blackness that smelled like…

A black head rose from the black wetness on the blanket, as if whatever had been underneath it was seeping *through* it. It was a woman's head, with long, wavy black hair. And a black face…and neck, and body, and even wings.

Utterly black…and most definitely *not* Valtora.

"Who…?!" he gasped, scrambling backward in horror. He let out a shriek…and then the woman was upon him!

The woman lunged on top of him, putting a hand over his mouth and nose. A wet hand…or a hand made of wet something. It smelled like ink…and when Chauncy tried to take a breath in, ink flowed into his nose and mouth.

He choked, coughing and sputtering…but the woman's hand remained where it was, preventing him from breathing.

Chauncy kicked at the woman – no, at the *creature* – but his foot went right through her belly, instantly drenched in ink. He wrapped his hands around her wrist, but they merely went *through* it, covered in more ink. He thrashed, his vision starting to darken, his lungs burning.

*No!*

He tried to scream for help, but couldn't. Tried to fight, but it was hopeless. There was nothing he could do. Nothing that mattered, anyway. So it was that his vision went utterly black, and the world slipped away from Chauncy.

And the last thing he heard before he passed into oblivion was Valtora somewhere in the distance, calling his name.

# Chapter 20

Whilst King Pravus the Eighth had flown on his fiery dragon to the border of Borrin on metaphorical wings of heroism, he returned to Cumulus in the ghastly grip of terror. For the mere thought that Zella Trek might have tricked him – and attacked the very heart of his kingdom in his absence – made him sick with fear. Not for his stuff, which he was not *too* overly fond of, but for his people.

"Faster!" he urged the fire dragon, spotting the wall surrounding Cumulus a few miles ahead. "Make haste, noble steed!"

He felt Templeton's arms tighten around his waist, but at the moment he wasn't in a state of mind to enjoy it. His eyes were too busy scanning his kingdom, searching frantically for the telltale signs of mayhem.

It wasn't long before he found what he was looking for.

For as they drew nearer, Pravus spotted the castle in the middle of the city, within the bounds of a second wall. And twisted around its tallest tower, an all-too-familiar black, serpentine shape.

"Fang!" he blurted out, gripping the front edge of his saddle tightly. So tightly that, with his unmatchable grip strength, it snapped. He made the motion of drawing a sword from his back, and lo-and-behold, his golden sword appeared as if by magic. No…it *was* magic. Just like the vile serpent that dared slither in his home.

"The dragon, sire," Templeton stated. "It can aid us in our fight!"

"Indeed cousin," Pravus declared valiantly, glaring down at his foe. "Serpent against serpent, in a battle to the death!"

"And I daresay yours is far bigger," Templeton noted zestily.

"It is indeed," Pravus agreed.

The fire dragon flew them closer, soon passing over the outer wall of the city. As Pravus watched, the black serpent Fang slithered all the way to the top of the castle's tower, to its gold-plated peak.

"What do you suppose that snake is up to?" Templeton wondered aloud.

"Mischief," Pravus answered grimly. "Of the most dastardly kind!"

And before their eyes, Pravus's prediction came terribly true. For Fang flexed his long, coiled body around the tower...and its stone walls began to crumple inward under the beast's terrible grip.

"He's squeezing the tower with all his might," Templeton exclaimed. "It can't withstand that terrible grip much longer!"

"Hurry!" Pravus urged the fire dragon. "Fell that serpent before my tower falls!"

But it was too late. For even as they soared toward the tower at breakneck speed, the vile serpent continued to squeeze. And to Pravus's horror, the base of the tower crumpled inward so completely that there was no saving it. Fang slithered down to its base, even as the shaft of the tower began to tip over, falling toward the castle roof below.

"Egads!" Templeton cried.

And then the tower struck the roof below, demolishing a sizable portion of the castle.

Pravus watched as the section of the castle disintegrated into rubble...and felt something inside him snap. And out of whatever had broken within him came red-hot, blind rage.

He *roared*, standing up on the saddle, gripping his sword's hilt tightly in both hands. The fire dragon flew a good hundred feet over the serpent as it slithered across the intact castle roof away from the carnage it'd caused. Pravus leapt right off the dragon, plummeted forward and downward toward it.

"FANG!" he bellowed, lifting his sword overhead as he fell rapidly toward the beast. The serpent stopped, twisting its inky black head around to look at him. Its eyes widened at the impossible sight...of a king wielding a massive golden sword falling out of thin air toward it.

Pravus swung his blade downward with all his considerable strength, engaging his lats, triceps, and rear deltoid muscles as only he could. His blade struck Fang right between the eyes...

...and split the vile serpent's head in two.

Pravus's feet struck the roof of the castle, and he smashed right through it, and then through the floor of the room beyond. He landed on his side on the following floor with a *whump*, rubble falling all around him with a horrible clatter. He felt not a hint of pain, his magical uniform and crown protecting him from harm.

He grunted, then rose slowly and agonizingly to his feet. For while a hundred-foot fall into sheer stone couldn't harm him, there was no magic powerful enough to prevent the pain of leg day.

Directly above, the huge, black head of Fang hung limply through the hole in the ceiling, inky black blood spurting from its split. And showering Pravus in the process, as he was quite unfortunately standing right under it.

"Pffftpphhhthh," he spat, accepting this downpour, then wiping the ink from his face. There was a loud *thump* from somewhere outside of the castle, followed shortly thereafter by the rapid patter of footsteps. Soon, none other than Templeton appeared, rushing toward him.

"Sire!" his cousin cried, skidding to a stop before him. "Are you hurt?"

"Only my heart, cousin," Pravus replied. He eyed the rubble all around him. The unmoving bodies of a few guards were half-buried under it.

Then one of the half-buried guards stirred, spotting them…and crying for help. Pravus sheathed his sword by pretending to put it back on his back. It vanished as if by magic, because it was.

"Come Templeton," Pravus prompted, limping toward the sound. "Our guards have spent their lives preparing to protect us. It's about time we repaid the favor!"

139

# Chapter 21

Gavin Merrick had nearly fallen asleep under his lean-to when a shrill scream woke him. He jerked upright instantly, his hand going automatically to his suit pocket. But of course, he wasn't wearing his magical Evermore suit…and that was no longer where he kept his magical golden coin. One that could turn anything but him into solid gold.

Gavin rose to his feet in one smooth motion, emerging from his shelter and triangulating the source of the shouting. It'd sounded like a woman's voice screaming…and had come from Chauncy and Valtora's lean-to.

"Harry, Nettie!" he barked, rushing toward the lean-to. For in times of danger, having the back-up of experienced wizards was valuable indeed. As he neared the lean-to, he spotted Valtora running away from it and toward the woods. "What's going on?" he asked. "I heard a woman screaming!"

"That was Chauncy!" Valtora gasped, sprinting into the forest. "They've got him!"

Gavin followed behind her, catching up to her quickly…and Rocky rose to his blocky feet, stomping after them. Nettie brought Harry on a stream of flowing water, and even Peter joined in, galloping after Valtora.

"Who?" Nettie asked, surging past Gavin to reach Valtora's side.

"Something dark," she answered. "It vanished into the woods this way!"

"Which way?" Nettie pressed.

"I don't know!" Valtora replied, continuing to weave through the trees frantically. Nettie blinked.

"What?" she blurted out. "What'd'ya mean you don't know?"

"It was really dark," Valtora explained, huffing and puffing. Nettie stopped, staring at Valtora incredulously.

"Then why in blazes are you running?" she demanded. Valtora slowed, then stopped, turning to face her.

"What else am I gonna do?" she shot back.

"Not run randomly through a damn forest in the middle of the damn night," Nettie answered, putting her hands on her hips…and sucking the water from the stream back into the magical stone she wore around her neck. The Water Stone, or Wet Stone, she'd called it. Gavin couldn't quite remember.

"But they took Chauncy!" Valtora pressed, her eyes growing moist. Her lower lip trembled, and she glared at Nettie, her hands balled into fists at her sides. "We have to do *something!*"

"Honey, you feel anything?" Nettie asked, turning to Harry. Harry frowned, kicking off a shoe and digging his big toe into the ground. He paused a moment, as if deep in thought.

"Somethin' moving fast," he answered. "About a half-mile this way," he added, pointing to Gavin's right.

"Let's go!" Valtora exclaimed. Peter neighed, rushing to her side, and she mounted him, grabbing fistfuls of mane.

"Hold your horses," Nettie told her. Then she turned back to Harry. "Any idea what's got the kid?"

"Something with two feet," he answered. "Must be dragging him."

"Wait, is it one thing or a lot of things?" Nettie pressed.

"One," Harry replied.

"Well go on," Nettie ordered. "Lead the way already!"

Harry paused.

"Uh oh," he warned.

"What?" Nettie pressed.

"Can't feel 'em anymore," he explained. She glowered at him.

"What'd'ya mean?"

"Must've taken to the air," he reasoned.

"It can fly?" Nettie asked.

"Guess so."

"Well great," she grumbled. "What the hell are we gonna do now?"

"We have to save him!" Valtora urged. Nettie rolled her eyes.

"No shit," she muttered. "How, genius?"

Valtora furrowed her brow, rubbing her chin. Then her eyes brightened.

"His staff!" she exclaimed.

"What about it?" Nettie pressed.

"He can call it to himself," Valtora reasoned. "Maybe if we attach it to something too heavy for it to pull to him, we'll be able to see which way it's trying to go."

"Like a compass," Gavin stated. "It's a sound plan."

"Actually, that ain't half bad," Nettie agreed reluctantly. "Good thinking."

"Aww, thanks," Valtora replied.

"Rocky should fit the bill," Gavin reasoned, eyeing the stone giant. He was the heaviest of them, after all. "Where is Chauncy's staff?"

"I'll get it," Valtora offered. And with that, she turned Peter around, galloping back the way they'd come. Everyone followed after her, eventually reaching the camp again. Valtora had already retrieved Chauncy's staff, and handed it to Rocky.

"We should tie it to Rocky," Gavin stated. "That way, it won't fly out of his grasp if it's recalled when he's sleeping."

"Good idea," Valtora agreed. Nettie eyed Gavin with reluctant approval.

"Well you're not useless at all, are you," she mused. "Kinda strange having a competent wizard around for once."

"Might wanna take notes, honey," Harry replied. Nettie ignored him.

"Anyone got a long enough rope?" she asked. "Or any rope at all?"

"Nope," Harry answered.

"Um…no," Valtora replied.

"I believe I can help," Gavin offered.

"Oh yeah?" Nettie inquired. "How?"

Gavin retrieved his twin golden knitting needles from their holsters, smiling at her.

"With these," he replied.

She just stared at him blankly, as if he were a complete idiot.

"What, you gonna knit Rocky a sweater or something?" she asked. Gavin didn't bother to entertain her quip, sitting down instead. He tapped the ends of his needles together, then drew them apart…and a line of bright red wool appeared between them.

"Ooo," Rocky breathed. Nettie rolled her eyes, but Gavin ignored her, starting the process of knitting. He focused on the wool, and soon found himself lost in shaping it. One strand looping back on itself over and over again. And over and under, over and under. Each section becoming part of a network, each warp supporting the woofs, and each woof supporting the warp.

One thing of many things, a continuous thread. Of itself, supporting itself, without a single section left to itself. It was, like the universe, a thing of many things, with every part an essential part of the whole, supporting everything else. There was nothing out of place. Nothing that *could* be out of place.

And as he knitted, Gavin felt himself returning to that wondrous place in his mind, becoming one with what he was doing. With only a small portion of his attention on the end result. For the end was not what he treasured, but the process. The knitting, not the knitted. He trusted the process to create the product, and therefore he was free to enjoy the *now* of its creation.

He realized he was finished, and looked up, seeing everyone seated around him. How long had passed, he hadn't a clue. But when he looked down, he saw a giant red vest, fashioned with holes like a fishing net.

"Here Rocky," he offered, handing the sweater to the giant. Who took it, turning it about in his hands for a bit to figure out how it should fit, then pulling it on. It stretched over the giant's chest and back, fitting quite well.

"Liiiike," Rocky declared, beaming down at Gavin.

"Great," Nettie said. "Now he looks as stupid as you do."

Gavin ignored her, grabbing Chauncy's staff and handing it to Rocky.

"Put this under, at your lower belly," he instructed. "If it's close to your center of gravity, it's less likely to tip you over when Chauncy summons it."

"Okkeeee," Rocky agreed, doing just that. The vest held the staff tightly to the giant's body, preventing it from flying out.

"Now you'll be able to feel where the staff wants to go," Gavin reasoned.

"Pretty clever," Harry noted, nudging Nettie. Who nodded grudgingly.

"Now we just gotta hope Chauncy's smart enough to summon it," she stated.

"It's likely he will," Gavin said. "It's his main weapon…it should be the first thing he thinks of."

"Should be," Nettie retorted, clearly unconvinced. Gavin frowned.

"What do you mean?" he asked. For he knew that Chauncy had not only helped defeat his former raiding party at the Great Wood, but had also single-handedly defeated The Dark One.

"Chauncy's a good boy," Nettie explained. "But sometimes he's…"

"An airhead?" Valtora offered.

"Right," Nettie agreed.

"Totally useless?" Valtora added.

"Occasionally," Nettie replied.

"A complete idiot?" Valtora pressed, seeming to enjoy insulting her partner.

"You're perfect for each other," was all Nettie said.

"Damn right," Valtora agreed. She paused. "Now what?"

"Now we wait," Nettie answered. Valtora's eyes widened.

"What?" she blurted out. "But Chauncy's in trouble!"

"He is," Gavin interjected. "But at this point, we won't know where he is until he summons his staff. There's no other way to find out."

"Unless we go back to the Order of Mundus," Nettie replied. "They've got all sorts of ways of finding people. But by the time we get there, it'll be days from now, if not longer."

"So there's really nothing else we can do?" Valtora pressed. Gavin shook his head.

"I'm afraid not," he confirmed. "At this point, Chauncy's survival is up to Chauncy. If he's alive – and has the presence of mind to summon his staff – then he'll have a chance."

"And if not," Nettie replied grimly, "...we won't be saving him. We'll be getting our revenge."

# Chapter 22

To Chauncy's surprise, he woke up. And to his further surprise, he found himself lying on a large bed, covered in silky black sheets up to his upper thighs, with his arms and legs bound in soft black restraints at each of four bedposts. He was staring up at a ceiling a good ten feet above his head.

One composed entirely of skulls.

There were human skulls and bovine skulls. Horse skulls and cat and dog skulls. All sorts of skulls, really. Fit together with inky black mortar. And in each of the many, many eye sockets, there were ruby-red crystals staring down at him.

He closed his eyes, then reopened them. But the view was the same.

Chauncy rubbed his eyes, then sat up, looking down at himself. To his surprise, he was naked. Or at least mostly naked. For when he checked down below, he found himself wearing something quite unexpected. And on a most unexpected place. For there, on his most prominent – and previously injured – part, was a little silver helmet of sorts completely covering the...head. Sculpted to look like a demon's wickedly grinning skull, no less...complete with ruby-red eyes.

"Do you like it?" a voice inquired from his right.

He jerked his gaze toward the voice, seeing a woman standing by a doorway there. She was tall, slender but curvy, and spectacularly beautiful. So beautiful, in fact, that she eclipsed even Valtora's bedazzled self. She had long black hair that was perfectly straight, and skin as pale as...well, as something very pale. Her eyes were large, purple, and hypnotically gorgeous. Intricate tattoos covered her hands, arms, neck, and even framed her face, but in an elegant way, if disturbingly so.

But Chauncy found his gaze dropping a bit, to even more intriguing matters below.

For the woman was wearing a shiny black sleeveless uniform, one so very tight that it left extraordinarily little to the imagination.

145

And, given just how intriguing her curves were, the imagination – without any work to do in guessing at anatomy – was left to imagine what it would like to do with it.

"Oh," he murmured, staring quite despite himself.

"I got the idea from a book I read in the Cave of Wonder," the woman told him, strolling into the room. Even the way she walked was suggestive. Badass, but in a "wowee" kind of way.

"Huh?" he mumbled, returning his gaze to hers.

"Mods for Rods," she stated. "It's all about magical codpieces and…little heads for your little head," she explained, her gaze dropping to his. He blinked, then looked down at himself, remembering that the sheet was still down below his waist…and that his…erm, demon was showing.

And furthermore, that it was now…ah…showing off.

"Oh!" he blurted out, moving to cover himself. But he couldn't, on account of his limbs being tied to the bedposts. The woman's lips curled in a smirk, her eyes locked on his…demon.

"Looks like I got your size right," she mused.

"I uh…who…where am I?" he stammered, blushing furiously.

"In my lair," the woman answered, gesturing at the room. "Do you like it?"

"Um…who are you?" he pressed.

"My name is Zella Trek," she answered. Which to be fair, was the answer he was both expecting…and dreading. "And you're my husband's bastard love child. The son of a dick."

Chauncy didn't quite know how to respond to that.

Zella went right up to the right side of his bed near his feet, gazing at him with her unnerving purple eyes.

"You look just like him, you know," she mused, putting a hand on his thigh. He resisted the urge to pull away. "It's really quite unnerving, actually," she continued. "When I saw you in that little shelter of yours, I thought you *were* him."

"Huh," Chauncy mumbled.

"So handsome," she mused, sliding her hand up a bit. He did try to pull away then, feeling awfully exposed. "And younger. And not a dick, not like your father." She smiled. "You're really just *perfect*."

"Um…thanks," he replied. Then he paused. "Perfect for what?"

"You'll see," she promised.

"I thought you were going to kill me," Chauncy told her.

"I was," she confessed.

146

"So…why haven't you?" he asked. "Not that I'm complaining," he added hastily. Bound to the bed as he was, she would have no problem murdering him if she chose to.

"I changed my mind," she answered.

"Oh," he replied. "Well that's good."

"It is for you," she agreed. "And for me."

Chauncy paused.

"Why's that?" he pressed.

"You'll see," she replied. With a rhyme, he noted. Which hinted that she was indeed a wizard. He squirmed, straining against his restraints.

"Why did you bring me here?" he demanded.

"To kill you," she answered breezily. "I could've killed you in your little camp, but I wanted to drag it out a bit."

"So you *are* going to kill me," he accused.

"We already discussed this," she retorted. "Don't put words in my mouth."

"I'm not putting words in your mouth," he retorted. She smirked.

"Wouldn't be the first thing you put in my mouth," she replied. He blinked…then blushed furiously.

"Th-that was you?" he stammered, his cheeks burning hot. He squirmed, her hand on his thigh even more discomforting now. Her eyes twinkled.

"It was my Inkling," she corrected, turning around to show him her back. Which, seeing as how her uniform was scandalously split in the back – nearly down to her anatomical split, in fact – was spectacularly displayed. He saw a large tattoo of a beautiful winged woman, one that looked just like Zella, but entirely black, like her shadow. And to either side of this, there was another pair of tattooed wings.

"Your…what?" he asked. She turned around.

"A very special creation of mine," she explained. "When I set her loose, I can control her as if she's me. I see through her eyes, feel through her skin…as if she were my body instead of my own."

"So you were the…ah, the one who…um…" Chauncy stammered. Her smile widened.

"Oh yes," she confirmed. "Glad to hear I haven't lost my touch."

Chauncy grimaced. She most certainly hadn't, as much as he hated to admit it. It'd been distressingly spectacular. He felt an immediate pang of shame at the thought of what had transpired. For even though he'd been fooled, the fact that he'd so definitively enjoyed the company of another woman was still a betrayal. In fact, he recalled having told her the unfortunate truth…that it was the best he'd ever had.

*I'm sorry poopy-dooz,* he thought.

"It's been a long while," she admitted. "Especially for me. I have to say, it…brought back memories."

"Let me go," he told her. In far less commanding a way than he would've liked.

"Goodness no," she replied. "Why would I do that?"

"Because it's the right thing to do," he explained.

She just stared at him for a long, uncomfortable moment. Then she burst out laughing. It was a melodious sound, and quite pleasant, which was jarring in the face of his position, the skull-ceiling, and her overall dark and badass look. At length she finished, shaking her head and smiling at him.

"Well aren't you something," she mused. "You really mean that, don't you?"

"I do," he confirmed.

"The right thing to do," she quoted.

"That's right."

"For whom?" she inquired. He paused.

"Huh?"

"How would you know what's right for me?" she inquired, arching an eyebrow.

"I…well, because it's just right," he answered. "There's right and wrong," he added. "This is wrong," he stated, yanking at his restraints. "And letting me go is right."

"And how many times in your life did you think you were doing something wrong when it was right?" she pressed, putting a hand on her hip. "Or something right…and then find out it was wrong later?"

Chauncy grimaced.

"Right," she concluded. "So you're wrong."

"How can kidnapping and tying up someone be right?" he argued.

"I didn't kill you," she pointed out.

"Well yes," he replied. "Thank you for that."

"You're welcome," she replied. "And you're welcome for my hospitality."

"Hospitality?" he blurted out incredulously, jangling his restraints. She smirked, eyeing his little demon.

"You know what I mean."

"I'm not thanking you for that," he retorted. "It's not so nice now that I know it was you."

"Oh I find that *very* hard to swallow," she retorted, sliding her hand up a bit further. "And that's not usually a problem for me…as you know."

Chauncy blushed. For the male brain was quite intelligent at times, but easily overruled by his far stupider brain…which awoke at the reminder of her proficiency. A fact that Zella, being ever the perceptive one, didn't miss.

"You look *so* much like him," she mused, giving him a mysterious smile. "It's uncanny, really. Only your personality gives it away."

"What?"

"You're…sweet," she explained. "Innocent. Just perfect, really."

"For what?" he pressed. She smiled.

"For this."

And then she slid her hand up further, and more to the middle, her fingertips brushing against his…happy place. Which was all-too-happy to accept her touch, to Chauncy's dismay. Sadly, happy places were happy to be happy, regardless of the circumstances.

"No!" he blurted out, struggling against his restraints.

"Shh."

"I'm taken!" he protested.

"That didn't stop your father," she argued. And was clearly not stopping her. For she continued to play with his toys, so to speak, despite his reluctance to share them.

"I'm not my father," he retorted, starting to squirm. For while his better angels made him struggle against his restraints, her strategy of pandering to his…little demon proved a distressingly successful strategy, at least as far as the demon was concerned. "Stop!" he cried.

She did stop then, smiling down at him with a very satisfied expression.

"That's only the beginning, Chauncy," she purred. "Just *wait* until you see what else I can do."

"Untie me," he told her.

"No."

"Release me!" he demanded.

"If you insist," she replied. And reached down to do just that.

"Not what I meant!" he protested, thrashing about some more. She laughed, then bent over him to gaze into his eyes.

"You're the best parts of your father," she told him, stroking his hair. "With none of the worst." She smiled. "You deserve good things, Chauncy," she told him, leaning down to kiss his forehead, then staring at him with those deep purple eyes. "And I'm going to give them to you."

# Chapter 23

After the fall of the tallest tower of King Pravus's castle, Pravus and Templeton spent the rest of the day – and the following morning – helping rescue survivors from the rubble. Pravus's unmatched strength – along with Templeton's help – allowed them to lift the rubble from more than a few guards, servants, and other victims. Victims who were rather amazed that their king had personally come to save them. Helping them had felt ten times as heroic as slaying the beast Fang, and after the last victim had been rescued, Pravus felt proud indeed. But this was soon replaced by an equal measure of shame and regret…for the ones who hadn't made it.

"I failed them," Pravus muttered as he stood before his throne, staring at the monstrous chair. He didn't feel worthy of sitting on it, seeing as how he'd brought devastation on his realm once again. "First those townspeople with The Dark One," he said, "…now this."

"It's not your fault," Templeton assured him, standing at his side.

"Everything is my fault," Pravus countered. "It has to be; I'm king."

Desmond – who'd been spared from the devastation wrought by Fang, thank goodness – eyed Pravus, standing at his other side.

"Your heart was in the right place sire," the old man declared. "But you're too trusting."

"As I was with Gavin, and the Chosen Ones, and now Zella," Pravus muttered, shaking his head. "And here I thought I was cynical and rude."

"You are," Desmond assured him. Which wasn't reassuring at all.

"Pardon?" Pravus stated, turning to eye the old man.

"You've got a cynic's mind and a hero's heart," Desmond explained. "And one often gets in the way of the other."

"Hmm," Pravus hmm'ed, rubbing his chiseled jaw.

"Truer words have rarely been spoken," Templeton agreed, smiling at Pravus. "You're a good man, my liege…and good men are prone to have their goodness used against them by evil men."

"And women," Pravus noted.

"Indeed," Templeton agreed.

"Well then," Pravus stated. "I suppose I need men – and women – with cynicism in their hearts to advise me, to balance my propensities."

"That would be me," Desmond replied. Pravus gave him a look.

"As I recall, *you're* the one who advised me to follow Zella to Borrin," he pointed out.

"I can't be right all the time," Desmond counter-pointed.

"So honestly, the deaths of all those poor guards and servants is on you," Pravus pressed. Desmond grimaced.

"The cynic's mouth has spoken," he grumbled.

"Well it's true," Pravus pointed out.

"We all have regrets, sire."

"Indeed," Pravus agreed.

"A man can only live without regret if he barely lives at all," Templeton philosophized. "To be a hero requires taking on risk…the risk of failure."

"Well said, Templeton," Pravus agreed.

"Quite," Desmond concurred.

"Are you implying that you're a hero?" Pravus snipped.

"Not until recently," the old man replied.

"Oh *really*."

"I did advise you regarding Gavin Merrick," Desmond pointed out. "And during The Dark One's rise."

"Quite successfully," Templeton pointed out. Rather irritatingly, which was an unusual sentiment for Pravus to have for his cousin.

"Words don't make heroes," Pravus shot back. "Deeds do."

"My words led to your deeds," Desmond argued.

"So you're saying *you* made me a hero?" Pravus pressed, putting his hands on his ridiculously narrow waist. And flaring his lats a bit, because he couldn't really help it.

"I helped bring out the hero I always knew was in you," Desmond replied.

Pravus frowned. For the wily old man had managed to craft a downright touching reply…one that had quite definitively ended Pravus's line of argument. And, seeing as how he was in an argumentative mood, this was *enormously* irritating.

"I hate you and go away," he ordered.

"At once, sire," Desmond droned. And with that, the old man did go away, leaving the throne room with irritating slowness. Pravus watched him go, then sighed, turning to Templeton.

"What now?" he wondered aloud.

"Might I make a suggestion, my liege?" Templeton inquired.

"Always," Pravus urged.

"I suggest we enlist some help," Templeton said. "From the Order of Mundus."

"They won't help," Pravus replied, still irritably. "They always defer to the Chosen Ones."

"True," Templeton conceded. "But Zella was impersonating a wizard of the Order…a fact I'm sure they'll want to know."

Pravus considered this, rubbing his chin.

"Why you're right," he realized. "They'll surely seek to censor her, at the very least. Can't have rogue wizards giving the Order a bad name, destroying castles and carrying on massacring and such."

"It simply wouldn't do," Templeton agreed.

"Well done, Templeton!" Pravus declared, beaming at his cousin.

"It is my pleasure to serve you my king," Templeton replied with a bow.

"Then I look forward to your continued servicing," Pravus stated with a smile. "In the meantime, we'll need a backup plan, in case the Order is as reticent as ever."

"A contingency for their well-known propensity," Templeton concurred. "And we'll have to coordinate the castle repairs, and the funerals for the tragically deceased."

"And the disposal of the massive corpse of Fang," Pravus added. For the serpent still remained where it'd fallen, its head split in two.

"Indeed," Pravus agreed. "To the office?" For he always felt a bit smarter there, surrounded by books. Ones he'd never read and never would, but it was the ambience that mattered.

"At once!" Templeton replied with gusto.

With that, Pravus leg-day-limped out of the throne room with Templeton hobbling at his side, eager to do the work of governing. For he'd learned the hard way that giving in to despair solved nothing, and that it was impossible to help oneself – or others – when one felt helpless.

He was King Pravus the Eighth, the leader of his people. And while he wasn't the best monarch – but hopefully not the worst – the people of Pravus deserved *his* best. As the gym had taught him, it wasn't the weight lifted that mattered, nor the number of reps. No, it was the effort that mattered, and having the courage to try.

The greatest failure was to give up. And that was the one thing Pravus could promise he would never do.

# Chapter 24

Chauncy stared up at the ceiling of skulls, feeling utterly drained. Zella had left him some time ago, for what purpose, he didn't know. And to be frank, he didn't particularly care. For it was clear that she had no intention of releasing him…at least not from her custody. He sighed, gazing up at those countless eye sockets with their ruby-red crystals imbedded within, all seeming to stare at him…while mocking him with eternal, horrible grins.

"Fuck," he declared. Which summed up his situation nicely.

He thought of his friends then. Of Nettie and Harry, and Rocky and Rooter. Of sweet Valtora…and little Chaos Little, all probably worried sick about him. He even thought of Peter, although those thoughts were of a darker tone. And Gavin, who'd inexplicably returned to their lives, as a creator of magic rather than a consumer of it.

They were probably looking for him right now, wondering where he'd gone. Wondering if he was even alive anymore.

Chauncy felt a lump in his throat at the thought of them mourning him. Of Valtora weeping over her lost love. Of Nettie and Harry shaking their heads…and blaming themselves for his death, just like they'd blamed themselves for their former apprentice Greg's death so long ago. His vision blurred with tears, and he blinked them away, feeling absolutely miserable.

"I failed," he muttered to himself, gritting his teeth against another surge of emotion. "I'm a terrible wizard," he added.

And that was truest of all, he realized. He was the worst wizard he'd ever met, in fact. Nettie and Harry were far better, and Imperius Fanning was beyond anything he could ever hope to be. Even Valtora was more confident in battle than he was.

Sure, he'd beaten The Dark One. But he knew damn well it'd been sheer luck that he'd done so. And now his luck had run out.

"This sucks," he muttered to himself.

So he lay there, staring up at the ceiling, waiting for whatever fate awaited him in the future. For there was absolutely nothing he could do now. Not against a real wizard like Zella Trek. With nothing to do, he closed his eyes, waiting to fall asleep.

And heard a baby crying.

Chauncy's eyes snapped open, and he pricked his ears, focusing on the sound. It was barely there…maybe not there at all. But regardless, he could hear it.

*It's not real*, he told himself, closing his eyes again. He felt himself drifting off…and then heard it again.

*Waaa…*

Chauncy opened his eyes, lifting his head to look around the room. But of course it was empty. Except for him…and his little demon helmet, grinning demonically up at the ceiling of skulls.

"Go to sleep," he told himself. And closed his eyes again to do just that.

*Waaa!*

"For the love of…!" he blurted out, opening his eyes and doing a bit of thrashing against his restraints. For it was clear what he was hearing. Or rather, what he *wasn't* hearing, but was still hearing, inexplicably.

*Phantom cries!*

He pictured Chaos then, cradled in his arms during their walk together. Just looking up at him with those big eyes, as if Chauncy was the world to him. Which, Chauncy supposed, was mostly true. He and Valtora *were* Chaos's world…and not just because they were Chaos's parents. For the little boy *was* Chauncy and Valtora, in that he was two lives continuing as one. He recalled his doppelganger's words to him then, in the Cave of Wonder:

*Where there's one, there's always two.*

Everyone was a continuation of the lives of two people, just as Chauncy was his father and mother, and Chaos was Chauncy and Valtora. Every one *was* two…and Chauncy's life would continue through Chaos, and through Chaos's children, and so on. Even if Chauncy died, his life would continue, in that most peculiar and clever of ways.

*The end of you is the end of* your *world*, Imperius had told him.

But the worlds in those who lived would go on. For in the end, that's all there was…the world as experienced by those living it.

If Chauncy died here and now – which was the only time it would happen, as it was the only time there was – *his* world would end. But the worlds within Valtora and Chaos and Nettie – and everyone else – would remain.

"Well I guess it's all right then," he decided. For Valtora would have no trouble at all finding another man to help raise Chaos. And oddly enough, as depressing as the thought could've been, Chauncy found it freeing. For if his own death wasn't the end of the world – or worlds, as it were – why, then everything *was* going to be all right.

Chauncy smiled, feeling quite suddenly at peace. And strangely enough, the realization that it would be perfectly okay if he died gave him the courage to try not to.

"The universe told me to play with myself," he declared, eyeing his little demon-helmet. "So that's what I'll do."

"Oh *goody*," the demon-head replied.

Chauncy blinked.

"Um…" he began, staring at the thing. For as the…helmet had spoken, its little mouth had moved, in a stimulating sort of way. "Did you just…"

Chauncy's…part rose, until it was standing straight up. Which was quite strange…but not as strange as what happened next. For the demon-helmet swiveled around on Chauncy's little head, its glittering red eyes staring at him.

"Holy…!"

"Hardly," the demon shot back.

"You *talk*?"

"You tell me," the demon replied. Each word sent a pleasant little zing through Chauncy's…thing, which was a bit distracting.

"You're…alive?" Chauncy pressed.

"I'm certainly sentient," the demon answered. "A magical mod for your rod."

"Oh," Chauncy mumbled. He took a moment to process this, and found himself having trouble doing so. Because it felt like he was talking to his…

"Tip," the demon said.

"Uh…excuse me?"

"My name is Tip," the demon clarified.

"Just Tip?"

The demon smirked.

"Doesn't seem like enough, does it?" he mused.

Chauncy just stared at the…Tip.

"Well go on," Tip urged.

"What?" Chauncy asked.

"You said you were going to play with yourself," Tip reminded him.

Chauncy blinked, then blushed.

"That's not what I meant," he told the demon.

"Uh huh."

"I meant I was going to do a little magic," Chauncy explained. Tip grinned.

"I've already got you started."

"Not *that* kind of magic," Chauncy protested. "Wizardly magic!"

"Aww," Tip replied. His…body even slouched a bit. "Shucks." Chauncy frowned.

"How are you doing that?" he demanded.

"Doing what?"

"Controlling my…thingy," Chauncy clarified.

"I'm your penis personified," Tip explained.

"You're my…uh, peepee?"

"That's right," Tip confirmed. "A mod for your rod. It's been modified. Permanently."

Chauncy blinked.

"Permanently?" he asked. Tip grinned evilly.

"Permanently."

"What do you mean?" Chauncy demanded. "Can't I just take you off?"

"You can try to get me off," Tip replied rather hopefully.

"That's not what I…" Chauncy began, then thought better of pursuing this particular line of conversation. "Why would Zella put you on me?"

"Look up at the ceiling," Tip replied. Chauncy did so, seeing the skulls staring down at him. Then he returned his gaze to the demon.

"And?"

"She's *totally* psycho," Tip explained. "But practical. After all, you're all tied up, and that can get…messy after a while."

Chauncy gave the demon a questioning look.

"Beds make poor toilets," Tip clarified.

"Ah."

"Luckily I magically live off of your waste," Tip continued with a grin. "So it doesn't go to waste. You'll never need to go to the bathroom again!"

Chauncy took a moment to process this.

"So I'm talking to my penis," Chauncy pressed, hardly believing he was having this conversation.

"Didn't see that one coming, did you?" Tip quipped. And began to chuckle, standing up straight again.

Chauncy just stared for a bit.

"Right," he decided. "Whelp, I've gone insane."

"Not at all," Tip countered. "Magic is your relationship with the world...including yourself," he reminded Chauncy. "And your relationship with *me* is magical indeed."

"Anyway, I want to get out of here," Chauncy stated. "So I'm going to play. But not with myself," he added hastily. Tip pouted.

"Perhaps later then?" the demon asked hopefully.

"Um...sure," Chauncy replied noncommittally. "Now be quiet," he added. "Please."

To his relief, Tip did just that, lying back down. And apparently to go to sleep, for his little demon eyes closed. Chauncy looked up at the ceiling then, at the innumerable skulls grinning at him from high above. He grinned back just as crazily as he could. For the only things that could give a man confidence were competence...and psychosis. And as he was chronically lacking in the former, he'd have to settle for the latter.

"It's *wizard* time, bitches!" he declared. Psychotically.

Then, with a most badass feeling indeed, he opened his right hand, splaying his fingers wide.

"Staff Tug!" he cried, willing his Staff of Wind back to him.

He waited then, knowing there was quite a distance for the staff to travel. And waited.

And waited.

A few minutes passed, and then considerably more than a few. And yet Chauncy's staff didn't come...no matter how many "Staff Tugs" he tried. At length, he slumped into the bed, feeling hopeless once more. He relaxed his right hand, for his staff wasn't coming...

...and felt it rest on something very soft and furry.

Chauncy yanked his hand away, jerking his head to look at what he'd rested his hand on...and found a large cat lying on the bed under his hand, big purple-pink eyes staring at him.

Sexily.

"ZoMonsterz?!" Chauncy blurted out, hardly believing his eyes.

"Reowrr," ZoMonsterz replied, licking his hand. While maintaining eye contact. Tip stirred.

"That's nice," Tip murmured, eyeing the cat the precise way that ZoMonsterz was eyeing Chauncy.

"I need to get out of here," Chauncy told ZoMonsterz, ignoring the demon-head. "Can you help?"

ZoMonsterz stopped licking, then got up, stretching her back luxuriously. Then she turned her purple gaze on the rope binding his right wrist…and extended a big paw, retracting her claws. Which were very long. And very sharp. And glowed faintly purple. Also, each had a slight wet sheen to them, as if coated in some sort of unhealthy substance.

ZoMonsterz swiped at the rope in an almost dismissive sort of way…and it snapped as if cut with a sword.

"Wow," Chauncy murmured.

"Reowrr," ZoMonsterz agreed.

And that's how Chauncy's escape began.

# Chapter 25

It was well past bedtime when Rocky was woken by a tug. He opened his eyes, seeing stars in the heavens above. Little Rooter was lying curled up in the crook of his right arm, sleeping peacefully. Rocky smiled at the sight of the little guy…then felt another tug. Specifically, a fair bit below his chest. Or even more specifically, within his vest.

He looked down at himself, seeing his pretty red vest…and Chauncy's little staff tucked within it. It had risen off his belly, and was trying to fly away.

He smiled, feeling quite relieved. For that meant that his good friend Chauncy was okay. Or at least alive; and with Rooter's help, alive *meant* okay.

Rocky jostled Rooter just as gently as he could, and Rooter's stony eyes opened. Rocky pointed to the staff, and Rooter broke out into a rocky smile, rising to his little feet. They exchanged not a word, for words were difficult for them both, each having gravely voices. Neither suffered for this lacking, for words only got between those speaking them. *Doing* communicated everything Rocky needed to communicate, unless dealing with humans. For they were astounded and hypnotized by endless songs they called sentences, like birds constantly chirping to each other. As a result, they tended to ignore what they were doing…or not doing.

So, in lieu of speaking, Rocky *did*. He rose to his feet, then picked up Rooter, placing the little golem – and his very best friend – on his left shoulder. Then he stepped up to Nettie and Harry's lean-to, reaching out with a finger and scratching at the angled roof. This made a loud scraping sound; within moments, it had its intended effect, and Harry woke up.

"Heya Rocky," Harry greeted. Rocky smiled, pointing to Chauncy's staff, still straining against Rocky's vest. "Oh goody," Harry said, eyeing the staff. Unlike most humans, Harry didn't use many words to communicate; perhaps it was his love of rocks that made the wizard this way. For rocks needed words even less than

161

giants and golems did. Harry woke Nettie, who made complaining-type noises, then got up reluctantly. She shot Harry a glare, then turned it on Rocky. Of course, glares didn't bother Rocky; he had a thick skin, both literally and figuratively. As such, he didn't mind them. Or pay them any mind, for that matter.

"Whelp, the kid's not dead," Nettie grumbled, eyeing the staff. She glanced at Harry. "Guess you better wake Valtora," she prompted.

"With a kiss?" Harry hoped.

"Do it and I'll drown you," she replied. "And the little hussy too."

Harry eyed Valtora's lean-to, rubbing his chin thoughtfully. Nettie rolled her eyes, stomping off toward the lean-to instead, gently nudging Valtora. Who woke up and got up, adorable little Chaos in her arms. Valtora turned to Rocky, spotting Chauncy's staff bulging out of Rocky's knitted fishnet vest, and broke out into a huge smile.

"Chauncy's alive!" she gasped, putting both hands to her mouth in shock. And dropping Chaos in the process. "Oh!" Valtora gasped, lunging to catch him. But he landed right on the ground with a *whump*, bouncing a little.

Chaos's eyes snapped open, and his mouth opened up wide. And, as Valtora scooped him up and clutched the baby to her chest, he burst out in an awful, heart-wrenching scream.

"Valtora!" Nettie complained.

Rocky lowered Rooter to the ground by Valtora, and the little golem made quick work of healing the poor child. And how convenient it was that Chauncy's magic – and Harry's – had combined to bring Rooter to life, so that Chauncy's son could withstand having Valtora as a mother. T'was the strange wisdom of destiny, Rocky supposed.

"Sorry baby-poo," Valtora cooed, rocking the child. Nettie just buried her head in her hands, and Harry chuckled, rubbing her back.

"What's going on?" Gavin asked, stepping out of his own tent. Rocky turned to face the man. He had no hard feelings about their former enemy. After all, Rocky himself had started off being enemies with Nettie, Harry, and Chauncy, before Harry had shown Rocky his heart…and Nettie and Chauncy had done so soon after.

"Chauncy's summoning his staff," Nettie replied, gesturing at it. Gavin said not a word, merely helping to gather everyone's belongings for the inevitable trip. A fact that Rocky had noted in observing Gavin; the man was a do-er…and a leader. Like Rocky and Rooter, he let his actions do most of the talking.

It wasn't long before they were all ready to go, and Rocky lowered himself onto all fours to accept Nettie, Harry, Gavin, and Rooter on his back. Valtora rode Peter, and off they went.

\* \* \*

Valtora bounced on Peter's back as he wove through the Great Wood, Rocky *thump*, *thump*-ing right behind them. She gazed down at Chaos, all snuggled up in his coot widdle wrap, his chubby cheeks smooshed against her boobies. A favorite place for any person to be, Valtora knew…herself included. She'd been concerned that he'd suffocate himself in said position, but his face remained nice and pink.

"My widdle Chaos Widdle," she cooed, stroking his hair lovingly. She felt the soft spot above his forehead pulsing, and made a face, withdrawing her hand. "Ew," she blurted out, deciding to keep her hands to herself.

It wasn't long before she spotted the end of the Great Wood less than a hundred feet away…and the great grassy plain that extended beyond it. She twisted around, seeing Rocky on all fours, Chauncy's staff bulging out of his vest rather suggestively, the tip pointing the way. She giggle-snorted at the sight of it…as she had countless times during this particular trip.

"Idiot," she heard Nettie grumble from atop Rocky's back. As *she* had countless times during the trip. Valtora ignored her, for she wasn't in the mood for an argument. A rare thing indeed; she suspected it was because her boobies ached, being that they were practically bursting with milk. As if on cue, Chaos's eyes opened, and he began to cry.

"Booby break!" she called out.

She reached down, tugging gently on Peter's multicolored mane. He stopped, and she unleashed the boobies, guiding Chaos to the fount. And with the eventual release of milk, she sighed in relief, then did a little shiver. After a few minutes, she shifted him to the other boob, letting him drain it. For Chaos was an impatient little bastard; the second the milk started to slow, he'd lose his figurative shit.

"Got your momma's temper, don't you," she mused, smiling down at him. He stared back at her with those unblinking eyes, and she felt her heart melt. "But you're so darn *coot* momma can't be mad with you."

"Except for that time you broke his arm," Nettie pointed out from behind. Valtora would've ignored her, but she was comfortable now...which meant she was in the mood for an argument.

"Shut up hag," Valtora snapped. "Or I'll break *your* arm."

"I'd like to see you try, hussy," Nettie retorted. "Whatcha gonna do, bedazzle me to death?"

"You could use it," Valtora argued, sensing a weak spot. "Crone!"

"Whore!" Nettie shot back.

"Shrew!"

"Slut!" Nettie snapped.

"Harridan!" Valtora retorted. There was a pause.

"Harridan?" Nettie asked. "What the hell's that?"

"Harridan," Valtora answered. "Noun. A scolding, vicious woman."

"Oh," Nettie replied. She paused. "There's something seriously wrong with you."

"Virago!" Valtora insulted gleefully.

"I'm done playing with you," Nettie grumbled. Valtora frowned. "Aww."

She realized then that Chaos was done, so she covered up, then patted Peter to prompt him to press on. They made it to the treeline, continuing onward across the grassy plain beyond. It stretched out as far as the eye could see, an endless rolling landscape between her and her destiny.

"Chauncy's out there," she told Peter, patting his neck. Peter snorted dismissively. "He'd come for you," she pointed out. Peter didn't reply. But he kept going forward, which was answer enough.

Onward they went, minutes passing into hours, and hours crawling by until they'd made up most of the day. The sun sailed across the sky, eventually dipping below the horizon for its nightly slumber. And right before it vanished, it seemed to dream in vivid color, setting the sky on purple-pink fire.

"Ooo," Rocky breathed, clearly impressed. Valtora smiled; for she knew as well as anyone how magical beauty could be...and that beauty could be found in just about everything.

Even The Dark One, rest his miserable, monochrome soul.

Valtora found herself gazing at her diamond hand, its facets glittering brilliantly in the light of the setting sun. With all the colors of the rainbow, in fact…which was a fact of white. For Valtora's hand served to split white into all of its component colors, turning what was plain into something beautiful.

That, she realized, was what wizards did. They took the world, plain as seemed to be to everyone else…and brought out its glory, proving that every last part of it was magic. Well, at least to someone.

Peter shook a fly from his head, breaking her from her reverie…and making her startle a little. Chaos squirmed, opening his eyes and looking up at her with nary an expression on his ugly little face. Utterly blank.

"Having some deep thoughts 'n shit," she told him, patting his head. They were the type of thoughts she never searched for, only accepting them when they sought *her* out. She enjoyed them when they came, but enjoyed *not* thinking even more. There was far more magic in experiencing life than spending it endlessly talking to oneself in one's head.

So, having had her revelation for the day – or week, or whatever – she gazed off into the sunset, perfectly content to do so. For as long as Chauncy's staff kept pointing the way, she knew that her love was alive. And if he was alive, then Rooter could make him well, no matter his current state.

And if that bitch Zella was behind his capture, then Valtora would end her like she'd ended Marie Merrick…and the last thing the woman would ever see was the flash of a gorgeous, multicolored diamond fist.

# Chapter 26

Having had his bonds severed by the glowing purple claws of his disturbingly faithful hellcat ZoMonsterz, Chauncy found his purple wizard's robe – and the special underwear Valtora had forced him to wear on their trip – on the floor. He put it on – after trying in vain to pull Tip off.

"Keep trying," Tip urged during the attempt. Chauncy ignored his newly sentient member, knowing full well that Tip was interested in one thing and one thing only. Something that involved getting off, but not from Chauncy's body. So Chauncy pulled on his robe instead.

Thusly dressed, Chauncy checked his pockets, and to his relief, he found his belongings still within. The Magic of Magic on his left, and the Sunstone on his right.

"Okay," he declared, eyeing ZoMonsterz, who was sitting on the floor at his side. "Zella could be anywhere," he warned. "And without my staff, I won't be able to beat her."

ZoMonsterz just gazed up at him lovingly, seeming unconcerned by this fact.

"If she recaptures me, I want you to run," he told her, struck by a sudden burst of heroic self-sacrificial sentiment. "Then find Valtora and tell her where I am."

"Reeowr," ZoMonsterz replied, whether in agreement or not, he hadn't a clue.

"Mffmm mmfff," he heard a muffled voice declare from the front of his pants. He frowned, lifting his robe a bit from his…bits.

"Say again?" he asked.

"If she captures you again, I'll distract her," Tip offered. "At least until Valtora rescues us."

"Um…okay," Chauncy replied.

"That way she won't kill us," Tip added. "It'll be hard work, but I'm up for it."

Chauncy ignored the demon-head, letting his robe fall back into place to muffle the guy. He strode across the room to the door, twisting the knob open. He cracked the door open, peering out…and saw a sliver of hallway beyond, with a skull-embedded wall similar to the ceiling of his room. He glanced down at ZoMonsterz…who darted out of the room, vanishing beyond. "Hey!" he whisper-yelled. But she didn't come back. He sighed, screwing up his courage, then opening the door a bit further and poking his head through. He saw a long hallway beyond, flanked by walls of skulls similar to the bedroom ceiling. The ceiling and floor were made of depressing stone, the precise hue of moldy tombstones.

And ZoMonsterz trotted right down the hallway, toward a stairwell leading upward a good forty feet ahead.

Chauncy eyed the two walls, but to his relief, there were no doors that might open up suddenly and scare the daylights out of him. And there was no daylight, for the only illumination was from skull-lanterns bolted to the walls at regular intervals. This cast the hallway in an extra-spooky light, shadows flickering menacingly.

"Wait!" he hissed at ZoMonsterz, hurrying behind her. The floor was awfully cold, which made him realize he didn't have shoes or boots. So he padded down the creepy hallway, catching up with ZoMonsterz right as she reached the bottom of the stairs. She stopped there, glancing back at him with her unusual eyes. "Okay," he told her. "We need a plan."

She continued to stare at him. Because she couldn't speak.

"Right," he stated, running a hand through his hair. "Um…" But there was really nothing to plan. He had no idea where he was, or where the enemy was, or what she was capable of. And two previous adventures had taught Chauncy that he really didn't even know what *he* was capable of. For his capabilities had often only revealed themselves when needed, and not a second earlier.

*You're a wizard*, he reminded himself. *Play!*

And that, Chauncy knew, meant letting go. For the surest way to kill play was to control it. In short, he needed to be ridiculous.

"Time to lose control, Chauncy-boy," he declared, putting his hands on his hips and executing a rather vigorous hip-thrust. Which was made a bit awkward by Tip's extra weight adding to his manly swing. But the fact that he was here surrounded by skulls, with a demonic mod on his rod, dressed in sparkly purple, and with a hellcat at his side, wasn't just ridiculous. It was *ludicrous*.

Which was precisely what he needed.

He took a deep breath in, then let it out.

"Well alright then," he declared, building up a big ol' dose of crazy. He started hyperventilating, then hopped up and down, wiggling his fingers and flailing his arms wildly. "Bliggity-blig! Yackety-shmack!" he blurted out.

ZoMonsterz blinked.

"Blarg blarg bliggity-blarg!" he continued, spinning like a top, then squatting down low and gritting his teeth. "Dragon fart!" he cried…and then pushed out a rather large – and wet-sounding – burst of flatulence. One that sounded precisely like wet fabric ripping…and made Chauncy stand up quickly and check the back of his wizard's robe, just in case.

"I got it," Tip reassured. "Spicy," he added unnecessarily.

ZoMonsterz wrinkled her nose, then bounded up the stairs. Which made Chauncy giggle…and follow after her with a bit less fear than he'd had before. For if it was his fate to climb these stairs to his death, by golly he was going to die like a wizard: ridiculously.

So, instead of sneaking up the stairs as a perfectly reasonable person would do, Chauncy bounded up them three at a time, grinning like a maniac.

"Weeee!" he cried. Or rather, battle-cried. For it was as good a battle-cry for a wizard as any. He reached the top of the stairs, finding a closed door there with ZoMonsterz standing before it. Without a care, he flung it open…and saw an all-too-familiar sight:

A shadow-woman shaped precisely like Zella, but with wings folded on her back.

Chauncy froze, his breath catching in his throat…and it was Tip's turn to wee.

# Chapter 27

It was a good hour's trek through the rolling fields beyond the Great Wood before Valtora, Gavin, Nettie, Harry, Rocky, Rooter, and Peter spotted something ahead: a swamp. To Valtora's practiced eye, it was really quite perfect, a model representation of its kind. For the swamp was covered with delightfully spooky mist, brambles sprouting densely out of the less-mushy spots of soil. Brambles with long, curved spikes on them, making the path ahead treacherous indeed. At least for a human. But for Rocky and Harry, spikes weren't scratchy at all. So they simply took the lead, plowing right through the brambles with ease.

Valtora rode Peter into the swamp, Peter's hooves sinking inches into the mushy muck underfoot. Chaos was all bundled up at her chest, carried as usual in her wrap. A most convenient invention, the wrap; if she'd had to carry the baby with her arms this whole time, Valtora would've surely left Chaos behind.

"Ooo!" she blurted out, leaping down from the saddle and landing in the muck with a satisfying *squelch*. Chaos startled at the quick maneuver, but settled soon after. Apparently he was becoming accustomed to her spur-of-the-moment bursts of activity, more out of necessity than anything else. For she sure as hell wasn't about to change, not for some kid. Not for *anyone*.

Valtora giggled as she lifted her foot up to take a step, and the sucking vacuum left by her foot made a satisfying farting sound.

"That poor baby," Nettie grumbled from atop Rocky's broad back, shaking her head. Valtora ignored her, not currently in the mood for an argument. For she was busy enjoying the silly sounds of sucking muck, and didn't have time for insulting old ladies.

Peter snorted, eyeing the muck with disgust, clearly unhappy that his fine white coat was being sullied. Or it might've been the stink of rot that was bothering him. Either way, it was clear he wasn't happy.

"Don't worry Peter," she whisper-reassured, patting his flank. "I'll make it up to you."

Peter snorted again, but with a far happier tone, his trudge becoming more of a prance.

Onward they went, Harry and Rocky forging a path through the brambles for what seemed like forever, but was probably a half-hour. At length, they came to an island of relatively dry earth in the middle of the swamp, one where dead-looking trees stood with twisty branches hanging over deep brown dirt. Not that far ahead, Valtora saw gravestones jutting up from said dirt, row after irregular row of them. It was a graveyard, in terrible disrepair. The dead buried in a dead land.

"Momma *likey*," Valtora said, smiling at the place. For while she loved brightness and cheer and color and such, she also found beauty in its absence. And after being with The Dark One for so long, she had an expert's eye for evil aesthetics.

"You're cracked," Nettie grumbled.

"This has to be where Chauncy was taken," Valtora reasoned, ignoring her. "It's like, *totally* evil lair material."

"You would know," Nettie pressed.

"Sure would," Valtora agreed, pleased at this acknowledgement of her expertise.

They reached the tombstones, and everyone dismounted Rocky, who had an easier time navigating the densely packed headstones when walking rather than going on all fours. Soon he – or rather, Chauncy's staff – led them to a huge mausoleum in the center of the graveyard. It was one story tall, wrought of bone-white stone, with dead vines crawling all over it. But while it wasn't tall, it was quite broad, extending over a hundred feet wide, and goodness knew how long. There were no windows, which made sense, considering corpses couldn't usually see. And the entrance was an open doorway with no door, because corpses couldn't usually walk either.

Usually.

Rocky stopped before the entrance, pointing to it.

"Thaaarrrr," he boomed.

"No shit," Nettie replied, putting her hands on her hips. "Well you're not fitting in there Rocky."

Rocky grunted.

"Neither is Peter," she added. "Guess you two can stay out here and stand guard."

"Okkaahhh," Rocky agreed.

"Bye Peter," Valtora said. "Bye shmookie tookums!" And with that, she turned to go into the mausoleum.

"What are you *doing?*" Nettie snapped. Valtora stopped.

"Huh?"

"You're gonna take a damn baby into a damn crypt to fight a damn evil wizard?" Nettie asked incredulously. While giving her a look as if she was a complete idiot, rudely enough.

"*No,*" Valtora lied, unwrapping the wrap. She handed Chaos to Rocky then. "Idiot!" she added. Which was an excellent defense, for Nettie clearly thought *she* was an idiot. It was classic evil tactics to accuse your opponent of precisely what you were guilty of...a fact that politicians, in particular, were well aware of.

"You're an idiot!" Nettie shot back, falling right into the trap.

"What are you, *five?*" Valtora retorted. "Come up with your own insults."

"You..." Nettie began, then stopped, thinking better of it. Valtora pouted.

"Aww."

"Better get goin'," Harry prompted. "Gonna need Chauncy's staff, and Rooter." He gestured at Rocky, who pulled Chauncy's staff free from his knitted vest, then handed Rooter to Harry, who gave the adorable little golem a piggy-back ride.

"I'll take the staff," Gavin offered. Rocky handed it to him. "Ready?" he asked everyone.

"Ready," everyone replied.

"I'll go first," Harry offered. Valtora nodded; being the most invincible among them, it seemed like a good choice.

"Good idea," Valtora replied, never one to hold back a thought.

So Harry did just that, limping up to the mausoleum entrance and stepping right through. Nettie went next, followed by Gavin, then Valtora, who took up the rear. They entered a large room of bone-white stone, with cobwebs hanging in the corners and dust swirling in the air. Skull-shaped lanterns bolted to the walls gave off a dull light, barely up to the task of illuminating what lay within:

A statue of a man in a wizard's robe, right hand stretched high overhead, carrying the moon.

One that looked exactly...*precisely*...like Chauncy.

"Chauncy-poo!" Valtora gasped, clutching her hands to her chest. She rushed up to the statue, gazing up at it in horror. It *was* Chauncy, no doubt about it. "They turned him to *stone!*"

Harry limped up to the statue, touching it with one big, calloused hand. He close his eyes for a moment, then shook his head.

"Ain't him," he replied. "Just a statue."

171

"Oh," Valtora mumbled. Then she frowned. "Why'd Zella make a statue of him?" Her eyes widened. "She must be like, *obsessed* with him."

"Maybe," Nettie replied.

"Uh oh," Harry warned, his hand still on the statue.

"Well what is it now?" Nettie asked.

"Trouble," Harry answered.

And with that, black goo oozed out of a hole in the bottom of the moon, dripping down the statue's arm and chest. It oozed all the way down the statue's legs to the pedestal it stood on, then to the floor, forming a rapidly growing pool there.

"Back," Nettie ordered. Everyone backed away, even as the black pool's edge expanded slowly outward toward them. "Get ready," she added, putting a hand to the Wetstone. Harry stuffed his hands in his pockets and kicked off a shoe, and Valtora curled her diamond hand into a fist. Gavin reached into his holsters for his golden knitting needles, withdrawing them and holding them like swords.

"Let's *do* this," Valtora declared.

The black pool rose upward in the middle, engulfing the statue of Chauncy completely…then shaped itself around it. Black curved horns sprouted from the sides of its head, its face forming a glaring skull. Spikes grew from its back…and from the moon it engulfed, a long black chain extending from the bottom of the moon and wrapping around the figure's arm.

The black skull turned slightly, its hollow eye sockets seemed to look right at them. Then it pulled away from the statue, tendrils of goo stretching from where they'd touched the stone…then snapping back into the black skeleton-figure as it pulled away completely.

It stood before them then, its flesh seeming to harden. The black spiked ball it held in its right hand rolled off, falling to the ground with a loud *whump*. Dust stirred from the impact, the ball's spikes digging holes into the stone floor.

"Oh *shit*," Valtora swore…right as the creature yanked on the chain, swinging the huge spiked ball right at them!

\* \* \*

Nettie burst into action as the inky-black skeleton-beast attacked, connecting with the ocean of water within the Wetstone. She willed

172

it outward as if it were her own body, and water surged out of the Wetstone, shooting in a powerful jet at the spiked ball hurtling toward them. The jet struck the ball, blasting it with enormous force…and managed to stop it in its tracks in midair. It fell to the floor with a *clang*.

"Go Nettie!" Valtora cried. "Kick that thing's ass!"

The creature jerked the ball backward, then swung it forward again in a big arc…one that threatened to smash into Harry, who was the first in its deadly path. He just stood there, his skin turning as gray as steel right as it struck. With another loud *clang*, making Harry stumble to the side a bit…but harming him not at all.

Harry gave a hollow-sounding chuckle, reaching down to grab the ball's chain. But it merely turned to goo in his hands, dripping off and re-forming the chain again.

"Huh," Harry murmured.

The creature yanked the ball backward, so that it hurtled all the way to the opposite wall. Then it swung it in a circle in the opposite direction…right at Valtora this time. Nettie summoned more water from the Wetstone, ready to blast the ball again, but Valtora beat her to the punch.

Literally.

Valtora lunged right *into* the path of the ball, swinging her diamond fist at it with all her might…and making a huge dent in it, even as the force of the impact sent Valtora hurtling backward. She would've smashed into the wall at the corner of the room behind her if it hadn't been for Gavin…who had somehow made a knitted red safety net behind Valtora. One that had each end of its thread attached to golden knitting needles, which had somehow embedded themselves in either wall. Such that the net was well enough supported that it caught her safely in its soft embrace before she smashed her pretty face.

Gavin extended his hands, and the knitting needles flung out of the walls, flying into his hands. And the red net unraveled into a single thread…one that vanished when the needles struck his hands.

"Well shit," Nettie swore as she beheld this unexpected development. Even the inky-black creature stared for a moment, clearly as surprised as she was. But it recovered quickly…and the dent in its big spiky ball turned to gel, healing itself, then solidifying once again.

"Well shit," Harry stated.

"That's what I said," Nettie agreed. "Quit playin' around hon," she added. "Kick that thing's ass already!"

"Oh alright," he agreed, as agreeably as ever. Nettie chuckled, taking a few steps back and watching as Harry limped toward the enemy. And as usual in these situations, she settled in, prepared for quite a show. For while the enemy they faced was big and powerful, and could heal on a whim, she could guarantee it'd never met a wizard quite like him.

\* \* \*

Harry limped toward the black skeleton-goo thing, knowing full well that it was a magical tattoo made by Zella Trek. The stone of the statue and this room had told him as much, having witnessed it a while ago. How long, he couldn't be sure, for stone didn't sense time the way people did. In any case, he knew it was by nature ink, and as such, couldn't be killed in the ordinary way. Which wasn't a problem at all for Harry; he'd just have to find an extraordinary way to do it instead. Or at least an odd way.

The creature turned its inky eye sockets to face him, fixing him with a baleful glare. Which didn't bother Harry one bit, of course. He'd been subject to countless glares in his life – the vast majority from his wife – and not a single one had caused him any lasting harm.

"Hello," he greeted. "Wanna be pen pals?"

The creature pulled its ball and chain closer to itself, giving him a gurling hiss.

"Guess not," he decided.

The creature swung the ball right at Harry, and Harry merely fiddled with the piece of steel in his pocket, bringing its essence into himself…and giving himself to it. He felt it squirm with his life force, and at the same time, felt himself stiffen.

The spiked ball struck Harry with a *clang*, the sound *waaangwaaangwaaang*ing through his skull like a gong. He released the essence of steel, requesting his own essence back from the fragment in his pocket…and then he wiggled his bare great toe on the cool stone floor, giving himself to it instead. He grinned at the creature as it prepared to strike again, waving at it good-naturedly.

"Bye now," he told it.

"Oh boy," Nettie stated with a cackle. "He's about to get it!"

And with that, Harry expanded his *self* into the stone of the room, until he was all of it. The walls, the ceiling, the floor, and even the strange statue of Chauncy.

Then, with a thought, he fell apart.

The ceiling caved inward over the ink-creature, hunks of stone smashing down on its head. The sheer weight of the rubble crushed the thing, burying it completely…while leaving everyone else intact. Except for the statue, of course. Moonlight shone through the hole in the roof, casting the rubble – and Harry and the rest of them – in its gentle silver glow.

Harry sensed the creature struggling to get free from the rubble, and felt it give up. Instead, it did what he knew it must; turn back to ink to seep through the cracks.

And that's when he executed the second step of his simple plan.

Harry shifted the pieces of rubble as if they were parts of his own body – which in a way, they were – and scooped up the inky goop in a stony sphere. Then he simply told the room to go back to its…well, its room. And so it did.

The ceiling rose back up, re-forming itself, as did the statue. And held in the statue's upwardly-extended hand was the sphere of the moon…with the goopy ink trapped inside.

Harry put his shoe back on, then limped up to the statue, putting a hand on it. And he rearranged the minerals of the moon such that they were enormously strong…and so that no liquid could make an escape from within.

He turned to Nettie then, flashing her a grin.

"Good job hon," she told him.

"Do I get a reward?" he inquired. She gave him a look…but was still smiling.

"Can't say ya didn't earn it," she replied.

"Oh boy," he declared.

"Good job Harry," Valtora congratulated, beaming a gorgeous smile at him. Along with a truly astonishing hair-toss…one that, like Nettie's rewards, never got old, no matter how often Harry experienced it. He realized he'd stopped to gawk…and that everyone else had too. Nettie was the first to recover, clearly upset that she'd been dazzled by the bedazzled display.

"All right hussy," she grumbled. "Let's go get your boyfriend."

"My *fiancé*," she corrected.

"Whatever."

They all turned to Gavin.

"Lead the way," Nettie prompted him. Gavin grimaced.

"Chauncy's staff flew away when I dropped it to grab my knitting needles," he confessed.

"Well where'd it go?" Nettie demanded.

"I'm not certain," Gavin replied. "But there are only two possibilities: it either went back outside, or further inside," he reasoned. "Rocky and the others may have seen it fly out if it went that way," he added. "We should check there first."

"Makes sense," Harry replied. "Very reasonable."

"That's because he's from Borrin," Nettie shot back. "They do things regular there."

"I do things regular," Harry offered, shooting her a grin.

"Not that crap!" Nettie shot back.

"Well that's what I was talking about."

"Shut up Harry," Nettie grumbled. He chuckled, but did as he was told. Gavin left the building, followed by everyone else. For magic was the connection between a wizard and the world, and Chauncy's staff was therefore connected to him. Wherever it went, Chauncy would be, whether outside…or in the mausoleum.

# Chapter 28

Chauncy stood there at the top of the stairs, staring wide-eyed at the shadowy winged woman. The same one who'd abducted him in the first place...after fooling him into fooling around. Just the sight of her made his sphincter spasm, for he knew that Zella's dark doppelganger was essentially *her*. That Zella could see through its inky eyes and feel what it felt. And do what it...did.

"Uh..." he blurted out, taking a step back...and nearly falling backward down the stairs. He stumbled, catching himself. "Hi?"

The doppelganger folded its arms under its compelling chest.

"I was looking for...the uh...bathroom," he stated.

She didn't justify this with an answer.

"Right," Chauncy stated, squaring his shoulders. "Guess we're gonna have to do this the hard way."

"Oh boy!" Tip declared.

Chauncy cocked his fist back...just as ZoMonsterz leapt right at the Inkling's face...and clawed the hell out of it. It shrieked, an awful gurgling sound that made the hair on Chauncy's neck stand on-end. Ink-blood splattered under ZoMonsterz's brutal assault, coating the hellcat's fur.

Then ZoMonsterz leapt off, landing beside Chauncy again. And Chauncy, already having his fist cocked back, punched the thing in its ruined mouth, sending it stumbling backward. It fell on its back on the floor, and despite having done very little to accomplish this, Chauncy's heart swelled with that badass feeling he'd rarely experienced in his life.

"That's right," he declared, shaking the ink off his fist. "Get up and I'll..."

The Inkling did start to get up.

"Crap!" he blurted out, sprinting around the Inkling and charging down the hallway beyond. ZoMonsterz zoomed ahead of him, leading the way...and leaving little inky pawprints on the bone-white floor. "Wait up!" he called out after her. But ZoMonsterz ignored him in typical cat fashion, turning left around the corner at the end of the hallway and vanishing from sight. So Chauncy did the only thing he could do, which was to run after her.

He made the mistake of glancing back as he did so…and saw the Inkling rising to her feet, her face seeming to melt – and then heal – before his very eyes.

"Crap!" he blurted out a second time. Right as the Inkling broke out in an all-out sprint after him.

Chauncy pumped his legs as fast as he could, rounding the corner ZoMonsterz had turned down and continuing down yet another long hallway. To his dismay, the hellcat was nowhere to be seen…and there were doorways spaced every twenty feet or so on either wall. The hallway was a dead-end…which meant ZoMonsterz must have gone into one of the doorways.

"ZoMonsterz!" he cried, hearing wet footsteps catching up to him from behind. He charged forward, glancing sideways at each of the doorways as he passed them. They each led to crypts with stone coffins in them…but no ZoMonsterz.

He continuing running, glancing back a second time…and immediately regretting it. For the Inkling was running with terrible speed, closing the distance between them slowly but surely.

"Zo!" he yelled out, turning forward again…right before he collided with the wall at the end of the hallway. He skid to a halt, his shoulder slamming into the stone with a *whump*. Then he turned around…and saw the Inkling skidding to a stop before him.

"No!" he blurted out as she stepped closer, only a few feet away now. "Don't hurt me!"

She shoved him in the chest with one black hand, pinning him against the wall with formidable strength. Far more than Chauncy's spindly arms could muster, he soon discovered. For in his pursuit of magic, he'd neglected his muscles.

"Stop," he gasped as she loomed ever-closer, her inky face only inches from his now. "Please, I'll come quietly!"

"That'd be a first," Tip quipped.

"Shut up!" Chauncy snapped.

The Inkling's lips drew up into a smirk…and its free hand traced a line all the way down to his…

"Oh," Chauncy gasped.

"Oh," Tip murmured. "I enjoy that."

Then came the meow of a cat.

The Inkling turned around, and Chauncy saw none other than ZoMonsterz sitting a few yards away.

Then, to his surprise, the Inkling *shrieked*.

She unhanded him, flattening herself against the wall and staring wide-eyed at ZoMonsterz, who merely stared back at her. Then the cat sauntered up to Chauncy...and the Inkling shoved him toward the cat, continuing to shriek.

"What...?" Chauncy asked, backpedaling away from the Inkling, until ZoMonsterz was between them. It took him a moment to remember her magical powers. Not only to somehow be wherever his hand was whenever she wanted, but that when she scratched someone, they would live in mortal fear of her for precisely two years.

He broke out into a smile then, feeling enormously relieved.

"Not so tough now, huh," he mused, crossing his arms over his chest and glaring at the Inkling. "I'll be leaving now." He lowered his gaze to ZoMonsterz. "Come on Zo," he prompted. "Let's go."

And so they did, leaving the Inkling behind. She stepped forward after them, then backpedaled quickly when ZoMonsterz threw her a feline glare...while extending a paw in the air and retracting her vicious-looking claws. The Inkling flattened herself against the wall, absolutely terrified...and didn't dare take another step toward Chauncy and his hellcat.

"Now where's the exit?" Chauncy wondered aloud.

"Reowr," ZoMonsterz replied, trotting down the hallway, then turning left through one of the doorways. Chauncy followed her, entering into a creepy crypt with stone coffins against each stone wall. And even more creepily, with mummies lying in long cubbies inset into the walls. It was the perfect place for a cracked wizard like Zella to live...an evil lair filled with the dead.

Ahead, there was another doorway, one that led to another long hallway. ZoMonsterz sniffed the air, then turned right down the hallway, trotting confidently forward. Chauncy chose to trust her, knowing that her senses were far keener than his. His trust was soon rewarded, for she turned leftward through another doorway...and through a small room into a much bigger one. This had the same bone-white stone floor, walls, and ceiling as the rest of the place, but there were no bodies or coffins, to Chauncy's relief...just a statue of a man with one hand held overhead, holding what appeared to be the moon. Chauncy followed ZoMonsterz around it...and toward a large doorway serving as the exit to the building. Made obvious by the fact that beyond it, he could see outside.

And to his surprise, none other than Harry, Nettie, Valtora, and Gavin were striding through that doorway into the building.

"Chauncy!" Valtora gasped, sprinting toward him. She threw herself at him with abandon, slamming into him and nearly knocking him off his feet. He stumbled backward, then caught himself. Valtora leaned in for a kiss, which he happily accepted. It was, per her usual, a highly *un*usual kiss to give in public...and Chauncy enjoyed every second of it.

"Ooo," Tip murmured from below. "That's *nice*."

Valtora pulled away, giving Chauncy a confused look.

"Who said that?" she asked.

"T'was I, fair maiden," Tip answered gallantly. She blinked, then looked down.

"Huh?" she pressed.

"It's um..." Chauncy stated. "Uh...you see, what happened was..."

"Show her Chauncy," Tip urged.

"No!" Chauncy blurted out, blushing furiously and covering his bits, even though his robe was doing a somewhat adequate job of it already.

"Turn around everyone," Valtora demanded. And, sensing that it was in their best interests to do so, everyone did. She pulled up Chauncy's robe, then pulled down his special underwear...and gasped. "Ohmygod!" she blurted out as Tip revealed himself. The demon grinned at her, even throwing a wink in for good measure. A sleezy one at that.

"I'm a mod," Tip explained. "For his rod."

"Like in that book," she stated. "Mods for Rods, in the Cave of Wonder!"

"I remember that one," Harry called out, still with his back to them, thank goodness. He chuckled.

"Bet ya do," Nettie grumbled.

"You chose the demon!" Valtora gasped, clutching her hands to her chest. "That was my *favorite*!"

"Really?" Chauncy asked.

"Oh *hell* yeah," she confirmed. "I almost went back into the Cave of Wonder to get it," she added. "For The Dark One."

"Oh," he mumbled.

"I'm glad I waited," she continued with a big smile. "Once you put it on, it doesn't come off."

"It doesn't?" Chauncy asked.

"She could try," Tip offered.

"Shut up Tip," Chauncy grumbled. Valtora frowned prettily.

"Wait, how did you get this?" she asked.

"Zella put me on him," Tip explained. "And upon our union, I was given life!"

Chauncy's cheeks burned, and Valtora arched an eyebrow at him.

"I...she...I woke up with it!" he blurted out.

"He did," Tip confirmed. "She put it on when he was knocked out."

"Oh *really*," Valtora stated. "Why would she do that?"

"She's psychotic," Tip explained.

"Makes sense," Valtora replied, seeming relieved. "She has good taste in mods," she added, a bit reluctantly. "And evil lairs."

"Yes, well," Chauncy stated. "Anyway, we should..."

"She also wanted that extra feedback," Tip interrupted with a grin. "A little verbal confirmation that she was doing the right thing, if you know what I mean."

"Wait, what?" Valtora asked.

"Nothing!" Chauncy snapped, shoving his robe downward to cover – and smother – the demon. He cleared his throat. "We should get going," he warned. "Zella's Inkling is here...and she might come back."

"So this *is* Zella's lair," Valtora stated, thankfully going with the abrupt change in subject. "I knew it!"

"Can we turn around now already?" Nettie asked.

"Yes," Chauncy answered. And with that, everyone turned to face them.

"Let's go kick her ass," Valtora prompted.

"I don't think she's here right now," Chauncy countered. "Her Inkling was guarding my...uh, cell."

"Her Inkling?" Nettie asked.

"One of her magical tattoos," he explained. "It's her...doppelganger. She can see through its eyes and control it and stuff. It's the thing that, uh, kidnapped me," he added, eyeing Valtora with a fresh flushing of his cheeks. He left out the sordid details of that kidnapping, fully committed to taking them shamefully to his grave.

"We fought one of 'em," Nettie noted. "Tough little shit."

"Big shit," Harry corrected.

"I advise against fighting Zella here," Gavin piped in. "She has the advantage on her territory."

"It's five wizards against one," Valtora pointed out.

"But she's powerful," Gavin argued. "A former wizard of the Order of Mundus is not to be underestimated."

"Well so are you two," Chauncy countered, gesturing at Harry and Nettie. Nettie shook her head.

"He's right kid," she stated. "From what the Order told us, Zella's real dangerous. She's psycho, but she's a genius in battle."

"Like me," Valtora stated. Nettie gave her a look.

"Zella's a *real* psycho," she retorted. "She makes you look like a fairy princess in comparison."

"I can vouch for that," Chauncy agreed. Valtora shot him a glare. "I mean, she's *mean* psycho," he clarified. "You're *nice* psycho, darling."

"Aww," Valtora replied, giving him a hug.

"Let's go," Nettie prompted.

"Where to?" Chauncy asked.

"I'll tell you after we get outta here," she replied. "Where Zella won't have Inklings listening in on us."

"Oh," Chauncy replied. "Good idea."

"Of course it is," Nettie agreed with a smirk. "I came up with it."

With that, everyone turned to the exit of the building, ready to head on out. But before they could take a single step, someone else stepped through the doorway into the room. A tall woman dressed in a tight black uniform, her skin covered in intricate tattoos. She stopped, putting a hand on her hip, and smirked at all of them.

"Why hello there," she greeted. "Welcome to my home. I would've tidied up if I'd known you were coming."

"Zella!" Chauncy gasped, terror gripping him.

"In the flesh," she confirmed. Harry rubbed his chin, looking her up and down.

"Nice flesh too," he mused.

"I know, right?" Valtora said. "I mean, *damn*."

"Focus you idiots!" Nettie snapped.

Zella ignored them, her eyes on Chauncy.

"You've been a naughty boy, Chauncy," she scolded. "Up and leaving a girl after all the fun we had. Tsk *tsk*," she added.

Valtora blinked, then turned to look at Chauncy questioningly.

"Right," he stated, gripping his staff firmly. "Attack!"

And with that, he wound up, and swung his Staff of Wind at Zella just as hard as he could.

# Chapter 29

King Pravus's office was considerably larger than was strictly necessary for its day-to-day purposes, much like Pravus himself. But he found himself not minding its opulence on this particular day, a few days after Zella's attack. For he was struck with the sudden realization that the bare minimum was not to his taste. Muscles just big enough to do the work of eating, walking, and sleeping would adequately attend to the necessities of life, but hardly to the zestful enjoyment of it.

So, sitting here at his desk, surrounded by ginormous shelves lined with books, Pravus felt quite pleased indeed. For the beauty of life was in its excesses, and excesses were in abundance all around them.

"Do plants have a single flower?" he asked Desmond and Templeton, who were seated in chairs opposite his desk. "Do fish lay a single egg? Do grasses set a single seed to soil, to serve as the next generation?"

"No sire," Desmond droned, clearly not enjoying Pravus's philosophizing. Which only made Pravus want to do it more, just to torture the old man.

"Is there a single star in the sky?" he continued. "Or a vast overabundance, far more than strictly necessary?"

"The latter, I suspect," Templeton answered jovially.

"Indeed!" Pravus agreed. "A lesson from nature, one of exuberant excesses!" He smiled, leaning back in his chair and folding his arms in his lap. Both men stared at him, Desmond with a far less agreeable look.

"We were meeting to discuss Zella Trek," the dour old man reminded him.

"Yes yes," Pravus grumbled. "Her."

Both men continued to look at him, no doubt expecting him to do kingly things. Like leading and such. He frowned, rubbing his chin thoughtfully.

"Perhaps that's the problem with our approach," he stated. "Up until now, we've been doing the bare minimum," he explained. "Defending when Zella attacks." He gazed at the ridiculous number of books on his shelf, then up at the inappropriately high ceiling far above. "Why, that's it!"

"What's it?" Desmond pressed.

"We can't be practical," Pravus stated. "That's something Borrin would do. Are we Borrin?"

"No sire," Desmond droned, although he was boring indeed.

"Clearly not," Templeton agreed.

"Damn right!" Pravus exclaimed, struck by a sudden surge of rousing speech. He stood up from his chair abruptly, really feeling it now. For when high emotion struck, it was terribly important to let it carry one away, rather than resist its flow like practical – and safely sad – people did.

"Here it comes," Desmond sighed. Sadly.

"We are the magical kingdom of Pravus!" Pravus proclaimed, thrusting a fist into the air valiantly. "When evil rises to threaten our lands, do we send armies of soldiers against them?"

"We should," Desmond noted.

"No!" Pravus answered, ignoring the man. "We summon a handful of wizards to save the day!"

"The Order of Mundus does," Desmond corrected.

"Powerful wizards that can destroy entire armies with a wave of their magic wands!" Pravus proclaimed, pantomiming this very act. "An exuberant excess of unimaginable power!"

"Not so much in these particular Chosen Ones," Desmond argued.

"Now evil rises again to attack us," Pravus continued, fully in the sway of his speech, feeling as kingly as he'd ever felt. He glared down at Desmond imperiously. "Do we cower in fear, tucking our head and limbs in our proverbial turtle shells and hope for the best?"

"It's an option."

"No!" Pravus cried, so loudly that Desmond flinched. Pravus made the motion of drawing a sword from his back, and lo and behold, his magical golden sword – ludicrously large – appeared. He thrust it into the air. "We attack the way nature intended!"

"Excessively?" Templeton guessed.

"Precisely!" Pravus confirmed. "We're not going to counterattack. We're going to counter*obliterate!*"

"Shall I inform the generals of this detailed plan?" Desmond inquired. Snarkily.

"Plan?" Pravus scoffed. "We don't need a plan."

"As your advisor, I advise that we actually do," Desmond countered.

"Very well," Pravus replied. "Let exuberant excess be our plan!"

"Not a plan," Desmond pointed out.

"We'll mobilize the might of the kingdom to find and destroy Zella," Pravus stated.

"An overwhelming force!" Templeton exclaimed.

"Indeed Templeton!" Pravus exclaimed. "We're a kingdom, not a victim. It's time we stopped worrying about merely surviving…and started thriving!"

"With excessive exuberance!" Templeton declared, standing up from his seat.

"For Pravus!" Pravus cried. And it was as much for himself as the kingdom. And to his delight, even grumpy old Desmond stood from his chair stiffly, nodding grudgingly at his king.

"For the people," he piped in.

\* \* \*

Possessed of goals but not a plan, King Pravus, Templeton, Desmond, and a number of other advisors – as well as a few of the highest-ranking lords in the kingdom – got together in the conference room. A room for conferring, which was all fine and good. After all, discussion had its merits, and in matters of great importance, getting the opinions of respected and intelligent people had a way of conferring confidence in one's plans. The issue that Pravus had, of course, was that in lieu of respected and intelligent people, Pravus had to settle for politicians. People like Lord Ballister, the highest-ranked lord of the land.

So Pravus found him sitting at the head of a long, rectangular table, staring at Lord Ballister as he blabbity-blabbed on and on. Not at the man's lips, which were so thin they practically didn't exist, nor at his ghastly pale skin dotted with splats of freckles. But at the insufferable man's hair. Great sprouts of thick, curly red hair. It gave Pravus the willies to look at, honestly.

"…is far too great an expense for the lords to bear right now," Lord Ballister concluded, leaning back in his chair. Pravus found his gaze dropping to the man's hands, resting as they were on the table.

185

There were even small, curly red hairs on the backs of the lord's fingers, to Pravus's dismay.

He shuddered at the sight of them.

"Your majesty?" one of his advisers inquired. Not Desmond, but another generically mousy, bespectacled man. In a suit, naturally. The uniform of a serious and important man, the suit. But take the clothes off of all these men, Pravus knew, and the illusion of power would dissolve. For underneath these costumes were bodies wholly neglected, like so many pasty, half-melted candles hidden from sight.

A consequence of the inane belief that intellectual pursuits were the most important in life, and that the body was merely an inconvenient vehicle for the mind. Anyone who ventured to take the time to care for their body – to love it and love using it and developing it – quickly realized the truth: that the body evoked the mind as much as the mind evoked the body. It was mutual, a relationship that couldn't be denied.

"Sire," the advisor pressed, glancing nervously at Ballister, then back at Pravus.

"Hmm?" Pravus inquired.

"Lord Ballister's points," the advisor pressed. Pravus sighed, turning his gaze reluctantly back to Ballister.

"Ah yes," he replied. "Something about being a useless greedy coward with no plan other than saying 'no' to everything," he stated. "Was that your argument, or did I miss something? I fell asleep somewhere in the middle."

Lord Ballister grimaced.

"Honestly, it amazes me you can sit upright without a spine," Pravus mused. "How *do* you do it?"

"King Pravus," Ballister retorted indignantly. "My points are valid!"

"You mean vapid," Pravus retorted.

"Pardon me my liege," another lord stated. Lord Doxbury, a short, smarmy pudge of a man with a black handlebar mustache. One as greasy as he was. "I fail to see how insulting the good Lord Ballister helps us."

"Hardly surprising," Pravus mused.

"His points have some validity," Doxbury pressed, with an appropriately apologetic smile. "Sending massive armies to fight a single wizard…?"

"That smashed up my castle," Pravus pointed out.

"It's just that it's a rather large expenditure of resources for the task at hand," Doxbury continued. "Perhaps a smaller, more effective application of force?"

Pravus grimaced, irritated at the man's penchant for making every statement a question. It was Doxbury's preferred method of escaping accountability, in that it allowed him to state a contrarian opinion without getting in trouble.

"It's only a question," Doxbury insisted, as if on cue.

Desmond raised a hand then. The semi-advisor was seated close to the head of the table, much to the irritation of the lords seated further away. Most of whom Pravus didn't want to hear from anyway. The most annoying people he had sit in the back, where they could barely be heard.

"Yes Desmond?" Pravus inquired.

"The optics of Lord Doxbury's idea are sound," Desmond stated. Pravus shot him a withering glare, but the old man proved quite resistant to this visual violence, and had the audacity to continue. "Mobilizing a massive force will be expensive...and the kingdom has endured massive expenses already, with The Dark One's attacks and the damage to the castle."

"So?" Pravus snapped.

"If a massive force succeeds, Zella will be defeated, but the kingdom will be left weakened," Desmond reasoned. "If it fails, the kingdom will be devastated...and it will embolden our enemies."

"So you want me to use a spindly force?" Pravus inquired. "So that if they fail, it's no big deal?"

"A force that costs nothing," Desmond corrected. Pravus frowned, crossing his huge forearms over his thick slabby pecs.

"Go on."

"The Wilds has magical creatures like the fire dragon," Desmond stated. "We can ask for their help. After all, we saved the Great Wood from falling."

"True," Pravus conceded.

"They may also have ways of divining the location of Zella Trek," Desmond continued. "Ways that we do not possess."

"That was precisely my idea," Lord Doxbury agreed triumphantly, twisting his greasy mustache-tip with one hand. Which was almost certainly not true.

"Everyone's ideas are your ideas," Pravus grumbled. "Funny how they always come up with them first."

"I *say*," Lord Doxbury gasped with a glare, feigning terrible offense. Pravus rolled his eyes.

"Can we trust these wild creatures?" one of the other advisors inquired. "After all, they're not loyal to the crown."

"Neither are the Chosen Ones," Pravus pointed out.

"The Chosen Ones are chosen by destiny," Lord Ballister argued. "Or rather, the Order of Mundus."

"Honestly, this is the Order's fault," Doxbury piped in, always eager to assign blame, while taking none for himself. It was the only thing the man loved to give away. "She's their responsibility."

"That may be," Pravus replied. "But the Order has no obligation to the Kingdom of Pravus. If they don't want to help, they won't...and there isn't much we can do about it."

"What of the Chosen Ones?" the first advisor inquired.

"What of them?" Pravus shot back.

"Shouldn't we try to contact them?" the man asked. "If anyone could defeat Zella, it'd be them."

"Two of them are wizards of the Order," Pravus pointed out. "The other two are in Borrin, last I heard." Which was nine months or so ago. "Zella is after Chauncy Little, the wizard from Southwick."

"Ever more reason to contact the Order of Mundus," Lord Ballister pointed out. "Even if the Order itself won't help us, perhaps the two Chosen Ones there will."

"Perhaps," Pravus conceded. "Perhaps not."

"Perhaps it would be best if we sent the hardest person to say 'no' to," Desmond proposed. Pravus frowned.

"And who is that?"

"Why, you sire, naturally," Desmond answered. Pravus frowned, considering this with a rub of his chiseled chin. Then he sat up a bit straighter, puffing out his chest.

"You're right," he realized. He stood with enormous difficulty then, towering over the others. "Let it be so," he declared. "For when it comes to the King of Pravus, the Order can hardly say no!"

Everyone found someone to glance at besides him.

"Come, Templeton!" Pravus prompted. "Let us go astride the fire dragon, and make way to the Isle of Mundus!"

"At once, my liege!" Templeton cried gallantly. With far more vim and vigor than the dried-out husks that were the other personalities in the room. Serious men in serious suits, seriously lacking any semblance of play. Which was the most important element when it came to saving the day, Pravus knew: *heroic* play.

"But what of contacting the beasts of The Wilds to help?" Lord Ballister asked, looking alarmed. For he knew that once Pravus was swept up in heroism, that would be that.

"Make it happen," Pravus replied. "Don't ask how," he added before the man could. "Heroes find a way," he lectured.

"But…"

"Away!" Pravus prompted. And with that, he hobbled out the room, Templeton limping right behind him. Without a single glance backward – or a falter in their stiff steps – the two men made their way toward the castle exit, and toward the destiny they made for themselves.

# Chapter 30

Chauncy swung his Staff of Wind at Zella Trek with all his might, even getting his hips into the motion. A blast of wind shot out from it, smashing into Zella with the force of a hurricane.

By all accounts, she should've flown backward with enormous speed, careening through the air and tumbling across the graveyard beyond with bone-shattering force. But instead, she merely stepped out of the doorway – and hid behind the wall beyond – and as such, Chauncy's attack did nothing at all.

He'd swung so hard he lost his balance, stumbling to the side. Zella stepped back into view, smirking at him.

"You really think a little breeze is going to stop me?" she inquired.

"Oh we got more than that," Nettie shot back.

"And we're gonna do it to *you*," Valtora added, clenching her diamond hand into a threatening fist.

Zella just stood there, a hand on her hip. She arched an eyebrow. "I'm waiting," she stated.

"Harry, kick her ass," Nettie ordered.

"Well alright," Harry agreed.

He kicked off a shoe, then limped toward Zella, his hands in his pockets. She merely watched as he approached, her smirk never fading.

Then the ground opened up beneath her, fingers of earth rising up to grab her legs!

The earthen digits closed on Zella's lower half…and went right through her inky black suit, vanishing into her legs.

"Huh," Harry said, scratching his head. "Didn't expect that."

"Tsk *tsk*," Zella told him, wagging a finger disapprovingly. "Don't you think you're a bit old to be fingering me?"

"No," Harry replied.

"Shut up Harry!" Nettie snapped. She grabbed her Wetstone, summoning a rapidly expanding globe of water. One that she threw at Zella, connected to Nettie's hand by a thin cord of water. And through that connection, she flash-froze the globe at the last minute, sending an ice-sphere hurtling at Zella's head. But big black wings sprouted from Zella's back at the last second, folding forward around her. Armored wings, with metallic-looking feathers...that took the brunt of the impact, shattering the ice. She flung her wings open then, sending ice shards flying outward at them all.

Chauncy flung his arms up to cover his face, feeling sharp bits of ice pelt him. He stumbled backward, then felt himself back up into someone else. It was Valtora, he realized.

"Go on baby," she encouraged. "Pound that bitch!"

"Oh yes Chauncy," Zella purred. "Please *do*."

"Um..." Chauncy mumbled.

"It's a sound plan," Tip piped in, piping-in being his preferred method of attack.

"Come on Chauncy," Nettie prompted. "Be a damn wizard already!"

"Right," Chauncy replied.

He recalled his last foray into ridiculousness, and dug deep to find that energy within him. And, feeling it surge to the surface, he thrust his chest out valiantly, gripping his staff with steely resolve.

"Gusty thrust!" he cried...and thrust the butt of his staff at Zella. It struck her right in the face, snapping her head back. She stumbled, then caught herself, putting a hand to her mouth...and smirking.

"Right in the mouth," she mused. She sighed wistfully. "Reminds me of when we met."

Chauncy blushed furiously, suddenly realizing that Zella had a secret weapon. A weapon that was literally a secret: the knowledge of what he'd let her do to him. If she told Valtora...

"Die!" he cried, thrusting his staff again and again. This time, however, Zella was prepared, bringing her armored wings in front of her to block the blows. Then she flapped her wings together as if she were clapping her hands, creating a powerful gust of her own. Everyone stumbled backward. Except for Harry, of course.

He limped toward her...even as he summoned an earthen golem to rise from the ground behind her. The golem wrapped its arms around her, pinning her wings – and her bare arms – to her sides. Harry stopped a few feet in front of her.

"Stay," he ordered.

"Why?" she inquired. "So you can have your way with me?"

Harry paused, then turned to give Nettie a hopeful look.

191

"Focus Harry!" Nettie snapped. His face fell, and he turned back to Zella.

"Guess not," he replied.

"Then what *are* you going to do, hmmm?" Zella inquired. "Tie me up and have me put away? Kill me right here and now?"

"We'll let the Order of Mundus figure that out," Nettie answered. "Come on," she prompted the others. "Let's get out of here."

"Unhand me!" Zella gasped, throwing her head back dramatically, her long black hair draping over the golem. Nettie ignored her – while Valtora and the guys stared, for Zella had arched her back quite provocatively – and led the way out of the mausoleum. Everyone followed behind her, and the golem holding Zella stomped out with them. All while Zella thrashed. Also dramatically, and to little effect, other than to put her in various other provocative poses, limited as they were by her captivity. When Chauncy exited, he saw the graveyard stretching out before him, an array of tombstones followed by murky swamp and swirling mist.

Valtora stopped then, looking around and frowning.

"Where's Peter?" she asked. "And shmookie tookums?"

"And Chaos?" Chauncy added, struck with a sudden burst of fear.

"My baby!" Valtora gasped. They looked around some more, but the two were nowhere to be found. Everyone turned to Zella, who gave them the fakest innocent look they'd ever seen.

"All right toots, where'd you take 'em?" Nettie demanded.

Zella's eyes widened, and she blinked rapidly.

"Me?" she asked.

"Yes you, idiot!" Nettie snapped. "I know you're up to something. Tell us where we are, or that golem's gonna snap your little arms in half."

"Torture?" Zella inquired. "Tsk tsk. Aren't you supposed to be the good guys?"

"I'm not a guy," Nettie shot back.

"And I'm not good," Valtora added, making a fist with her diamond hand. "Tell me where you took my friends, or I'll crush your gorgeous little skull!"

"Well then I won't be able to tell you where they are," Zella pointed out.

"So you *did* do something with them," Nettie deduced.

"And you're doing something with me," Zella replied with a shrug. "And I did something with Chauncy," she added, flashing Chauncy a satisfied little smile. "Tit for tat, mmm?"

"Tit for tattoos," Harry quipped.

"Got those too," Zella told him with a wink. He grinned...and Nettie elbowed him.

"Quit flirting dolt," she snapped. "We have to find Peter and Rocky and the baby!"

"Oh all right," Harry replied.

And then the ground rumbled under their feet, and the earth in front of them rose up in a huge dome. One with a big cave entrance, oddly enough. And none other than Peter himself came trotting out, followed by Rocky, with little Chaos safely swaddled in his arms. The dome sank into the earth afterward – with more rumbling of the ground under Chauncy's feet – erasing any evidence that it'd existed in the first place.

"What the...!" Nettie blurted out, turning to Harry. "You knew they were there all along?"

"Well sure," Harry replied. "I put 'em there."

"Well why didn't you say so?" Nettie pressed.

"Wanted to see what Zella would do," he answered. "Seeing as how she thought her Inklings took 'em hostage."

Everyone turned back to Zella, who was staring at Harry, looking rather stunned. A fact which clearly pleased Nettie, who put her hands on her hips, smirking at the woman.

"Not such a hot shit now, are ya?" she mused, shaking her head. "Ha!"

"Good job Harry!" Valtora congratulated, detaching herself from Peter – who'd been rather clearly enjoying her hugs – and flinging herself at the old man. He didn't budge with the impact, hard as he was. Then she went to Rocky, happily taking Chaos from him and tucking the baby securely in her wrap. Chauncy smiled at the two, feeling quite relieved...and turned to Harry.

"Wait, so Inklings attacked Rocky and Peter?" Chauncy asked him. Harry nodded.

"While we were fightin' that thing in there," Harry confirmed, pointing back at the mausoleum.

"So you...beat that thing while fighting off the other Inklings and protecting Peter and Rocky?" Chauncy pressed.

"Sure did," Harry replied.

"How'd you know they were being attacked?"

"Ground told me," Harry answered with a wink, wiggling his toes. Chauncy shook his head in wonder...and Zella's shock faded, replaced by a stony stare.

"Well done," she stated. "What did you do with my Inklings?"

"They were bad," Harry replied. "So I grounded 'em."

"Good one Harry," Nettie said with a cackle, nudging him with her elbow. Zella gave a tight smile.

"Bravo," she congratulated. "At least *one* of you is a competent wizard."

"Ooo boy," Harry replied with a grin. "Ya hear that? I'm competent!"

"Don't let it get to your head," Nettie grumbled.

"Nicest thing a woman's ever said to me," Harry mused. Nettie rolled her eyes.

"All right, let's go," she grumbled.

"Where?" Chauncy asked.

"Where else?" Nettie answered. "The Isle of Mundus!"

* * *

So it was that Chauncy found himself sitting on Rocky's back with Gavin, Harry, and Nettie, while Valtora rode Peter...and Zella remained in the stony grasp of Harry's golem. One they named Shackles, for obvious reasons. Valtora had come up with the name, of course, being fond of giving nicknames to just about everything. Zella didn't say much of anything as they traveled, for which Chauncy was grateful. Though her limbs were trapped, there was still a great deal of damage she could do with her mouth. Most of which involved revealing to Valtora the trouble Zella's mouth had gotten Chauncy into. The fact that Zella was keeping her mouth shut for once was little consolation to him, of course. He knew full well that she might be saving that tidbit for later, when it could do maximum damage.

In any case, out of the graveyard they went, through a misty swamp to rolling grassland beyond. And, seeing as it was night-time – and they were all quite exhausted – they decided to set up camp. Unfortunately, most of their stuff was back in the carriage near the Great Wood, which meant that they were without tents to pitch. Once again, Harry came to the rescue, making domed earthen shelters for each of them...and then getting to work building a big campfire. All the good humans but Harry and Chauncy stayed within their huts for the moment, Valtora feeding Chaos and Nettie doing whatever it was she was doing. Zella remained in her own domed hut…one without a door, but only a man-sized hole in the ceiling to allow air in and out. Harry had crafted the dome around her, trapping her inside with Shackles the golem.

Chauncy offered to help Harry set up the campfire, feeling rather useless compared to the old wizard. For it seemed that, no matter the situation, Harry always came in handy…and solved problems with a calm assurance that they *could* be solved, and not with the usual gnashing of teeth and biting of nails that problems usually invoked in people.

"There aren't any logs or sticks," Chauncy pointed out as Harry gathered big stones to put in a ring around the eventual fire. They'd made camp in the middle of otherwise barren grasslands, after all.

"That's alright," Harry replied good-naturedly. "Make some."

Chauncy blinked.

"Huh?" he asked.

"Use grass," Harry explained. Which wasn't an explanation at all, in Chauncy's estimation.

"Grass?" Chauncy pressed. "Won't that burn too quickly?"

"Well sure," Harry replied, grabbing a handful of long grass blades and yanking them free from the earth. He started twisting them around each other then, forming a kind of rope. In no time at all, he was done, and handed it to Chauncy. "Do this."

"Uh…"

"Stuff burns quick when it burns all at once," Harry explained. "Force it to burn outside to in, it'll burn slow."

"Huh," Chauncy murmured, studying the grass-rope. "You've done this before, I take it."

"Nope," Harry replied with a grin. "Just came up with it."

"Really?"

"Yep," Harry confirmed.

"Wow," Chauncy murmured. "You're pretty alright, you know that?"

Harry just chuckled, continuing to gather stones. So Chauncy studied the rope for a bit longer, then set about pulling handfuls of grass from the ground…and doing his darndest to reproduce what Harry had made. Which was considerably harder than he'd expected. After more than a few fumbling, failed attempts, he went back to Harry.

"Not doing so well," he admitted, feeling rather embarrassed that he was so useless. "I kinda suck at this."

"Well sure ya do," Harry replied evenly. "It's your first time."

"It was yours too," Chauncy pointed out.

"Well I've been making stuff my whole life," Harry countered. "That's a long time."

The old man showed Chauncy his technique again, going slowly this time, step-by-step. Chauncy followed along until he'd gotten it right a few times, and then Harry sent him off to do it himself. All without a trace of impatience or any hint of belittling. Chauncy felt himself rather empowered by this. For one thing that Chauncy had learned in the last thirty-five years was that most people had their own particular default relationship with the world, and with other people. Harry's was one of positive regard…and simply to be around him was to absorb that mindset. Thus, after a half-hour of making grassy ropes and stacking them for the fire, Chauncy's relationship with the world was mighty fine…as was his relationship with himself.

He sat down beside Harry before the piled-up rope, watching as Harry tossed loose grass atop the pile for tinder, then used a piece of flint on his odd pebbly vest to start the fire.

"Is there anything you can't do?" Chauncy asked.

"Whatever I haven't put my mind to," Harry answered.

Chauncy considered this.

"But have you ever put your mind to something and found you couldn't do it?" Chauncy pressed. Harry paused, considering this.

"Not that I can remember," he answered at last. "Then again, my memory might be going," he added with a grin. Chauncy chuckled.

They sat there as the fire spread over the loose grass, then expanded to eat at the ropes Chauncy had made. And sure enough, the fire burned steadily, just as Harry had prophesized. They sat before it, enjoying its warmth and light. It wasn't long before the flames drew everyone else from their dome-homes, like a moth to candlelight. Except for Zella, of course.

With evil safely stowed out of the way, everyone else sat in a circle around the fire, Valtora sitting next to Chauncy, and Nettie next to Harry. Valtora held Chaos for a bit, then offered him to Chauncy, who happily accepted a bit of father-son time. Having just drank, Chaos was quite content to lie in Chauncy's arms, staring up at his father with unblinking eyes.

"Hello you," Chauncy greeted, smiling down at him. Valtora snuggled against Chauncy's shoulder, wrapping an arm around his shoulders. After what'd happened with Zella, he felt more than a little guilty...and he felt undeserving of her unreserved affection and trust. At a time when there would've been complete connection between them and this moment, the memory of what he'd done – or rather, what had been done unto him – served to disconnect.

"You okay?" Valtora asked him. Chauncy sighed.

"Sort of," he replied.

"Snort him," she ordered. He frowned.

"Huh?"

"Chaos," she clarified. "Snort him. It always makes me feel better when I do."

"Um…"

"Just *do* it already," she urged. Chauncy paused, then lifted Chaos dutifully, leaning in to the side of the baby's neck and sniffing.

"Yeah," Valtora purred, stroking his back. "Take it in *deep* baby."

Chauncy did so, and to his surprise, Chaos smelled *amazing*. It was a scent he couldn't describe, like the most pleasant flower in the world times ten. It smelled so good, in fact, that he snorted again. And again…and again.

"Oh my," he breathed. "Wow."

"Right?" she stated. "Fucking *amazing*."

"It sure is," he agreed with a smile. He snorted again, then sighed, letting his breath out slowly. But this time it was a sigh of contentment, for it appeared impossible to harbor any ill thoughts with the scent of Chaos in his brain.

"Give me some," Valtora urged. Chauncy held Chaos up to her, and she did a few snorts, after which she sighed contently, just like he had. Then they both sat there, quite content, watching the fire crackle merrily.

"All right," Nettie grumbled. "Hand him over."

Chauncy did so, handing Chaos off to Harry, who took a snort or two, then from Harry to Nettie, who took more than a few. Even Rocky took a turn, and Peter leaned his nostrils down to sniff…and the effect on all was the same. Eventually, Chaos made it back to Chauncy's arms, and he took one last big ol' huff before giving it a rest.

"This is nice," he declared, smiling contentedly at the fire.

"It's the best," Valtora agreed.

They sat there by the fire, baking in its heat. No one said anything for a while, which was just as well. For words would have distracted from the experience. Of being so marvelously alive, of being one with the moment.

And it occurred to Chauncy then that moments like these were the few that he remembered vividly, when all was said and done. Years later, most of his life would fade away into hazy memory, barely recalled, and even then in a kind of pieced-together reproduction of what had really happened. But moments like *these*, where he felt truly present, would remain crystal clear in his mind's eye...and would be, in the end, what he considered the very finest moments of his life.

Most of which, he realized suddenly, had been at night, sitting by campfires, in the presence of the people he loved.

It was a simple recipe, costing nothing but the effort and risk of connecting. Yet, in contrast to the lies propagated by the Republic of Borrin, which insisted that true happiness lay at the end of a sale – or the profit made from one – Chauncy couldn't recall a single purchase that had given him as much pleasure as right here...and right now.

He found himself giving Harry a sidelong glance, and Harry caught his eye, being ever the perceptive sort. The old man inclined his head, smiled, and had a twinkle in his eye...and Chauncy returned the gesture in kind.

A while later, when all had had their fill of the campfire's flames, they retreated to their respective domed homes to go to bed. Snuggled up in Valtora's arms, with Chaos by her side, they fell fast – and happily – asleep.

# Chapter 31

The next morning, Chauncy woke to find Valtora hovering over him...and Chaos fast asleep by his side. Valtora's eyes were locked on him, not on his eyes, but rather on matters below. He realized with a start that his wizardly robe had been pulled up to his belly, and that he was naked from the waist down. And what's more, that Valtora had unleashed Tip, his demonic dong personified.

"Oh!" Chauncy blurted out, reflexively pulling down his robe. But Valtora prompted pushed it up again, giving Chauncy an irritated look.

"We're *talking*," she scolded. Then she lowered her gaze to Tip. "So then what happened?"

"Well that was that, really," Tip answered. "All in all, a marvelous experience I'd say. Don't regret a thing."

"What...?" Chauncy began.

"Shush," Valtora shushed, putting a finger to her lips.

Chauncy swallowed nervously, glancing at Tip...and was struck with sudden horror at what they might've discussed. He thought about talking again, in a desperate attempt to change whatever subject they'd been discussing, but decided against it. If Tip had revealed his secret shame – what had happened between him and Zella, quite against his will – it was too late to defend himself. The truth was the truth...and if Valtora didn't know the truth yet, it'd only be a matter of time before it got out anyway.

"What did Chauncy do?" she asked Tip. He rolled his eyes.

"Whine and whimper and resist of course," he replied. "But he came 'round in the end." Tip smirked. "He giggles every time afterward," he added...which pretty much proved that they'd discussed what Chauncy feared most.

"I can explain!" Chauncy blurted out, unable to help himself. Valtora put her hands on her hips, glaring down at him.

"So you *liked* it huh?" she accused.

"No!" Chauncy exclaimed.

"Yes," Tip retorted.

"Shut up," Chauncy snapped.

"I'm just telling the truth," Tip countered.

"Yeah, well you don't have to be a dick about it!" Chauncy argued.

Tip just raised an eyebrow-ridge.

"Tip says he remembers everything your pee-pee has ever done," Valtora interjected. "Even since before he was put on you."

"I *am* your penis personified," Tip reminded him.

"He told me *all* about your little tryst with that Inkling in the lean-to," Valtora continued, sending a fresh bolt of terror through Chauncy. "I came as fast as I could when I heard you scream, but it turns out you did too."

The blood drained from Chauncy's face, and he lowered his head in shame.

"I'm sorry poopy-dooz," he told her, shaking his head miserably. "I thought...I thought it was you. But that's not an excuse," he added, suddenly filled with grim resolve. He lifted his gaze to stare her right in the eyes, setting his jaw firmly. "I don't deserve to be your fiancé, or your husband."

Valtora stared back at him, her expression stony. Then she stood, crossing her arms over her chest.

"You're right," she told him. "You don't." A tear came to her eye then, and her lower lip trembled. "It's over Chauncy," she declared. "We're through."

And with that, she turned and fled their dome, leaving Chauncy all alone.

"That went well," Tip mused. Chauncy glared at him, suddenly furious at the demon.

"How can you say that?" he snapped. "She's leaving me!"

"Yes, but there's always Zella," Tip pointed out. "And let's be honest, Zella's even hotter than Valtora. We both know you feel that way."

"Shut up!"

And to his surprise and relief, Tip did.

Chauncy sighed then, resting his head back on his pillow and staring up at the ceiling of the dome.

"Great," he muttered. "Just great."

He thought of Chaos then, and their home back in Southwick. Of his perfect life, of what had once been. It was all ruined now, his world destroyed. Imperius Fanning had been absolutely right, but not in the way that Chauncy had expected. He'd assumed that the end of his world would be his death…but this was far worse. For in death, he no longer had to live with regret. There would be no suffering or pain. In the end, he'd suffered far worse a fate: a life of perpetual shame.

*It's over.*

And what's worse, not only was his future with Valtora over…but now his future with Chaos might be too.

It was enough to drive Chauncy to tears. So he rolled onto his side, pulling his knees to his chest, and sobbed.

"Awww," a voice said.

He cut off his sobs abruptly, scrambling to sit up…and was shocked to see Valtora standing there, her hands clutched in front of her chest.

"My widdle Chauncy-poo!" she gasped, throwing herself at him. She struck him with a *whump*, throwing him backward onto his pillow. She showered him with smooches then.

"What…?"

"I'm sowwy baby," she cooed, pulling back from him. "I was just pwaying a widdle twick on you."

Chauncy blinked.

"Huh?"

"I was only *kidding*," she told him. "Duh," she added.

"You were?"

"Well *yeah*," she confirmed. "So Zella had a little fun with you," she added with a shrug. "We already talked about this."

"What?"

"About not living like everyone else," she clarified. "We're wizards, remember? We do things different."

"Differently," he corrected.

"Whatever."

"But…" he protested.

"Now we're even," she interjected, breaking out into a satisfied smile. "You can't be mad at me for Peter. So this is like, *perfect*."

Chauncy frowned, then remembered precisely what'd happened with the unicorn. Something he'd totally forgotten about, surprisingly. But, having been remembered, his mind's eye did its usual thing, reproducing the event in all its rainbow-colored splendor.

"Right," he grumbled.

"Besides, she's *totally* hot," Valtora continued. "If I were you, I'd have hit it."

"I didn't," Chauncy protested. "We never…you know."

"Your loss," Valtora replied. "You totally could."

"Can we change the subject already?" Chauncy pleaded. For he was quite done with the topic at hand. Valtora pouted.

"Awww," she said. "Alright. Hungry?"

He broke out into a smile.

"Starving," he replied.

And with that, she lend a diamond hand to help him stand up…and threw her arms around him, giving him the most passionate kiss he could imagine. He froze, then melted, turning to mush in her embrace.

She pulled away then, a mischievous twinkle in her eye.

"Gonna reclaim you," she vowed.

"Now?" he asked hopefully.

"Nope," she replied. "You've been a *bad* boy Chauncy," she scolded, wagging her finger at him. "I'm gonna make you *wait*."

"Ooo," Chauncy murmured. For a lifetime of waiting for such things had taught him that there was great pleasure to be had in anticipation. Which was quite the opposite of living in the moment, of course. But he'd found it impossible to live in the here and now constantly, as it appeared to be something a human could only do from time to time. Learning to enjoy there and then was just as important, as long as one also enjoyed what one had anticipated when it finally arrived.

After all, if he could only enjoy the future, he'd never enjoy it when it came. For his mind would already be on tomorrow when it did.

"Let's *feed*," Valtora declared. So they left the dome to do just that.

\* \* \*

When Chauncy and Valtora emerged from their dome, they found Nettie and Harry already up, having taken bread and soup mix from the packs Rocky helped carry and heated them by the refreshed fire. Harry handed them both some soup-soaked bread without a word, and each ate to their gut's content. And after perhaps twenty minutes, Chauncy found his mood quite improved. Such was the magic of sated stomachs that they soothed the brain; it made Chauncy wonder how many arguments and acts of violence were, at the root, caused by hunger rather than the logical loops people normal crafted to explain their moods and actions. A few days with Chaos had proven that beyond a shadow of a doubt. For without a full belly – and adequate sleep – Chaos was evil indeed. Goodness was only a booby away, it seemed…at least for babies.

"Where's Peter and Rocky?" Valtora asked. She didn't ask about Rooter, knowing that Rocky and Rooter were forever together.

"Went for a run," Harry answered, gesturing off in the distance. "Peter's getting antsy again," he added, giving Valtora a significant look.

"I'm on it," she told him. She turned to Chauncy then, giving him a look as if daring him to challenge her. Which, given the circumstances, he did not.

"So guess we'll have to wait for them to come back before we set off," Chauncy said. "I was hoping to get an early start."

"Wanna get it over with already, eh?" Nettie said, finishing her meager meal. "I don't blame you kid."

"The road's no place for a child," Chauncy mused, squinting off at the rolling grassland in the distance. He could barely make out Rocky and Peter running and galloping respectively back toward them, what seemed like miles away.

"Why not?" Nettie asked.

"Hmm?"

"Why isn't the road a place for a child?" she pressed.

"It's dangerous," Chauncy answered.

"So's meeting your destiny," Nettie pointed out. "You wanna keep Chaos safe and secure and desperately depressed like your grandma did?"

"Bless her heart," Harry added, for politeness's sake.

Chauncy hesitated, then shook his head. And it was true, he realized. Sure, if he kept Chaos at home, safe and snug, always protected from anything that could harm him, he'd have the best chance at living a long life. But it would be at the expense of a life worth living…a life of adventure, of great risks and great rewards. Of ups and downs, ecstasy and tragedy…a life truly felt. Without risk, Chaos's life would be numb. For pleasure was felt most keenly on a background of its absence, just as hunger was the best of spices. And thirst made water into a delicious treat, and warmth felt marvelous when chilled to the bone.

The people of Borrin were obsessed with quantity, whether of possessions, money, or years of life. But Chauncy had lived more in a few weeks of adventure than he had in a quarter-century of playing it safe. Playing it risky – to just the right extent – seemed to be the trick.

At length, Rocky, Rooter, and Peter made it back to camp, and Rocky got on all fours in preparation for being ridden. Harry and Chauncy put the packs on Rocky's back, then Harry turned to Zella's dome. With a bare toe wiggled into the earth, the dome sank into the ground, revealing Zella in the process of being embraced from behind by Shackles the golem.

"Mornin'," Harry greeted, flashing a smile at her. And a little wave.

"Don't be nice to her," Nettie scolded. "She's bad, remember?"

"That's why I'm being nice to her," Harry replied. "Maybe she'll be bad with me."

"Sorry," Zella replied, eyeing Chauncy. "Already taken."

"So is Chauncy," Valtora retorted, slapping Chauncy on the butt. And then squeezing for good measure.

"You get the back," Zella replied with a little smile. "I get the front."

"I get the whole package," Valtora shot back.

"And I got it yesterday," Zella countered.

"There's a story there," Harry interjected, seeming quite interested in where this was going.

"Story-time's gonna have to wait," Nettie interjected. "We're going back to the carriage, then taking this hussy to the Order of Mundus."

"Who, me?" Valtora asked.

"No, the other hussy," Nettie clarified.

"Oh," Valtora replied, seeming a bit disappointed that someone else had taken her nickname.

"Come on," Nettie grumbled. And with that, they did, Valtora retrieving Chaos and putting him in her wrap, then vaulting on Peter's back. Everyone else but Zella got on Rocky, while Shackles walked Zella dutifully behind them.

With that, they set out to the Great Wood to retrieve Harry and Nettie's carriage…and make the long journey to the Isle of Mundus.

* * *

It was a bit before noon by the time Rocky and Peter carried the Chosen Ones to their carriage, and Nettie got inside while Harry rode the horse pulling it. Valtora remained on Peter, while Rocky carried Rooter and Gavin and Chauncy. Chauncy found himself eyeing Gavin, who'd pulled out his golden knitting needles. The man touched their ends together, then pulled the apart...and a golden string appeared between them.

"So...knitting," Chauncy stated. "That's what's magic to you?"

"Yes," Gavin answered.

"How did you find out?" he asked.

"Before I met you, I'd spent my entire life using people," Gavin explained. "But when I visited the Great Wood, I realized that I'd been used too. By my grandfather and father, who'd groomed me to take over Evermore. And by society, who made me believe the money game was the only game in life that really mattered...and that my value as a person was the labor I contributed to Borrin's economy."

"Yeah," Chauncy replied with a smile. For he'd been beguiled in the same way, giving the best years of his life away doing something he hated, just so he eventually wouldn't have to do it anymore.

"I'd already won the game," Gavin confessed. "But I kept playing it, because I didn't realize that that's all it was."

"So when you went into the Cave of Wonder...?" Chauncy prompted.

"It made me confront myself," Gavin stated. "The things I hated about me...and how to be the 'me' I was meant to be."

"A knitter?"

"In a way," Gavin replied. "For me, knitting is magic. It's the universe explained in yarn."

Chauncy glanced at the yarn skeptically, not quite sure how this could be. Gavin must have noticed, for he smiled, starting to knit. It wasn't long before he'd knitted a rectangle of woven cloth.

"A single string," Gavin explained. "Every warp supporting a woof, every woof supporting a warp. Everything holding everything else up...to create something beautiful."

"How is that like the universe?" Chauncy inquired.

"The universe is a single thing like the string," Gavin explained. "Woven into countless things. Each supporting each other like the warp and woof. In a network of being where all is connected to all, no matter how far away they may be."

Gavin offered Chauncy the rectangle, and he took it. Then Gavin pulled on one corner...and the entire thing changed shape to stretch a bit. Chauncy smiled despite himself.

"Everything connected to everything," he murmured. He felt a chill run through him, and he lifted his gaze to the sky far above. He felt his consciousness expand, and suddenly he was keenly aware of the air around him, the grass and clouds and trees. All connected to each other by the distances between them, even by space, which was not nothing but *some*thing. For as he'd noted before, space had volume, and as such, couldn't be the absence of things. It connected everything even as it separated them…just as The Dark One had said of humanity.

That people placed things in categories, and that in being, they discriminated between things. But if all things were *one* thing…

"The universe is a string," he breathed, turning his gaze back to Gavin. Gavin inclined his head, sharing his sudden understanding.

"You're the one who taught me that," Gavin confessed. "You believed that I could be a wizard like you. I owe you a great deal, Chauncy."

"If you feel magic, then that's all I ever wanted for you," Chauncy replied. "I know what it's like to live without, and my dream is to do for others what I've done for you."

"In Southwick?" Gavin asked. Chauncy nodded. "They need you," Gavin agreed.

"My grandmother was wrong in a lot of ways, but in a few ways she was right," Chauncy mused. "Everyone needs A Little Magic in their lives."

"That they do," Gavin agreed. "Not to possess it like I did, but to feel it like I do."

With that, Gavin sheathed his magic knitting needles, falling into silence. But Chauncy didn't mind at all, being quite comfortable with having nothing to say. For when not putting out, he could take in…and he took in this very moment. Sitting on the back of a rocky giant with his former arch-nemesis, making his way toward the Isle of Mundus. At long last, he was going to visit the place where magic was most profound, where the most powerful wizards in the land resided. Perhaps they would be able to not only defeat Zella Trek, but solve the enigma that was Chauncy's past. Of his mother's fate and his father's whereabouts…mysteries that, after twenty-six years of wondering, might be solved at last.

# Chapter 32

King Pravus soared above his kingdom on the back of his very own fire dragon, Templeton behind him as always. The wind whipped through their black hair, making them squint their glacier-blue eyes as they made their way toward a wide shore in the distance. Beyond this was a great, rippling ocean...the Sea of Magi. The Isle of Mundus was a small island smack in the middle of this legendary sea. A sea – it was claimed – that hosted a mystical underwater kingdom, home of a god. Or a goddess, or whatever...no one could quite be sure. Because it was all probably poppycock anyhow, as legends tended to be.

"Almost there cousin!" Templeton exclaimed with his usual gusto, bringing a smile to Pravus's lips. For Templeton was forever impressed with the experience of life, enjoying each moment as it came. He was the type of person who made life better just by being in Pravus's, for like the sun, Templeton cast warmth upon everything his light touched. And his light was bright indeed.

Perhaps that was Templeton's magic, Pravus mused. That by relating to the world so fondly, he made others fond of it too. The magic of cheer...a powerful magic indeed. Not as destructive as a fireball, nor as epic as a hurricane. But to make men's hearts soar – to lift their spirits and evoke smiles from the most bitter of souls – was as constructive a power as any Pravus could imagine.

"Indeed," Pravus replied. "The Isle of Mundus," he stated, raising his voice over the shriek of the wind. "How I've longed to see it!"

"I hear it's spectacular," Templeton replied. "Soon we'll see."

"Assuming the Order lets us," Pravus said. For it was not guaranteed that they would. The Order of Mundus was notorious for its secrecy, rarely allowing strangers within its castle or even at its shores. But he had to believe they would at least entertain the king of Pravus...particularly given the circumstances.

At length they'd left the shore of their kingdom far behind, such that they could no longer see it behind them. The endless ocean extended outward in all directions below them, without an island in sight. It was a bit nerve-wracking, to have nothing for the eye to rest on. No visual to anchor them in a particular place, or to make it clear how fast they were going. Pravus found himself feeling lost, struck with the sudden fear that they'd never find their way back home. For with nothing to hold onto behind them and nothing ahead, there was no way to know where *here* was.

He glanced down at the dragon, who flapped its wings lazily, gliding over the ocean without a care. It certainly wasn't concerned; perhaps it was incapable of existential despair. Or more likely, it was confident in its ability to find its way home, even if it got lost. In either case, Pravus was no longer in control, which was almost certainly why he felt so disturbed. To let go of control – and trust in his dragon – took a special kind of courage. Not a confidence in oneself, which Pravus had in excess, but a confidence in someone or something else.

Pravus patted the dragon's back, smiling at the creature.

"Thank you," he told it. And to his delight, he saw it shoot a bit of fire out of its nostrils in reply.

He settled into the moment then, enjoying the sun baking his skin. Its heat contrasted nicely with the coolness of the wind, a feast for the senses. A slight tang of saltwater served as seasoning, and Templeton's arms around his waist were his dessert. Pravus found himself enjoying himself…and in that merging with the moment, his fears about what was behind him – and before him – faded away.

Now was nice, and that's all the mattered. So nice, in fact, that Pravus vowed to spend more time in 'now' from now on.

"There!" he heard Templeton exclaim, and saw his cousin point ahead and a bit to the right. This broke Pravus from his reverie, and he followed Templeton's finger, spotting an island barely visible there. As they drew closer, the island grew larger…as did Pravus's eyes. For it was beyond a doubt the most marvelous sight he'd ever laid eyes on.

"My *god*," he breathed, his jaw going slack.

For ahead was the Isle – and Order – of Mundus. And it quite literally took his breath away.

# Chapter 33

Day turned to night, and after making camp and falling asleep – and waking up to continue their trek, Chauncy decided to spend some time in the carriage instead of on Rocky. He felt like he hadn't gotten much time to talk to Nettie during this particular trip, after all, and he missed their conversations. So in the carriage he went, he on the left as usual, she on the right. And off they went…or rather, off-road. For no roads led to the Isle of Mundus.

"Because it's an island, that's why," Nettie explained when he asked. "Out in the middle of the Sea of Magi."

"Oh," Chauncy mumbled. "So uh…how are we going to get there?"

"You'll see," she replied. Mysteriously.

He fell silent for a bit, gazing out of his carriage window. Not confined to the width of a road, Valtora rode Peter beside the carriage. She waved at Chauncy, beaming the most gorgeous of smiles…and then blew him a kiss. He grinned, blowing her a kiss back…and she made as if to catch it in her diamond hand, reaching down to Chaos wrapped up in her wrap and putting it on his cheek.

"Aww," Chauncy said. "So cute."

"Sure is," Nettie agreed. "Getting cuter every day too." Which was true. For while Chaos had been born uglier than sin, his features were starting to take a more pleasing shape. Birth was traumatic to babies' heads, after all. But traumatic trials were a part of life; if babies were like many adults, they'd never suffer being born for fear of facing them.

"Yeah," Chauncy agreed. Nettie eyed him with a little smile. "What?" he asked.

"Just thinkin' about how far you've come," she told him. "I remember when we first picked you up. So stiff and uptight," she mused. "So desperate to get back to your depressing life, even though you hated it."

"I didn't know anything else," he admitted.

"And didn't want to, until we got through to you," she agreed.

"Until I learned to play," he recalled. For it hadn't been until he'd learned that magic was real that he'd agreed to let go of being respectfully dull…and start on the path to being a bit ridiculous. It was the horrible weight of public opinion that had held him back, like a ball and chain tied to his ankle, keeping him in a prison of propriety. Impropriety, it turned out, was far more fun…and allowed him to be not quite like everyone else, but more like himself.

Who he *really* was.

"Huh," he murmured.

"What?" Nettie asked.

"Magic is my relationship with the world," he recited. It'd been what she'd taught him, after all. "But the world isn't just the world," he continued. "It's *me*. And I discovered magic when I rediscovered myself."

Nettie patted him on the knee.

"Darn tootin'," she agreed. She gave a proud smile. "You're coming along, kid."

"Thanks."

"But you got a long way to go," she added, putting a damper on his joy. "Problem is, you keep forgetting you're a wizard."

Chauncy sighed.

"I know," he replied. "That's my problem."

"Only a problem if you think it is," she countered. Chauncy paused, then nodded.

*The solution to the problem is the problem itself*, he thought. One of the most important lessons he'd learned during his last adventure. His depression over not being a good enough wizard was precisely *why* he wasn't a good enough wizard. But every time he let go – every time he *played* – he proved more than adequate to the title. Indeed, it'd been in the spirit of play that he'd defeated The Dark One…his most impressive accomplishment yet. Other than siring a son, of course.

Or rather, that's what he was supposed to say. For siring a son was easy to do, requiring little risk or effort at all. But having the courage to face his fears of not being enough, and get past them to prove that he was…

"Let's spar," he blurted out, struck with the sudden urge to do so. Nettie blinked.

"Now?" she asked incredulously.

"Now," he confirmed. "And after I spar you, Harry's next."

"Oho!" Nettie declared. "Chauncy's feeling his oats!" She rapped on the front window of the carriage, and opened the sliding door to talk to Harry. "Stop the carriage," she ordered. "Chauncy's gonna spar us."

"Okie dokie," Harry agreed. And with that, he did.

\* \* \*

For their sparring match, Nettie chose a relatively flat bit of meadow, standing waist-deep in wildflowers. Which was knee-deep to Chauncy. To his dismay, there were bees buzzing everywhere, a distraction he hadn't anticipated. He was a bit terrified of bees, in that they could sting him and it would be painful. Not because the pain was particularly horrible, but because he never knew when it would come. Anticipation could be a terrible thing, particularly when it involved considering a future unpleasant event. And it served to take his mind out of the here and now, which unfortunately was where the rest of him was…and where his mind needed to be.

"Ready?" Nettie asked.

"Bees," Chauncy sort-of-answered, flinching away from one as it buzzed near.

"What about 'em?" Nettie pressed, seeming irritated at this delay.

"They're here," he explained. "They can hurt me."

"So can I," she retorted. "But if you're always anticipating the bad stuff that might happen in the future, it's far more likely to."

Chauncy grimaced.

*The solution to the problem is the problem itself.*

"Right," he declared.

And with that, he decided to be ridiculous. Right then, right there. Or rather, here and now. And not just a little ridiculous. *Absolutely* ridiculous.

"I'm gonna lose my frickin' mind!" he announced. And with that announcement, he went to that familiar place in his psyche, building up another heaping dose of crazy. With a giddy rush, he cackled at the bees around him, staring at them with wide, unreasonable eyes. "Come and *sting* me!" he cried…and then thrust his staff up high, bursting into a wild yodel. If he wasn't going to run from his fears, by golly he'd run right *toward* them.

Nettie buried her face in her hands, almost certainly at his yodeling, and shook her head. Which was precisely the opening

Chauncy needed. But instead of telegraphing his next move with a loud battle-cry, he did it in his head.

*Thrusted Bust!*

He jabbed the butt of his staff at her chest…or more specifically, her Wetstone. The resulting bullet of wind struck her…and sent an explosion of water blasting outward from the magical stone.

"Ha!" he cried as Nettie flew backward. She wrapped the water around her, creating liquid armor to soften her fall. Then she got to her feet.

"Oh ho!" she exclaimed. "Bet you're a clever little shit, don't'cha?"

"I'm a big ol' *nasty* shit," Chauncy shot back, eyeing the bees nestled in the flowers all around her. "Stinging swarm!" he cried jubilantly, swinging his staff in an arc at her. A blast of wind shot outward, flattening the wildflowers in a wide swath between them…and flinging bees right at Nettie. A big swarm of them…all of whom, having been pulled from their pollen, were understandably upset. So they went right after Nettie, dive-bombing her.

"Ow!" she blurted out as they stung her. She squeezed her Wetstone, creating a dome of water outward all around her. One that protected her from the bees…and drowned many of them to boot.

"Bee killer!" Chauncy gasped. "I shall avenge thee, sweet bees!"

"He's lost it," Harry observed.

"That's why I have it!" Chauncy shot back.

"Good job baby!" Zella called out. It took Chauncy a moment to realize she was talking to him. Valtora glared at her.

"He's *my* baby," she shot back. "Pound her ass, Chauncy!"

"Then mine," Zella added with a villainous grin.

Nettie ignored both of them, shooting a big glob of water at Chauncy, attached to a rope-like stream connecting her to it. Which meant, he knew, that she was going to freeze it. Or try to drown him. He'd seen it before, and in his present state of mind, being bludgeoned or drowned didn't seem like something to worry about.

"Big Staff Smash!" Chauncy cried, executing a powerful overhead chop. The top of his staff struck the ground, the impact releasing a massive amount of wind. Wildflowers and clumps of soil shot upward and forward in front of him, and a vertical shockwave shot toward Nettie, flattening the flowers in a narrow line leading right to her. She froze the dome of water still around her, flash-freezing the bees still stuck within…and protecting herself from his blast.

The wind struck her shield, cracking it…but it held. Until Chauncy followed up immediately with another silent attack, swinging his staff in an upward arc. Another blast struck Nettie's shield…and this time, the shield caved. But to his surprise, its interior was filled with water, suspending Nettie within…and absorbing the force that'd penetrated her ice.

She melted the shield, then sucked the water back into her Wetstone, smirking at him.

"Nice try," she called out.

"Nice DIE!" he shot back, whipping his staff around in a flurry of attacks, as if battling the air itself. A barrage of windy blasts shot toward Nettie, many of them missing by a fair margin. But it forced her to stay put instead of trying to dodge, for dodging would've dodged into the blasts that'd missed. So she created another icy shield, one thicker than before…and that easily absorbed the blows.

Eventually Chauncy tuckered out, stopping his mad swings…and Nettie reabsorbed her shield, still smirking at him.

"You done now?" she inquired. He rolled his shoulders a few times, then cracked his neck from side-to-side.

"Just getting warmed up," he assured her. Which, in truth, was a lie. For it turned out that crazy took an unexpectedly large amount of energy…and Chauncy was in terrible shape.

"Uh huh," Nettie grumbled, putting her hands on her hips. "I'll wait."

He gave in, bending over and taking a breather. After a while, he stood up straight…right as a jet of water struck him dead-on in the face. His head snapped backward, and he fell, landing on the ground with a *whump*.

Then the ice froze, covering his face in an icy mask. One that wrapped all the way around his head…and covered his nose and mouth.

"Mmmff!"

He scrambled to his feet, clawing at the icy mask. But it was terribly slippery, and as hard as rock. There was no way for him to take it off. And it certainly wasn't going to melt before he was asphyxiated. So, seeing no way out, he raised his staff above his head in surrender.

Chauncy waited then, expecting something to happen. For he couldn't really see that well through the ice, not much more than a blur. But as his lungs started to burn – and his skin quickly and painfully froze – the something he was expecting didn't happen.

*Come* on *Nettie*, he thought, thrusting his staff up a few times to make his surrender clear. But again, his ice-mask didn't melt away. And now his lungs were *really* starting to burn…and the realization that help wasn't coming was the only thing that did come.

That's when the desperation hit.

*Crap!*

Chauncy pulled at the mask, but again his fingers slipped right off. Then he got on his hands and knees, trying to find a stone with his free hand. But there was only grass and flowers…so he started banging his head against the ground. It was too soft, and the ice didn't crack…and now his vision was starting to fade. Desperation turned to terror, one that threatened to overwhelm him right before the very end. So he rose from the ground, his staff in hand, charging toward where he thought Nettie was.

*Staff!*

He stopped, slapping his ice-covered forehead with his hand…and then wound up, smashing it with his staff instead.

The ice shattered, a blast of wind snapping his head back, and he flew through the air, landing on his back. His breath burst from his lungs…and then he sucked air in, sweet air! And laid there, dousing the fire in his lungs with it.

"Oh…god," he gasped. "That's…the…stuff!"

He heard cackling from ahead, and an old man's chuckle as well. And even a giggle-snort from Valtora, and a snorting-snort from Peter. But Chauncy didn't care, seeing as how he was alive. As long as he was, his failures weren't too big to learn from.

At length, he got to his feet, brushing flower petals and grass from his wizard's robe.

"Well done," he conceded, bowing at her. "You win…this round."

"'Course I did," she replied. "I was playing. You were…whatever the hell that was."

"I was playing too," he retorted.

"Crazy's not the same as playing," she pointed out. "How are ya gonna play with your mind if you've lost it?"

"Oh," Chauncy mumbled, scratching the back of his head. His cheeks flushed, whether due to the fact that were thawing out or due to embarrassment, he wasn't sure.

214

"You can be playful without being an idiot," she lectured. "Try having fun, not a mental breakdown."

"Alright," he agreed rather sheepishly. For he'd once again screwed things up. And he'd never be much of a wizard if he didn't start learning what Nettie was teaching.

"*He* beat The Dark One?" Zella Trek asked from the sidelines, staring at Chauncy incredulously.

"Chauncy beat his ass good," Valtora confirmed proudly.

"How?" Zella pressed.

"He put The Dark One inside himself…" Valtora explained.

"Oh my," Zella replied.

"…and inside all of us," Valtora concluded. "His magic is to put things into things, and pull them out again."

"Oh *my*," Zella repeated, gazing at Chauncy with renewed interest. "Do a little of your magic with me next, darling."

"Not like that," Chauncy protested.

"And not with *you*," Valtora added.

"You mean not again," Zella corrected. Chauncy's eyes widened, a fresh bolt of fear striking him. And to his further horror, Valtora frowned.

"Huh?" she asked.

"He didn't tell you?" Zella asked, clearly enjoying watching Chauncy squirm. "I *truly* enjoyed our first meeting," she mused. "And I know that Chauncy did too. Didn't you darling?"

"Um…" Chauncy began.

"What was it you said?" Zella asked. "I think it was: 'That was by *far* the best you've ever done.'"

"Word for word," Tip confirmed. "And let me tell you, he meant it. I mean *wow*."

"Shut up!" Chauncy snapped at the demon.

"Honestly, it's not even close," Tip continued. "Sorry Valtora."

"Wow," Valtora muttered, crossing her arms over her chest. "Just…wow."

"You really should've told her," Zella mused, throwing Chauncy a little smirk.

"Oh he did," Valtora replied. Zella frowned.

"He did?"

"Sure," Valtora confirmed. "I mean, he didn't say it was the best ever though. What'd you do?"

Zella blinked.

"Excuse me?" she asked.

215

"Like, what'd you *do*," Valtora repeated. "Can you show me? I mean, if you're that good, I *have* to know."

Zella said nothing, clearly taken aback by Valtora's equanimity. And her enthusiasm.

"Come on," Valtora urged. "Just tell me."

"I'd rather show you," Zella replied with a smirk, eyeing Chauncy. Valtora considered this, then opened her mouth to reply. But Chauncy cleared his throat loudly to interrupt whatever she was going to say, turning to face Nettie.

"Again!" he cried...and swung his staff before she could respond, attacking her with a powerful windy blast. Thus began round two of their match...which Chauncy hoped would be their last.

# Chapter 34

Having gotten walloped by Nettie every single round, Chauncy ended their sparring session feeling defeated. Not just because he'd been beaten, but because his soul had been beaten down. Thus he'd declined to spar with Harry, continuing their journey instead. He rode atop Rocky in dejected silence, with Gavin sitting cross-legged beside him. Gavin left Chauncy alone, for which Chauncy was grateful. It was only proper for a man to lick his wounds alone, after all.

And lick Chauncy did, spending some time traveling down memory lane. A psychic journey that revealed the unfortunate truth: despite over a year and three adventures, he'd failed to self-actualize as a wizard.

He sighed, gazing up at the darkening sky, the sun close to setting in the horizon now. It was profoundly frustrating to want something – and to be willing to put in the work to get it – but have no idea what it was he was supposed to do. The way forward was hidden to him…and he despaired that he might not ever find it, no matter how many times destiny knocked on his door.

*Maybe it's not meant to be*, he thought. A thought that was followed by the sudden realization that after dealing with Zella, he could just go home to Southwick, and focus on being a husband and a father rather than a wizard. Valtora and Chaos were more than enough to make a man happy, after all. It would be a life most people would kill to have, having a successful business, a gorgeous wife, and a child to love.

The kind of life, in fact, that Grandma Little had wanted for him.

A strange thing, to think that she might have been right all along. Why should Chauncy need to be a wizard to be happy, after all? So far, it'd only made him feel as if he weren't enough.

The thought made him antsy. And being antsy made him want to do something, so he shoved his hands in his pockets…and felt The Magic of Magic in his left one. He pulled it out, eyeing the glittery purple cover, then cracked it open to a random page. One with an illustration of the night sky in perfect, inky black…with a full moon casting silver light down on a grassy field below. It immediately took him back to his experience in the Cave of Wonder, with his odd doppelganger there. About what it'd said when he'd asked it what he wanted.

*To not be me. To not be you.*

He pondered this for a bit, but soon gave up. It didn't make any sense at all. Of course, that's what he'd said about the other revelations he'd had in the Cave of Wonder the last time he'd been there. Which meant that it *did* mean something…he just hadn't figured it out yet.

The black carriage stopped ahead of Rocky, pulling to the right side of the road. Nettie got out, and Harry got down from his driver's seat, Rocky stopping just behind them.

"All right," Nettie declared. "We old farts need our beauty sleep. Go pitch a tent, Harry."

Harry got to work doing so, and Chauncy and Gavin got down from Rocky's back to help. With the former president of the Evermore Trading Company's help, the tents were pitched in no time. Gavin was competent in just about everything, it seemed, learning new skills far faster than Chauncy. The guy was taller, smarter, handsomer, stronger, and just all-around better than him…a fact that was monumentally depressing. Chauncy glanced at Valtora, who got down from Peter, meeting his gaze and giving him a happy wave. He wondered suddenly why she stuck with him, when she could so easily get a guy like Gavin.

The tents pitched, and night having fallen, Harry went to build a fire. Gavin helped…and without Chauncy's help, a merry fire was soon blazing.

"You alright?" Valtora asked Chauncy, standing at his side whilst feeding Chaos his nighttime meal.

"No," he confessed.

"What's wrong?" she pressed. He paused, then sighed.

"I think I need to go for a walk," he replied.

"Ooo, take Chaos," she told him, pulling the baby from her wrap and handing him to Chauncy. Chauncy grimaced, taking Chaos reluctantly in one hand. For he'd hoped to take a walk by himself. But he was a father now; doing things by himself was a luxury he could no longer enjoy very often. So he bid his goodbyes, walking away from the camp, making his way to the road. He followed it for a while, using his staff as a walking stick, then veered off to the left onto a relatively flat grassy field. Soon he left the road far, far behind…so far behind, in fact, that he couldn't see it.

He gazed upward as he walked, at the starry sky above…and the full moon glowing down at him. He stopped then, staring up at it. It brought him back to the day Grandma Little had died, when they'd made it back from the shop to her front porch. How she'd gone inside, and he'd gazed at the moon, looking just as it did now. He'd been struck by the irony then that, despite working all day in a magic shop, the moon had been the closest thing to magic he'd ever seen.

He remembered the moon hanging just above the great stone wall separating him from the kingdom of Pravus that day, as if guiding him to the Gate. To the greatest mystery in his life at the time…a place where his dreams of magic might come true.

"What do you want with me?" he asked the moon, clutching Chaos to his chest. He had the sudden sense of the vast space between himself and the moon, a distance beyond his comprehension. And at the same time, he was struck with the uncanny feeling that this unthinkable space not only separated them…but at the same time also *connected* them. It was just as The Dark One had said. The borders which separated things also connected them. It was true not only of categorizations, but of the universe.

And the universe *was* mostly space, a vast mystery that served to separate and connect all things.

With that revelation, Chauncy felt a chill run down his spine…and at the same time, something entirely unexpected occurred. For space itself seemed to *shift*…and he suddenly found himself standing on the surface of the moon.

* * *

"What the hell?" Chauncy blurted out, freezing in place. All around him was the bright gray, blighted surface of the moon…and high above, in precisely the same spot as the moon had been moments ago, was an entirely different sphere. One of brilliant blue and brown and green, with wispy white clouds all around.

"That's home," a voice behind him said.

Chauncy gasped, then spun around…and saw a man standing there before him. A man who looked like him, in fact, just like in the Cave of Wonder. But this man had graying hair at his temples, and a long straight beard. And he wore a wizard's robe of midnight black…with twinkling white spots like stars shimmering on its surface. Or rather, they seemed to *be* stars, for if Chauncy looked at the robe, it seemed to be composed of vast space…just like the sky far above.

"Who are you?" Chauncy asked. "How did I get here?"

"Here?"

"In the sky," Chauncy clarified. "Or in space, I mean. On the moon."

"You were always in the sky," the man replied. "It's not far above…it's right here," he added.

"But…"

"You were always in space," the man continued. "Everything is. And there's space in you."

"I…" Chauncy began.

"To answer your first question, I *am* Space," the man continued. "And thus the greatest part of you. For without me, there would be no you…and no anything to distinguish from anything else."

Chauncy frowned at this.

"You're…space?"

"Personified," the man confirmed. "I'm a Magus, Chauncy."

"A…what?"

"A Magus," he repeated. "A wizard who's become what he loves. By connecting with it so strongly that we become one thing, like The Dark One did with evil."

Chauncy blinked.

"The Dark One was a wizard once?" he asked. The stranger nodded.

"A wizard of the Order of Mundus, in fact," the stranger confirmed. "Long, long ago. He ascended to become a Magus, and made his home on Mount Thrall. For the very purpose of serving as a method of self-actualization for future wizards…wizards you now call Chosen Ones."

"Wait…The Dark One…what?"

"He rises to serve as a challenge, to make heroes of men and women," the stranger explained. "He serves the Order of Mundus in this way…for the greatest of the Chosen Ones that 'defeat' him are welcomed into the Order. And the greatest of these," he added, "…become Magi."

Chauncy stared at the man.

"Oh," he mumbled.

"I was a member of the Order," the man explained. "And still am, of course. I connected with space...and thus, connect all things."

"Wow," Chauncy murmured, not knowing quite what to say. So he just stared, feeling a steady breeze whip through his hair. He shivered, realizing it was awfully chilly. "Sure is cold on the moon," he stated, holding Chaos a bit tighter. "And windy."

"Actually, there's no air on the moon," the stranger – or rather Space – countered. "Your staff is releasing air. Or else you'd be dead."

"Ah," Chauncy replied. And felt suddenly terribly ill at ease. Space smiled.

"Don't fear," he reassured. "I won't hurt you, Chauncy. After all, we're family."

"Fam...ily?"

"Of course," Space replied. Chauncy frowned, furrowing his brow.

"I'm afraid I don't understand," he confessed. Space put a hand on his shoulder, giving him a kindly smile.

"Quite alright Chauncy," he replied. "Or should I say, Chauncy junior."

"Huh?"

"I'm your father, Chauncy," Space replied. "And I've been watching over you all this time.

# Chapter 35

Chauncy stared at the man who looked so much like him, only a bit older and scruffier. A man wearing a robe almost identical to his, only instead of glittering amethyst, it portrayed space and stars. He suddenly forgot entirely what the man had just told him. For the life of him, he couldn't recall it. So he just stared, feeling oddly numb.

"Huh?" he asked at last.

"I'm your father," the man apparently repeated.

"My what?"

"The 'spindly coward' who knocked your mother up, or so your Grandmother used to say," he replied. Chauncy continued to stare blankly. "The man who made you, with your mother's help of course," the man added with a wink.

"My father?" Chauncy asked.

"Right," he confirmed.

Chauncy stared a bit longer, then shook his head.

"But…you…"

"Left you and your mother, vanishing from sight?" his supposed father guessed. Chauncy nodded numbly. "In a way," he admitted. "I ascended, Chauncy. But I never left you. I was with you all along."

"You were?" Chauncy asked, still not quite believing any of this was happening. For he still felt strangely numb, as if this wasn't really happening to him. As if it were all a dream…and any moment now, he'd wake up. If his hands hadn't been occupied with Chaos and his Staff of Wind, he'd have pinched himself.

"As Space, I'm everywhere," Space replied. "And I've been with you." He paused. "Have you ever felt that?"

Chauncy frowned, remembering how he'd felt that night when Grandma Little had died. As if he'd taken the night sky for granted. That vast space, a beautiful mystery, magical in and of itself. And he remembered his last adventure, when he'd taken a walk during the journey to defeat The Dark One. How he'd realized that night-time was when he felt most alive. And how space connected everything, even as it separated everything.

"I guess I did," he realized, a chill running down his spine. The realization brought him into the moment, into the here and now. The numbness left him, and it suddenly became quite clear that what was happening was happening to *him*. And that he was standing before his father right now, right here. His lower lip quivered, and tears came to his eyes, blurring his vision. He lunged forward quite involuntarily, wrapping an arm around his father. "Dad!" he cried.

Space wrapped his arms around Chauncy, enveloping him in a warm embrace. Chauncy felt it not just with his father's arms, but with his entire being, as if his father were hugging every part of him.

"I love you son," his father murmured.

"I love you," Chauncy replied. And in that moment, he did. All of the bitterness he'd felt about his father – or rather, about the story Grandma Little had told Chauncy about his father – vanished in that moment, the fiction replaced by fact. He knew that his father *did* love him. That he always had.

"I'm sorry," Space added, pulling away to arm's length, his hands on Chauncy's shoulders. "If I'd stayed human, you would've had a father. But Imperius told me that this was ultimately the better way, so I trusted that he was right, as painful as it was."

"But what about Mom?" Chauncy asked. For Grandma Little had told him his mother had died when he was nine. Space sighed, letting go of Chauncy's shoulders and turning away, his jawline rippling.

"She ascended too," he confessed. "She didn't want to, of course. She wanted to stay with you until you were grown, and then ascend. But Imperius warned her that if she did so, you would die young. So she made the decision to ascend instead."

"Wait," Chauncy protested. "She's alive?"

"Yes," Space replied, turning to face Chauncy again. "She is."

"Really?" Chauncy pressed, another chill running through him. "Where is she?"

"All around you," Space answered. Chauncy frowned.

"What?"

"She's touching you right now," Space explained. "She's everywhere you can see."

"I…don't understand," Chauncy confessed.

"She's light," Space revealed.

Chauncy blinked.

"What?" he asked.

"She's light," his father repeated. "Light incarnate," he added. "She connected with light completely, because it was magical to her."

"She's alive?" Chauncy blurted out.

"She is," Space confirmed with a smile. "As I am."

Chauncy stared at his father – his honest to goodness father! – and felt his legs turn to mush. They wobbled, and he would've fallen if his father hadn't reached under his armpits to hold him up.

"Let's get you back home before you run out of wind," Space told him. And with that, Chauncy felt a *shift*. In a blink of an eye, he was standing back in that grassy field, precisely where he'd been before going to the moon.

"Wo*wee*, he breathed, hardly believing this was really happening.

"Right?" his father replied with a smile. "Being a Magus has its perks."

"Sure does," Chauncy agreed.

"But it also has its downsides," the man added, his expression growing grim. "I can only assume my original human form for short periods of time, and only when you truly connect with me. Soon I'll fade away, Chauncy."

"But why?" Chauncy asked.

"A Magus connects with what they love," he explained. "They merge with it. Become it, forevermore. But in becoming something more than human, we lose the ability to *be* only human for long. That's just the way it is."

"But I just met you," Chauncy protested, feeling a sudden burst of fear. "Will I see you again?"

"I'll be all around you, and in you," his father answered with a smile. "As space, I'll *be* most of you."

"Will we ever talk again?"

"If fate wills it," Space replied, putting a hand on Chauncy's shoulder. He slid it down to touch Chaos's head, gazing at the child. "Congratulations, Chauncy," he murmured, caressing Chaos's scalp. "Enjoy everything you have while you have it."

And with that, his father began to fade, his body dissolving before Chauncy's eyes.

"Wait!" Chauncy protested. But it was no use. "Dad!" he cried.

"We're always with you," Dad assured him. "Your mother and I. Where there is space or light, we're right there with you."

And with that, he was gone. Space once more. Returned to being what he loved, what loved him was all that remained. And so

Chauncy stood there, alone yet *not* alone in that grassy field, surrounded by space…and light.

His parents, always with him. For light was upon him in its silvery glow, and space was around and within him.

Chauncy stood there, another chill running through him, Chaos the only source of warmth he could feel.

"W*owee*," he breathed.

And promptly passed out.

* * *

Chauncy woke to find himself lying on his back, Chaos cradled in his arms. And Chaos was *shrieking*.

"Oh!" he blurted out, scrambling to his feet. He looked Chaos over in a panic, searching for bruises and breaks. But the baby seemed fine. Which was odd, because the kid was still screaming. Chauncy turned around, looking frantically for a bit of light in the distance from Harry's campfire. He spotted it, and nearly broke out into a run…until Valtora's triple-check came to his mind.

*Booby, booty, bedtime.*

Having no boo…er, breasts, Chauncy peeked in Chaos's diaper. It was both wet and poo-filled, to his dismay…and he had no diapers with him.

"Sorry Chaos," he apologized, hurrying back to camp. "You're just going to have to wait."

At length, they made it back to the road, crossing it to get to the camp. Everyone was around the fire, even Zella, still held by Shackles. She winked at him as he approached, eyeing him with what could only be described as a hungry look. A look he'd seen before, to unfortunate effect. He looked away quickly, turning to Valtora instead…who stood when she spotted Chauncy, rushing up to him and the still-crying Chaos.

"My baby!" she gasped, reaching out for her son. Chaos gladly gave him over.

"Booty," he informed her. She nodded with instant understanding.

"Got it," she replied, turning and rushing toward their tent.

"I can do it," Chauncy offered, following her inside. She set Chaos down, then stepped aside, handing him a new diaper. And with his face all scrunched up with the thought of poop – though that poop strangely had no smell – Chauncy changed his first crappy diaper. It wasn't nearly as bad as people had made it seem when they'd told stories back at the shop; in fact, Chauncy didn't mind it at all.

*Maybe I can do this,* he thought, smiling at Chaos. He picked his son up, leaning down to give him a kiss, then rocked him gently.

"Aww," Valtora cooed, smiling at them both and giving them both a peck on the cheek. "My *men.*"

"Shucks," Chauncy replied with a smile of his own.

"How was your walk?" she asked. "Feeling better?"

"Quite a bit, actually," he replied. And then he told her the tale of what'd happened. Of how he'd met his father, who just so happened to be Space. And that his mother was in fact still alive, the personification of light.

"Wow," Valtora breathed.

"I know, right?"

Valtora stared at him.

"Wow," she repeated. She eyed Chaos, then him. "Damn, did I ever get lucky," she mused.

"Sure did," he agreed. "Um…why?"

"Your parents are like, fucking *powerful* and shit," she explained. "Your seed's gotta be potent as hell."

He blinked.

"I mean, what more could a girl ask for?" she asked. "Chaos's grandparents are practically gods."

"Well, not gods exactly," Chauncy countered. "They're Magi."

"Whatever."

"It explains everything," he realized. "Why both of my parents left. Why Grandma Little never told me what happened to Mom. Grandma couldn't have known Mom became a Magus, so she probably thought Mom was kidnapped or something."

"Or that she just up and left, abandoning you," Valtora offered. Chauncy gave her a look.

"My mother loved me," he countered.

"And I love Chaos," she replied. "But sometimes I want to leave him."

"Or throw him down the stairs?" Chauncy asked with a guilty smile.

"Hell yeah," she replied with a smile of her own, though considerably less guilty. And the fact that they were both smiling and saying such terrible, awful things proved that they were really not good people. Or at least, not very good parents. But in lieu of being very good, they'd have to settle for being good enough.

Chauncy's stomach growled then, for he hadn't eaten dinner.

"What's for dinner?" he asked.

"The usual," she answered. Which meant bread and soup. But while it was boring and plain, hunger had a way of transforming one's relationship to food, and had the power to turn boring and plain into a feast. So it was that Chauncy, Chaos, and Valtora exited the tent together to dine as a family. As Chauncy stepped outside, he found himself gazing up at the heavens, at the moon and countless stars. Chauncy gazed down then, at little Chaos's gremlin-face, a bit cuter than yesterday. Moonlight cast Chaos in a silver light, and Chauncy was struck with a sudden insight. That the light was touching Chaos – and him – just as space did…a fact he'd never thought of much. Which meant its illumination and warmth were not merely dumb rays cast by a ball of fire in the sky, but his mother's loving touch.

With a newfound joy in his heart, Chauncy joined the others by the crackling campfire, sitting down next to Valtora…and as it happened, Zella Trek. In the moment, he hardly minded, for he was too happy to care about the darkness in his past.

"Gimmee," Valtora ordered, reaching for Chaos. Chauncy gave him over…and then Valtora reached for his left hand with her free hand, holding it gently. He smiled at her…and then felt someone hold his right hand. He turned, seeing Zella there beside him. She flashed him a smile.

"Hey there," she greeted, giving his hand a squeeze. And to his horror, Tip stirred.

"Hey yourself," the demon greeted, standing up for the occasion.

"Uh…" Chauncy blurted out, pulling his hand away. He glanced at Tip, who'd pitched a tent, then Valtora, who clearly noticed, arching an eyebrow at him. He gave her an apologetic look. "I…can't help it," he stammered.

"It's okay," Valtora reassured, squeezing his hand as well. "Let her hold it."

"My…?" he asked, glancing at Tip's obvious ascent. But in lieu of Tip, Zella held his hand instead, squeezing it just like Valtora had. He swallowed in a suddenly dry throat, utterly abashed and confused.

"How was the walk Chauncy?" Nettie asked, clearly deciding to ignore this development. He hesitated, glancing at Zella, then clearing his throat nervously.

"Fine," he replied.

"Just fine?" Nettie pressed. "Any revelations?"

"Nope," he lied.

"Well shoot," Nettie replied. "At least you're not so depressed," she noted. It took Chauncy a moment to remember why'd he'd taken the walk in the first place: to take his mind off of his abysmal sparring performance. Which didn't bother him at all, now that he thought about it. For his parents were alive…and in relation to that, everything else seemed relatively minor.

Chauncy realized then that this was the way of life. Everything in relationship to everything else, which meant everything was relative. Hot was only hotter in relation to colder, relief relative to pain. Harder to softer, darker to lighter, taller to shorter, and so on. A single event could feel like a catastrophic, life-ending failure…or a minor inconvenience. The key was his relationship to what happened in the moment…and a moment later, that relationship could change.

As it had for his relationship with his father, who he'd assumed was a deadbeat dad. A lifetime of feeling that way had shifted without a moment's notice, to feeling anything but.

*Magic is my relationship with the world*, he recited. A lesson Nettie had taught him long ago. But until now, he hadn't realized that the world included *him*…and that his relationship with himself could be magical too.

With that thought, Chauncy's being opened, seeming to spread outward to everything he saw. His friends – and enemies – and the starry sky, and even the moon far above. Until he felt an uncanny feeling that he wasn't so different from all of them.

Nettie eyed him with a knowing look, a smile curling her lips.

"Got that feeling again, eh?" she asked. He smiled back.

"Sure do."

She spoke not a word more, knowing it was pointless to do so. For words could not hope to give justice to the experience of revelation; it was something felt more than thought. Chauncy found in that moment that he'd failed to become a wizard not because of his relationship with the world, where he thought magic came from. But because of his relationship with himself. Not only that he was so hard on himself…but that he saw himself as just regular ol'

Chauncy. The same kid who'd followed Grandma Little around day after day, doing whatever she told him to do instead of following his own heart.

*I'm a wizard*, he realized. And though it was hardly for the first time, it was a thought that – this time – was accompanied by a feeling. One of utter sureness, of absolute conviction.

He was a wizard...an honest-to-goodness *wizard*...just like he'd always dreamed he'd become.

It wasn't sometime later that he'd find his power and become a badass wizard like Imperius. It was right now. For the most part because he believed he could.

*That* was the secret, right there. The thing that he'd missed all this time. The only person stopping him from being him was him...and he didn't have to do it anymore.

So he let go of that tension, that fear – not just of failure, but of success – and embraced his *self*.

"Hoo boy," Harry breathed, eyeing Chauncy with a twinkle in his eyes. "You see it?" he asked Nettie, nudging her with an elbow.

"Yup," Nettie confirmed.

"I could take you right now," Zella declared, squeezing his hand tight. Chauncy blinked, turning to look at her. She'd leaned in to him, and to his surprise, she seemed to be snorting him like he'd snorted Chaos before.

"Ooo, then you can show me that thing you do!" Valtora exclaimed, clapping her hands excitedly.

"Um...no?" Chauncy interjected.

"Shhh," Valtora shushed. "Just go with it babe."

"I will not," he retorted. Valtora glared at him.

"But I wanna learn the *thing*," she insisted. "You'll be glad I did, right?"

"But...I can't..." he stammered, glancing at Zella. Both women looked down at Tip.

"Pretty sure you can," Zella replied.

"Definitely can," Valtora agreed.

Chauncy stood up then, hiding his growing...problem and backing away from them.

"Right," he declared. "Going to bed now. Goodnight."

"Coming," Valtora said. She stood suddenly, handing Chaos off to Nettie. "Come on Shackles," she added, turning to the golem holding Zella. "She's coming with us."

"Oh *boy*," Tip declared.

"Don't even *think* about it," Chauncy scolded the demon. Even as Valtora grabbed his arm – with her ultra-powerful diamond hand – and hauled him toward their tent.

"Too late," Tip replied.

"I've changed my mind," Zella stated.

"Huh?" Valtora asked, turning to face her.

"I'm the best he's ever had," Zella explained. "And I'm going to keep it that way."

Valtora's eyes narrowed.

"Bitch!" she swore. Zella shrugged.

"And?" she replied.

"You *will* show me," Valtora vowed, clenching her diamond hand into a fist.

"You'll just have to accept being second-best," Zella mused, shaking her head sadly. "Poor Chauncy. He'll always think back to our moments together, and secretly wish he felt that way with you."

"Bitch-ass bitch!" Valtora spat, stomping toward Zella. Clearly with the intent to murder her. Chauncy got between them.

"Now now poopy-dooz," he scolded gently.

"Get out of my way!" Valtora snapped, shoving him aside. Rather easily, to his dismay.

"But if you kill her, she'll never be able to teach you," he pointed out.

"Let her live!" Tip pleaded.

Valtora paused, then sighed.

"Fine," she muttered. She put her hands on her hips then, narrowing her eyes at Zella. And executed perhaps the most terrifying jawline-ripple he'd ever seen. Even Nettie and Harry's eyes widened, and Rocky looked away. And poor little Rooter covered his eyes with his hands. "You *will* teach me," Valtora vowed. "One day, before you die, your secret shall be mine!"

"Uh huh," Zella replied.

But Chauncy knew not to take Valtora's declaration so lightly. For she'd rhymed when she said it, making it carry the weight of a wizard's tongue. And when Valtora went all declarative – especially when using the word "shall" – what she said almost always came to pass.

"Right," Chauncy muttered. "Whelp, I'm going to bed."

And with that, he did.

# Chapter 36

King Pravus sat on his lofty perch atop a fire dragon steed, gazing down in wonder at what lay far, far below: the legendary Isle of Mundus, home to the Order of Mundus. He'd heard of it, and even seen a sketch or two. But any art he'd seen had been a poor imitation of what greeted his gaze now. It was beyond words to describe.

So he just sat there, staring down at the island, mesmerized.

It was a sight that was quite literally magical to behold. For it could not exist *without* magic. The Isle of Mundus existed not as a landmass rising from sea level, nor even as an island floating high in the air. Rather, it was *under* sea level. In that there was a hole in the ocean like a miles-wide cylinder, with massive waterfalls falling to a lower ocean a few hundred feet below. And *there* was where the fabled island stood. Or rather, floated. For it *was* levitating a good hundred or so feet above the water at the bottom of the cylinder.

A fact that made it practically unreachable, except by air. Except that there was a perfectly translucent dome that covered all but the island's sandy beaches, making it impenetrable as well as all-but-unreachable.

"Oh my," Pravus managed to exclaim.

"A spectacle beyond imagination!" Templeton declared with his customary exuberance.

"Indeed," Pravus agreed.

"Look at that castle!" Templeton urged, pointing at the middle of the sunken-but-floating island. Pravus did look, seeing a fine gray stone castle atop a tall white cliff that jutted straight up. Also utterly unreachable, unless by air or magic. Stately towers stood taller than any in Pravus's personal castle, much to his dismay. For he'd assumed his tower to be the most impressive of them all. Still, some of them were rather crooked, particularly one of the tallest ones, with a roof of the most eye-catching tone of blue. A fact that made him feel quite better about his, as his were ramrod straight. Save for the one that'd been felled by that black-hearted devil-serpent Fang, of course.

"How do you suppose we get in?" Templeton inquired. Pravus eyed the bit of beach extending beyond the glassy dome, realizing it was their only landing spot.

"First we land," he decided. "I'm a monarch riding a fire-breathing dragon," he added. "Someone's bound to notice."

"Quite so," Templeton agreed. "We make a fine sight I'd wager."

"A wager you'd win," Pravus prophesized.

The dragon flew them downward and forward toward the gigantic hole in the ocean, eventually diving into it. The roar of oceanic waterfalls was deafening, a fine spritz of saltwater assaulting them from behind.

"A refreshing spray!" Templeton shouted zestily, bringing a smile to Pravus's lips. For the man never failed to find something wondrous about his life, no matter the circumstance. A lesson to learn, that life was good or bad not merely on the basis of what happened, but how one happened to relate to it. Happiness was more a way of being than something to be gained, he supposed. To some it came quite naturally, while for others it was a struggle to maintain.

Ever forward and downward they went, until they neared the island's shore. The dragon landed upon it, a few yards before the translucent dome. Pravus leapt off, floating down gently to the sand by virtue of his magical king's attire, while Templeton unfurled a ladder and went down the old-fashioned way. At length they both found themselves standing before the dome, staring through it to the rest of the shore – and a lush tropical-looking forest beyond. They waited there for a bit, until Pravus began to fidget. For as king, he wasn't accustomed to being made to wait.

"Hmm," he murmured, tapping his chiseled chin.

"Perhaps if we knocked?" Templeton inquired.

"Or had the dragon roar," Pravus proposed.

"At the risk of seeming a bit overbearing," Templeton warned.

"And impatient," Pravus agreed. "I suppose knocking will have to do."

So he stepped forward and did just that, rapping his royal knuckles on the dome.

To Pravus's surprise, a *ding* rang out from the impact, vibrating across the surface of the dome and reverberating as it did so. Rather magically, he noted, and for some reason this gave him goosebumps.

It was a marvelous sound, one unlike any he'd heard before. It hinted that he was in a mystical place, one that would surprise him at every turn. In the way that some people supposedly felt about *his* kingdom.

"My *my*," Templeton murmured.

"You felt it too?"

"In my soul," Templeton concurred. He got a wistful look in his gorgeous blue eyes. "We stand at the very precipice of our childhood hopes and dreams," he declared.

Pravus nodded, saying nothing, because Templeton had said it all. Childhood was that sacred time in one's life where every last bit of the world was new, and enjoyed for what it was rather than what it could do for you.

"Right on time," a deep male voice declared. From behind them. Pravus whirled around, magically unsheathing his big golden blade…and found himself found face-to-face with an old man. He was tall and quite slender, and dreadfully old-looking. Skin all drooping from knobby bones, riddled with liver-spots and skin tags and other horrifying blemishes. The man's back was stooped, almost certainly due to neglect of his scapular muscles and his lower back, buttocks, and hamstrings. It was clear his muscles had atrophied to the point where they were only barely up to the task of keeping him upright. He had a long, thin white beard which contrasted rather nicely with his bright blue robe and pointed hat…and rather pretty blue eyes. The only feature the man possessed that Pravus preferred. Other than his impressive staff, of course.

The old man – clearly a wizard – eyed Pravus's oversized sword with a raised eyebrow.

"Sorry," Pravus stated, putting the sword magically away. "Heroic reflex."

"Ah," the man replied. "Hello Pravus," he greeted. Pravus arched an eyebrow, puffing out his pecs a bit.

"That's King Pravus," he corrected. "You know of me," he noted.

"I've met you," the man revealed.

"*Really.*"

"When you were a small boy," the man explained. "I visited your father. You took one look at me and gave such a look of disgust…much as you are now."

Pravus frowned, then realized he *was* grimacing at the man. He considered fixing his face, then decided against it. Honesty was the best policy, or so parents claimed…even as they desperately tried to beat the honesty out of their children by making them bearable to be around.

"As I recall, you ran away to your room and started doing push-ups," the old man stated.

"You *have* met me," Pravus declared. He furrowed his brow. "You're Imperius Fanning!"

"In the flesh," Imperius confirmed. Though it was flesh Pravus would never want to be in. Honestly, why the man didn't use a potion of youth or something was beyond him. He had to have access to such things, after all.

"We come with terrible news," Pravus began, preparing for a dramatic monarchal monologue.

"Zella Trek wrecked your castle and you want us to deal with her," Imperius interjected. Pravus paused, irritated at being interrupted.

"Correct," he grumbled. "You're an impatient one, aren't you," he snipped, feeling snippy. He hadn't eaten in some time on account of his flight, having forgotten to bring a pouch of beef jerky like he normally did. After all, muscles were ravenous things, and he had more to feed than most.

"My gut told me to interrupt you," Imperius replied. "And my gut is always right."

"Is it now," Pravus replied testily. "The villagers lying in mass graves after The Dark One's attacks might disagree. You know, if they weren't dead."

"Perhaps there would have been more dead had it not been for my gut," Imperius countered evenly.

"We'll never know," Pravus shot back. "How convenient."

"The few times I haven't followed my gut were disastrous," Imperius declared authoritatively. "The Great Purge, the War of Langsroth, the Vermillion Massacre, the…"

"Right," Pravus interjected. "Fine. So what is your gut telling you now?"

"It told me to be here at the moment you arrived," Imperius replied. "And it's telling me to continue this conversation as I am."

"I mean about Zella," Pravus pressed.

"My gut does not always say anything about a particular thing," Imperius explained. "It is not a crystal ball used to answer questions. It merely tells me what feels right in the moment, and in trusting that, disasters are averted."

"So…" Pravus prompted, arching an eyebrow.

"So we wait," Imperius replied. Pravus frowned.

"For what?"

Imperius merely smiled. And it was at that moment that Pravus spotted something over the decrepit wizard's underdeveloped shoulder. Something that made him blink rapidly, then rub his eyes, then blink again. For it was precisely the last thing he would have expected to see here and now. Or rather, precisely the last *who*. But it answered his question quite nicely, and he knew now just what to do.

# Chapter 37

The next morning, Chauncy woke up to find himself alone in his tent. He stood up, then did a yawn-and-stretch, still dressed in his wizard's robe. For he hadn't had the opportunity to undress the night before, as Chaos had been quite needy throughout. Thus, he'd been denied the opportunity to discharge the night's built-up energies, much to Tip's dismay.

He sighed, rubbing his eyes wearily, then exiting the tent. It was quite bright, the sun already above the horizon. He expected to see Harry and Nettie already outside, but apparently they weren't. Neither was Gavin, he discovered; only Rocky sitting by the carriage with Rooter on his shoulder, and Peter grazing nearby. And Valtora of course, who was busy stroking Peter lovingly with her diamond hand. His mane, to Chauncy's relief.

"Well," he stated to himself, putting his hands on his hips. "You had quite a night." And that was an understatement. For now he knew his parents were alive, and what's more, that they were always there with him. Which made him feel suddenly uneasy, for it occurred to him that this meant they were *always* there. Even when he didn't want them to be. He grimaced, shoving this unfortunate thought out of his mind and focusing on the salient point.

He was the son of a great wizard, and his father loved him. The guy wasn't a bad father at all; he'd just Spaced out at Imperius's request. Which meant that Chauncy might not end up being a bad father either. He wasn't destined to up and run when things got hard. There was no terrible darkness in his soul that would doom him to fail.

He was Chauncy Little, wizard of Borrin, son of Space and Light. He was the father of one Chaos Little…and by golly, everything was going to be alright.

At that moment, he felt fantastically calm, as if every last bit of anxiety had been drained from him. It was also the moment when he heard Chaos crying…not from his tent, but from Nettie's.

He strolled up to their tent, rapping his knuckles on the front door flap. It opened up, revealing a tired-looking Nettie carrying a crying Chaos.

"Take him," she told Chauncy, and Chauncy was all-too-happy to oblige. For that wonderful calm was still with him. He held Chaos cradled in his right arm, and stroked the boy's head with his left. Chaos gazed back up at him with those cute, unblinking eyes, just like he always did.

It was at that moment that Chauncy was struck with the sudden, inexplicable feeling that Chaos *was* him…or rather, that he was both of them. That Chaos was himself looking at himself. He smiled, feeling an affection so powerful it brought him nearly to tears.

"I see you in myself," he declared. "And I see myself in you."

And at that moment, something strange happened.

The world *shifted*, and suddenly he found himself lying on his back, looking up at a giant's face. Or rather, his *own* face, but far bigger than it had any right to be. He frowned, watching as that face scrunched up in confusion.

And then whatever Chauncy was lying on dropped out from underneath him, and he fell. He was so surprised that he didn't have time to cry out.

*Whump!*

Pain shot through the back of his head, and then he *did* cry out. With a sound that was quite odd, for it sounded precisely like a baby shrieking. Chauncy stopped abruptly, blinking in confusion…and watched as the giant *him* standing over him cried out in a slightly more manly voice, toppling over and landing on top of him. So that Chauncy's body was trapped underneath the giant's shins.

"Help!" Chauncy cried out. But it only came out as another baby-shriek. He flailed his arms, trying to push the giant shins off of him. But his hands were all wrong. His arms were too short and fat and his fingers too stubby. And what's more, they wouldn't seem to work right.

It was then that Chauncy realized that they weren't his arms at all. Or at least they hadn't been up until now. They were *Chaos's* arms…because he was in Chaos's body.

Which meant that Chaos was inside of *his*.

"Waaah!" Chauncy called out, which should've come out as Valtora. "Waaa, waaah!"

Omygodmy*baby!*" he heard Valtora cry from somewhere ahead. He gasped, managing to grab his original body's shin with one hand.

His left hand, in fact. The same hand he'd stroked Chaos's head with before they'd switched bodies. That feeling of being *one* came to him again…and suddenly he was lying face-down on the ground, his nose aching and bloodied.

"Ow!" he blurted out. He scrambled to his feet just as Valtora reached them, blood pouring down the front of his robe.

"What happened?!" Valtora cried, rushing to pick up Chaos. And then cradling Chaos to her bosom and giving Chauncy the dirtiest look he'd ever seen, as if *he'd* been the one to drop the baby. "Rocky, get Rooter!" she called out.

"I can explain," Chauncy began.

"Poor wittle *baby*," Valtora interrupted, bouncing the baby up and down a bit. "Did the big widdle man *hurt* you?"

"I didn't," Chauncy protested, pinching his hemorrhaging nostrils shut. To his irritation, she didn't seem at all concerned about *his* injury, which was worse than Chaos's. And he would know, having experienced both of them.

It was at that moment that Rocky arrived, lowering Rooter to the ground. In moments, both Chaos and Chauncy's wounds were healed, to Valtora's relief. Only then did she seem at all receptive to what he had to say…as was everyone else. For everyone had gathered 'round to see what all the fuss was about. So Chauncy told his side of the tale, informing everyone of his newfound ability.

"You can switch *bodies?*" Valtora asked, her eyebrows shooting up.

"I can," Chauncy confirmed. "At least I *did*," he added. "With Chaos. But I couldn't move very well, and every time I tried to talk, it came out like a baby crying."

"Nothing new there," Nettie quipped.

"Shut up Nettie," Harry scolded. She blinked, then glared at him.

"Stealing my lines, eh?" she accused.

"Only fair," he replied. "You stole my heart."

Her expression softened, and she leaned in for a kiss. Which Harry, being Harry, was only too happy to give.

"Sweet-talker," she told him.

"It's why you married me," he replied.

"That and a whole lot more," she agreed with a mischievous grin.

"So anyway," Chauncy interrupted. "New magic power."

"The power to be a baby?" Nettie asked.

"My *hand* is magic," he corrected. She smirked.

"Bet it is," she replied. Harry chuckled.

Valtora opened her mouth to say something, then apparently thought better of it. Which for her was a highly unusual thing to do. But she stared at Chauncy with an intensity that was sudden and rather disturbing.

"Well, I suppose it makes sense," Nettie stated. "Chauncy's power has always been putting things in other things. Putting himself in someone else – and someone else in him – fits right in."

"Now there's a visual," Harry quipped.

"Shut up Harry!"

"Something everyone can get behind," Harry added, ignoring her command. She elbowed him, then yelped, glaring at him.

"I outta beat *your* behind," she grumbled. "Anyway, enough lollygagging," she added. "We gotta get going if we wanna reach the Sea of Magi by tonight." She glanced at Harry. "Think we can make it?"

"Sure," he answered. "Just in time to set camp by the shore."

"Ooo," Valtora exclaimed. "Sounds *nice*."

"Romantic," Harry agreed.

"Let's pack up and get rollin'," Nettie prompted.

So with that, they did.

\* \* \*

As it turned out, Harry and Nettie were exactly right, for they reached the shore of the Sea of Magi precisely at night. The sun had just fallen below the horizon, the first of the stars opening their sleepy eyes to gaze down at Chauncy and his friends from the black shroud of the sky. Valtora was the first to see the sea, bolting forward when Peter sniffed the air and snorted twice, their not-so-secret signal that they were close. Peter galloped her ahead of all the others, his rainbow mane and tail rippling majestically in the breeze. Chauncy smiled; one of the greatest joys in his life was watching *her* enjoy herself. And seeing as she did so almost constantly, his life was joyous indeed with her in it.

At length Rocky and the carriage caught up with her, with Shackles trailing behind, Zella in his faithful grasp. They reached the sandy shore where Valtora had stopped, exiting their various modes of transportation and walking to the edge of the water. Chauncy stopped beside Valtora, who'd hopped off Peter and was gazing at the sea, her hands covering her mouth. Waves lapped at the sand, hissing and foaming before retreating back into the ocean. It was a sight Chauncy had never seen, having spent his life in a non-coastal city.

"Wow," he breathed, taking it all in.

"Right?" Valtora agreed, snaking her hand into his. He smiled at her, then returned his gaze to the sea, marveling at it.

"I don't see a boat," Zella noted, crossing her arms under her chest. Still in Shackle's arms, of course.

"I suspect Nettie will use her connection with water to get us across," Gavin ventured. Nettie nodded.

"Darn tootin'," she agreed. "Nice to have a smart one in the bunch, eh?"

"Nah," Harry replied, adjusting his glasses. "Now I got competition."

"Ha!" Nettie said. "He's handsomer too."

"And richer," Valtora added, always up for a bit of controversy.

"And he's a bad boy," Harry noted, taking sides against himself.

"But nobody rocks like *you* do," Valtora countered, switching sides abruptly. For she preferred the underdog, whoever it might be.

"Well that's true," Harry agreed.

"Except Rocky," she added, knocking him down a peg.

"All right, all right," Nettie grumbled. "Nettie needs her beauty sleep."

"That's for sure," Valtora quipped. Nettie shot her a glare, then pointedly ignored her, to Valtora's chagrin. "Aww."

"Let's set camp," Nettie stated. "Then we'll be off in the morning."

They did so with practiced ease, pitching their tents. Gavin decided to sleep outside, and Zella slept in a rocky dome made on the spot by Harry. Nettie and Harry went to their own tent, leaving Chauncy and Valtora to theirs.

"Finally," Valtora said, closing their tent flap and setting Chaos down. She fixed Chauncy with an intense stare, crossing her arms over her chest. He blinked.

"What?" he asked rather defensively.

"Get inside me," she ordered.

"Um...?"

"Do the thing you did with Chaos," she clarified, stepping up to him. "Go in me."

"Like...switch bodies?" he asked.

"Right."

"I don't know if I can," he warned.

240

"Try."

He eyed her suspiciously.

"Why?" he pressed.

"Because I wanna *try* it," she answered, stomping her foot. And transitioning to putting her hands on her hips.

"Okay, okay," he replied. He put his left hand on her shoulder then. "Ready?"

"*Hell* yeah."

He focused then, imagining switching places with her. Which didn't work at all. So instead he recalled that feeling he'd had…that she was really him, and he was really her.

He felt a *shift*…and with that, they were.

Chauncy blinked…and then realized he was looking at himself. Or rather, that he was Valtora looking at Chauncy. It was precisely like looking in a mirror, except that it wasn't a mirror-image of himself.

"Ooo," Valtora said, in his voice. Which was weird.

"Hi," he replied. In Valtora's voice, which was even weirder. He glanced down at himself, seeing Valtora's body. And then went from a glance to a stare…and then a full-on ogle. He glanced up at Valtora.

"Have *fun*," she told him. And promptly followed her own advice, beginning a rather targeted exploration of her new body.

"What's this?" Tip inquired, waking up.

Chauncy hesitated.

"I can?" he asked.

"Yes," she answered. "Ooo, she added. "That feels *weird.*"

"And now I'm up," Tip declared.

Chauncy paused, then began his own exploration. But he felt more than a little self-conscious doing so with his body's owner right there. Not that Valtora had any such reservations, but still, he liked to think of himself as a gentleman.

"Let's *do* it," Valtora urged.

"Um…uh…" Chauncy stammered, glancing at Tip. Who Valtora had freed from her sparkling purple robe. Tip was staring at him with those little demon eyes…with a look that Chauncy didn't particularly like. "Let's not," he decided.

"Come *on*," she pressed, grabbing him by the shoulders. Rather roughly, which was rude.

"No means no," he told her.

"Uh huh," she replied, pressing up against him. So that he could *feel* it. Meaning Tip. He grimaced, trying to push her away.

"You're a guy now," he reminded her. "You can get away with forcing me when you're a girl, but when you're a guy, it's bad."

"Bad?" she asked.

"Really *really* bad," he confirmed. With a grave tone. She pouted, pulling away a bit, to his relief.

"Aww," she complained, stomping her foot. Which was quite a bit less cute than when she did it with her own body. Still, she gave him a determined look. "We *will* try it one day," she vowed.

"Uh huh," he replied noncommittally.

"Hmph," she hmphed, looking down. For he'd left her quite the opposite of hanging. "Well what am I gonna do with this?" she demanded, gesturing at her rather threatening-looking appendage.

"Anything but that," he answered.

"Fine," she grumbled. And, having discovered treasure in her explorations, focused on enjoying it.

"Um…this is awkward," Chauncy confessed. For it felt like he was watching himself…do things. "Can I have a little privacy?"

"Sure," she replied at once. "Bye," she added, giving another little wave. Then she left the tent. Chauncy frowned, surprised at the rapidity with which this occurred.

"Huh," he mumbled, looking down at himself once more. Or rather, herself. And, with the privacy he needed, he found himself far more willing to continue his explorations. So, as anyone would in this particular situation, he did.

# Chapter 38

Chauncy opened his eyes, finding himself spooning Valtora in the dark.

He smiled, cuddling up against her playfully, enjoying her warmth and softness. While reaching around and being playful in quite another way.

"Hey baby," he purred, being all sexy-like.

"Mmm," she murmured, snuggling against him. He snuggled back.

"Chauncy's feeling *frisky*," he announced. Which was an understatement. For, after becoming accustomed to discharging his frisky feelings at least once a day, the last few days had built up quite a reserve of naughty thoughts. As such, he made it unmistakably clear just how frisky he was feeling…and what he intended to do about it. By doing it.

"Oh," Tip murmured before being muffled.

"Oh," she replied, accepting his…communication. Which went from the physical version of a word to a sentence, and then to a lengthy paragraph. It wasn't long before he neared the end of their particular conversation…one they both punctuated with enthusiastic exclamation marks.

Then, quite spent, he sighed, feeling marvelously content.

"That was *amazing*," he murmured. And it had been, although why he couldn't say. It just felt wonderful and right, and mind-blowing to boot. "Top three," he added. "Easily."

Still spooning, he caressed her in a place he was fond of, feeling lovey-dovey. But something was off, he soon discovered, for the particular perky parts he'd chosen to play with felt rather strange. In that they were altogether different than what he was accustomed to.

He blinked, eyeing Valtora's long black hair. Which was odd, because Valtora's hair was golden brown. It was quite dark in their tent, but not *that* dark. Yes, her hair was most definitely black…and her skin much paler than his love's. And, incidentally, now that he paid attention to it, covered almost completely in various tattoos.

"Oh!" he blurted out, unhanding what he'd been handling. The woman stirred, rolling to face him. With absolutely gorgeous purple eyes.

Chauncy's eyes widened.

"Uh!" he stammered, freezing in place. For it was none other than Zella Trek. She smiled at him.

"That was *nice*," she murmured.

"I came to the same conclusion," Tip concurred.

"I uh," he mumbled, scrambling to his feet. "Uh," he added. And promptly fled. Or at least he tried to; for he found himself not in his tent, but in Zella's earthen dome, the one Harry had made for her to sleep in. And as such, there was no door to go through to get out. Only a hole in the ceiling to let air in.

"What's wrong lover?" Zella inquired. He glanced down at her, realizing she was quite nude…and spectacularly so. He blushed, then eventually tore his gaze away. Then glanced back to look again, then blushed again, then cleared his throat.

"How did I uh, get in?" he asked. She smirked.

"Your staff, naturally."

He blinked, then looked down. Then blushed.

"I mean…"

"Your staff," she repeated, pointing to the floor. Where his Staff of Wind was lying.

"Ah," he mumbled, retrieving it. "Um…" he added, eyeing her, then blushing again. "Gotta go."

"Come again," she told him with a little smirk. "In fact, come as many times as you like."

Chauncy swallowed, then cleared his throat. Then he thrust his staff – his Staff of Wind this time – and flew upward out of the hole in the ceiling. He landed beside the dome, finding it still early morning. The sun hadn't yet risen over the horizon, but the sky was beginning to brighten.

Unfortunately, it hadn't been bright enough for him to realize what he'd being doing a few moments ago. Or rather, who.

*Fuck!*

He kicked himself mentally. And then slapped himself repeatedly in the forehead with the palm of his hand.

*Idiot idiot idiot!*

Chauncy stood there, cursing himself…and then turned to see his tent ahead. Terror gripped him, followed by a sickly, queasy feeling. The full weight of what he'd done came crashing down on him. The consequences of his unthinkable mistake. Having been assaulted by Zella was one thing, but this time he'd voluntarily made love to her. With particular delight, he recalled with dismay. Delight that he'd communicated with her, which was even more dismaying. For, once again, he'd told her quite honestly that what they'd done had been the best.

"Shit!" he swore. "Shit shit shittity shit *shit!*"

Then he took a deep breath in, letting it out. He set his jaw firmly, realizing that what was done was done. He'd screwed up, and now he'd have to face the consequences.

It was over. He'd violated the sanctity of his sacred relationship with Valtora. It didn't matter that it'd been a simple mistake of mistaken identity.

"So be it," he declared, squaring his shoulders and facing Valtora's tent. He strode forward then, facing his fate as bravely as he could. Better to get it over with now than to…

Valtora emerged from the tent, freezing in place when she spotted him. Her eyes widened…and then her expression went utterly flat.

*She knows!*

"Valtora," he began.

"Chauncy," she replied. "Um…where were you?"

He grimaced.

"Somewhere I shouldn't have been," he confessed. Which was true in more ways than one. She paused, then put her hand on her hip, fixing him with narrowed eyes.

"Oh yeah?"

"Yes," he replied. "I…"

"Spent the night with Zella," she accused. He felt another burst of fear, and sighed, nodding.

"I did," he confirmed. "But…"

"I heard," she told him. "Everything."

He gulped.

"Everything?" he asked. Her jawline rippled, sending fresh horror through him. His eyes immediately went to her diamond hand, which had clenched into a fist.

"Everything," she answered. Her lower lip quivered. "I hope it was *worth* it Chauncy," she added. "We had a family!"

Then she whirled about, retreating into her tent and shutting the flap.

Chauncy watched her go, feeling a truly awful sinking feeling inside. A feeling he'd only had once before, way back in his shop in Southwick. After Grandma Little had died, and life had ceased to have any meaning for him. He'd nearly hanged himself then, from the rafters of the shop. Only the fortuitous fact that Harry had happened to stop in had saved him.

"Howdy," a warbly voice greeted from behind.

Chauncy jumped, then whirled around, seeing none other than Harry standing there. The old man pushed his silver glasses up his nose, flashing him a grin.

"Oh," Chauncy blurted out.

"Looks like I interrupted something," Harry stated.

"Not really," Chauncy replied. "What's happened has already happened."

"What's that?"

"I'd...rather not say," Chauncy answered. The last thing he wanted to do was have Harry – a man he admired more than any other – know how royally he'd screwed up.

"Don't need to," Harry replied. "Ground already told me," he explained, tapping a bare foot on the sand. Chauncy blinked.

"Uh...?"

"That dome had a bit of me in it," Harry said, pointing to Zella's earthen hut. "I can sense what's going on inside."

Chauncy blanched.

"Oh," he mumbled. Harry grinned.

"Oh ho," he agreed.

Chauncy's shoulders slumped.

"I didn't mean to," he said in his defense. Harry chuckled.

"Ground told me that too," he replied. "Told me a whole lot of other stuff too."

"Like what?"

Harry's eyes twinkled, and he gave Chauncy a conspiratorial look.

"Bet you were real surprised when you woke up in Zella's hut," he said. Chauncy blinked. He hadn't even considered the mystery of how he'd done so, given how distracted he'd been by what had occurred inside of it.

"Now that I think about it," Chauncy replied. He frowned. "How *did* I get in there?"

"You did and you didn't," Harry answered.

"What?"

"What's the last thing you remember?" Harry asked.

Chauncy thought about it. Then he blushed. For he recalled having switched bodies with Valtora, and then doing what anyone would've done in that situation. Many times, in fact. Because unlike with his own body, he could. And then…

And then realization struck.

"Wait a minute," he blurted out. He whirled around to face Valtora's tent. "Valtora!" he barked.

There was a pause, and then her head poked out of the tent.

"Huh?" she asked, using her patented flatly innocent facial expression. The one she always used when she'd done something bad…or when she suspected she was about to be accused of such.

"What did you do!" he snapped.

"Huh?"

"I *know* you went with Zella last night," he accused. "You used my body with her?!"

"Well if you know that, why'd you ask me?" she retorted, glaring at him.

"Don't put this back on me," he countered. "You had *sex* with Valtora?"

"No, you did," Valtora retorted.

"My body did," he corrected.

"It sure did this morning," she pointed out. "Just a few minutes ago."

Chauncy grimaced…and, sensing weakness, Valtora pounced. Or rather, she stepped out of the tent, standing there with her hands crossed over her chest.

"How was it, *Chauncy?*" she sneered.

"I thought she was you!" he argued.

"Uh huh."

"It was dark," he added in his defense.

"Right."

"You started it," he insisted. She gave him a look.

"And you finished," she pointed out. "I heard it."

"Me too," Harry admitted.

"Everyone heard it," another voice declared. Chauncy turned to see Nettie hobbling up to them. "Gonna need to build thicker walls next time," she added, glaring at Harry.

"Well then I wouldn't be able to hear it," he pointed out.

Chauncy buried his face in his hands.

"Great," he grumbled. "Just great. Now everyone knows."

"Well you wouldn't have sex with me when we switched bodies," Valtora said in her defense. "And you said I could do anything but that."

Chauncy paused. And then realized it was true. He *had* said that. Which, knowing Valtora, had been an exceedingly dangerous thing to say.

"So I did Zella," Valtora concluded triumphantly. "And it was *great.*"

"It was," Harry agreed. Nettie gave him a look.

"How would *you* know?" she demanded.

"Sand told me," he replied.

"And the best part of all?" Valtora asked no one in particular. "She totally showed me that thing she did to you."

Chauncy blinked.

"She did?" he asked.

"Oh *hell* yeah," Valtora confirmed proudly. "She didn't even realize it was really me," she added with a cackle. "Totally gave it up just like I said she would."

"Um...wow," Chauncy replied.

"So anyway, now we're even," Valtora declared unilaterally. "Two wrongs make a right."

"Pretty sure that's not the case," Chauncy told her. She glared at him...and executed a perfect jawline-ripple. "But I agree," he added hastily. "Let's all just put this behind us." She relaxed, breaking out into a big smile. And lunged forward, leaping at him and nearly knocking him over with an enthusiastic embrace.

"I hate it when we fight!" she exclaimed. Which wasn't even close to true. For she loved fighting, as long as no one took it too personally.

"It's okay poopy-dooz," he replied. She pulled away, giving him a guilty look.

"I didn't think you'd wake up in your body," she admitted. "I was gonna go back to you before you woke up."

"We must've switched back while we were sleeping," Chauncy theorized.

"Wonderful," Nettie interjected. "Can we get going now?"

"After breakfast," Harry piped in.

"Good idea hon," Nettie told him. "I'll go fishin'."

"I'll build the fire," Harry replied. And with that, the elderly couple got to work. Chauncy watched them for a bit, then turned back to Valtora, giving her a little smile.

"Well that was interesting," he said.

"Sure was," she agreed. "*Totally* doing it again."

"Excuse me?"

"We're gonna switch bodies again," she informed him. "There's still so much I wanna try."

"With Zella?"

"Well duh," she replied. "Unless you're volunteering my body for it."

"Um…no. And no," he added. "I don't think it's a good idea."

"Why not?"

"You can't just have…relations with other people!" he exclaimed irritably. For it should have been obvious.

"Why not?"

"We're engaged!" he exclaimed. "We're going to get married! We have a kid!"

"So?" she pressed. "We should still get to do what we want."

He just stared at her, not able to comprehend how she couldn't get it. It was *obvious*.

"So we wanna live together," she stated. "And we're going to raise a few kids. Does that mean we have to just do everything the way everyone else does?" she asked, making a face as if she'd bitten into a fresh pile of dung.

"Well…no," he admitted.

"Right," she agreed. "We should do things the way *we* do them. And fuck all those other idiots," she added rather rudely. "There's a reason why they're not wizards. They're too focused on obeying the rules instead of getting what they really want. We're wizards Chauncy," she added. "We do things different. And that means we do different things."

Chauncy frowned. It made perfect sense. He'd spent most of his life living the life other people expected him to live, not imagining that there was anyway else to be.

"Maybe you're right," he realized. She beamed at him.

"Well duh," she replied, leaning in and giving him a kiss. The kind of kiss that woke up Tip, in fact. And wake up he did.

"Again?" the demon-head moaned. "I need rest!"

Chauncy frowned.

"How many times…" he began.

"So *anyway*," Valtora interrupted. "We should *really* be going now."

"For once I agree with her," Nettie piped in. "Enough with the drama. Let's move out."

With that, they got to work taking down their tents, and Harry took down Zella's prison-hut. She was, to Chauncy's relief, fully dressed. Or rather, dressed as scandalously as usual. He tried his very best not to stare, with little success.

"You're insatiable," Tip groaned, struggling to get up.

"Shut up!" Chauncy hissed.

With the camp taken down, Nettie walked right into the water...and the water beneath her froze. It formed a wide floating raft of ice for her to stand on. One that sank a bit when stepped on, so her feet got wet, but still quite able to support her weight. She closed her eyes, concentrating for a bit...and the ice expanded, forming a larger raft. One that soon grew so large it was practically a miniature iceberg.

"All aboard," she called out.

Everyone stepped on the ice – even Rocky and Peter – and to Chauncy's surprise, it held their weight. His surprise must've been obvious, for Nettie smirked.

"The ice goes all the way down to the sea floor," she explained. "When I set it afloat, it'll sink a bit. But as soon as we get further out, I'll make the ice a whole lot thicker, and it'll float better."

The ice-raft broke away from the shore, floating out to sea. And sure enough, it sank quite a bit, until they were immersed up to their knees in chilly water. Then – just as Nettie had claimed – the ice slowly rose as she made it extend much deeper, until they were once again above sea level.

"That's pretty creative," Zella conceded, inclining her head at Nettie.

"Gee thanks, hussy," Nettie replied.

"Hussy?" Zella inquired with an arch of her eyebrow.

"Hussy. Noun. A mischievous, impudent, or ill-behaved girl," Valtora recited.

"Ah," Zella replied. She frowned. "I suppose I *am* a hussy."

"Me too!" Valtora agreed happily. "A homicidal hussy."

"Well so am I," Zella replied. Valtora's smile broadened, and then she gasped, putting her hands to her mouth.

"We could be *besties!*" she exclaimed.

Zella gave her a doubting look.

"Well, seeing as how I'm floating on an iceberg toward my impending doom, it won't be a very long friendship," she pointed out. Valtora's face fell.

"Awww," she complained. She turned to Chauncy then, putting her hands on her hips. Which, as Chauncy was well aware, was a prelude to her dreaded – and patented – jawline-ripple.

"Chauncy!" she began.

"Yes darling?" he replied as charmingly as he could. Which wasn't much.

"Why are we killing my new bestie?" she demanded, her eyes narrowing. Chauncy eyed her jawline, just waiting for the inevitable.

"We're not," he protested. "We're just taking her back to the Order of Mundus."

"So they can kill her!"

"She tried to hurt me," he argued. Zella smirked.

"Pretty sure I did anything but," she replied. He grimaced. For it was technically true. She'd been remarkably hospitable to him, in a hostile sort of way. And most recently, in a rather kind and receptive sort of way.

"So she kidnapped you," Valtora stated. "So what? She thought she wanted you dead, but she liked you instead. Is that a crime, Chauncy?"

"Um…" he stammered, glancing at Nettie and Harry. Who were ignoring them. "No?"

"That's right," Valtora declared.

"But Imperius said she was going to destroy the world," Chauncy reminded her.

"No, he said she was going to destroy *your* world," Valtora corrected.

"Which is bad," Chauncy pointed out.

"Maybe," Nettie interjected. Chauncy blinked, then frowned, facing her.

"What do you mean?" he asked.

"Well, do you remember what I said about evil ending the world?" she asked him. "Back during our first adventure?"

"Um…no," Chauncy admitted.

"It's never really about the end of the world," Nettie recited. "No one wants it to end, or they wouldn't have any world for themselves."

"Pretty sure I was the one who said that," Harry pointed out.

"Shut up Harry!" Nettie snapped. "Anywho, Zella's just like every other black-hearted homicidal hussy," she continued. "She wants to end the way you like it so she can have it the way *she* likes it."

"Well that doesn't sound so bad," Chauncy stated. "I mean, depending on how she likes it," he added, glancing at Zella. "How um...*do* you like it?"

"You mean what do I want?" she inquired.

"Right."

"Well, before I met you, I wanted to kill you to get revenge on your father," she confessed. "I thought you shouldn't exist, because your father cheated on me to make you. So I was going to correct that mistake, knowing he would be able to see it happen. And I was willing to do anything to make it happen."

"Ah," Chauncy mumbled.

"Not helping your case," Nettie grumbled.

"But now I don't want to kill you," Zella continued. "Far more fun to have fun with you."

"But what about your revenge?" Harry asked. Zella smirked.

"Making sweet love to my husband's son over and over again – knowing he knows it's happening – is as good a revenge as killing him," she argued.

"It's even better," Valtora agreed quite happily. "Old-school evil. You just don't see it that much anymore," she lamented with a sigh.

Nettie stared at both of them incredulously.

"You're both cracked," she declared. "I can't tell who the villain is."

"Wanna be evil girlfriends and shit?" Valtora asked Zella.

"Surprisingly yes," Zella replied.

"Yay!" Valtora exclaimed, hopping up and down, then giving Zella a hug. "Ooo, we're gonna have *fun*."

"What do you have in mind?" Zella inquired.

"Hold your damn horses a minute," Nettie interjected, putting her hands on her hips and glaring at them both. "What the hell are we doing here?"

"Hmm?" Valtora asked.

"We're on a damn iceberg in the middle of the damn ocean..."

"Not really in the middle," Harry noted, gesturing at the still-visible shore.

"Shut up Harry!" Nettie snapped. "Anyway, we're on our way to the Isle of Mundus *right now*. And now you're saying we should just go back and let Zella go?"

"Yep," Valtora confirmed.

Nettie stared at her, then threw up her arms.

"So that's it," she stated. "All this for nothing."

"Not nothing," Valtora argued. "I have a *bestie* now."

"A bestie of darkness," Zella agreed.

"Oh yeah?" Nettie said. "What're you gonna do if we let you go?"

"Honestly, I have no idea," Zella admitted. "Get a tattoo, probably."

"Ooo," Harry said. "Where?"

"Gasp!" Valtora gasped. "Could you do me after?"

"You'll have to be more specific," Zella replied with a smirk.

"Tat me *up*," Valtora clarified.

"I've never tattooed anyone else before," Zella stated. "Except your father," she added, eyeing Chauncy. "A little wedding ring tattoo on his ring finger. The wuss wouldn't agree to anything bigger."

"Men are *such* pussies," Valtora stated, shaking her head at the entire gender.

"That's not right," Chauncy complained. "You can't just say that about *all* men."

"Don't get your thong in a bunch," Valtora replied. "It's just girl talk."

"Which is mostly about hating men," Zella added.

"Oh, and other women too," Valtora agreed. "Except our besties of course. That's how you *know* they're your besties," she added sagely. "You don't hate on them even when other people do."

"So back to the point," Nettie interrupted. "Are we going to the Isle of Mundus or not?"

"Ooo, I wanna see it!" Valtora exclaimed.

"Slightly less enthused," Zella piped in. "But willing."

"Actually, I kind of do want to see it," Chauncy admitted. Rocky grunted his agreement, and even Peter nodded his head, causing his rainbow mane to glitter gorgeously.

"Then that's the vote," Nettie declared. "We're going."

"Is Zella going to be alright?" Chauncy asked. "I mean, will the Order hurt her if she comes with us?"

"Nah," Valtora answered. "She hasn't done anything wrong. If they make a fuss, we'll say she's with us."

"Nice rhyme honey," Chauncy told her. Her eyes lit up.

"I *did* rhyme that time!" she said. Then she gasped, for she'd done it again. The sign of a true wizard, to play with words. For they were those wise enough to have a playful relationship with the world, instead of taking it all so seriously.

It occurred to Chauncy then that letting Zella live *was* the right thing to do. Or rather, it was the playful thing to do. For life would be far more interesting with her in it than locked away in some prison cell. It would be more complicated, sure, and he still didn't know what to think about what'd happened last night...and this morning. But wanting to kill someone – and then changing one's mind – was hardly an act worthy of being labeled a crime. If it were, he'd be guilty of it himself, what with the thoughts he'd thought on his first night with Chaos.

"Well I guess that's that," Nettie declared.

So they continued on their journey across the Sea of Magi to the Isle of Mundus, their course never having changed. But while their destination was still the fabled island, their goal was not the same.

# Chapter 39

Noon transitioned gradually to afternoon, Nettie's iceberg-raft zooming across the Sea of Magi with rather astonishing speed. It left a violent wake in its…well, wake, the wind shrieking and tearing at their hair and clothes as they went. A fact that resulted in Chauncy's Staff of Wind absorbing quite a lot of it, making it practically *hum* in his hand. More so, in fact, than it'd ever had. It made him feel like quite the wizard, carrying it atop the speeding iceberg. Quite the wizard was precisely what he was, particularly with his newfound power.

And even more importantly, he felt like quite the father, what with Chaos cradled in his left arm. A wizardly father and a fatherly wizard, like *his* father before him.

Yes, Chauncy Little was following his destiny, he could feel it in his bones. A feeling that what he was doing – right here, right now – was precisely what he wanted to be doing. Not what he should do, not an obligation or an answering of a call of duty, but what he *really* wanted to do. Riding an iceberg across the ocean with his friends and family, journeying to an ancient land of powerful magic. It felt precisely as awesome and mystical as his childhood dreams of the kingdom of Pravus had been, in that a great mystery awaited him.

"Gettin' close," Nettie announced. Chauncy frowned, peering ahead.

"I don't see anything," he replied.

"Me neither," she said. "I can feel the water, remember?"

"Oh. Right."

A few minutes later, Chauncy *did* see what Nettie was talking about. For, directly ahead, the ocean just…stopped. In a drop-off. And far, far ahead, easily miles in the distance, he spotted a massive waterfall. Which meant there must be *two* waterfalls…and they were approaching the first rather rapidly.

"Um…" he began, pointing at it.

"That's the edge," Nettie explained.

"The edge?"

"The Edge," she corrected. "With a capital 'E.'"

"Oh."

"That's where the most powerful magic is found," she stated. "Just beyond the Edge."

"Of the ocean?" Chauncy asked.

"Of normal," she replied. "Of the expected. The Edge is where most people are too afraid to venture near, much less go over. It's a sheer drop to whatever terror lies beyond," she added. "And most people stay comfortably – and miserably – clear of it."

"So it's a metaphor," Gavin stated.

"A magical metaphor," Nettie agreed. "To reach the Isle of Mundus, you gotta face your fear. You have to face the edge of what you're willing to do…and go beyond it to find the answers to the mysteries of life."

"So it's a sheer drop," Chauncy stated, having trouble getting beyond this fact. "How far, exactly?"

"Far enough to make your butt pucker," she answered with a grin.

"And to make it throw up in your pants," Harry added with a shit-eating grin.

"You said it hon," Nettie agreed.

"So we're going toward it?" Chauncy pressed.

"Yep," Harry confirmed.

"But we might die," he pointed out.

"Might," Harry agreed.

"That'd be bad," Chauncy pointed out.

"Only for a moment."

"But…" Chauncy began.

"Get ready," Nettie interrupted. "Here we go!"

And then, with what felt like far too little warning, they went over the Edge.

Freefall gripped them as the iceberg tipped over the edge of the massive waterfall, revealing what lay beyond: a sheer drop hundreds of feet to a watery bottom far below.

Chauncy screamed, then did the only thing he could think of doing. Which was to thrust the butt of his Staff of Wind down, and fly upward and forward through the air.

He left the others quickly behind as the iceberg continued to fall, plunging downward with terrible speed. He flew toward something else far below…an island, in fact. One inexplicably floating above the watery surface at the bottom of the inexplicable hole in the sea.

An island with a dome covering it almost entirely, save for a bit of sandy shore at the very edges. He spotted a most inexplicable sight at that shore: a massive red dragon, and next to it, three men.

He felt himself reach the top of his flight, then begin the inevitable plummet toward a watery grave below. He grimaced, realizing he'd abandoned his wife and son to die on that iceberg, all so he could save himself. In the heat of the moment, he'd proven himself the precise opposite of a hero: not a villain, but a self-serving coward.

But it was too late. The die was cast. So Chauncy thrust his staff backward and downward for another windy blast.

In this way, he soared toward the shore, eventually landing a bit roughly near the dragon and the three men. Who were, he found, instantly recognizable to him, for he'd met them all before. It was King Pravus, his cousin Templeton…and none other than Imperius Fanning, bestower of wizardly destinies. He stumbled to a stop, facing the men. And feeling like a puny little boy compared to the muscly might of King Pravus…and even Templeton, who, while not as large, was still quite impressive.

"Um…hi," he greeted, waving a bit lamely. But not a one of them paid him any mind. In fact, they were all looking off into the distance at something behind him. So naturally he turned around, facing the giant waterfall in the distance…and saw a huge water elemental – easily a hundred feet tall – wading toward them. "Holy…!" he blurted out, taking an involuntary step back.

"Hardly," King Pravus replied. For the monarch's gaze was not on the elemental per se, but on the people within a hollow chamber in the elemental's chest: Nettie, Harry, Rocky, Rooter, Gavin, Valtora, Shackles, and even Peter!

And of course, one Zella Trek. Who was precisely the person King Pravus – and Imperius, and Templeton – beheld.

"Ah, there we are," Imperius declared.

The elemental reached the shore, depositing everyone on it. Nettie sucked the water back into her Wetstone.

"Imperius," she greeted. "King Pravus. Not gonna kneel," she added before Pravus could make the request. "Bad knees."

"I see you've brought me Zella Trek," Pravus declared, ignoring her comment. He crossed ridiculously large and veiny forearms over his ludicrously developed chest. "You've done well to help me capture her. A bit late, as usual," he snipped. Nettie arched an eyebrow.

"Excuse me?"

"The vile villain destroyed part of my castle," Pravus informed her. "And killed many innocent men and women. All because of him," he declared, pointing right at Chauncy. Chauncy felt his sphincter tighten, and he blinked, pointing at himself as well.

"Me?" he blurted out.

"She threatened to destroy my kingdom if I didn't tell her where you were," Pravus said. "My treasonous advisor revealed your location, and I rushed to intercept her before she could harm you. And then she tried to destroy my castle anyway," he concluded, glaring at Zella. Who was still in Shackles' grasp, of course. She had the gall to smirk.

"Oopsy," she quipped.

"That wasn't very nice," Pravus told her.

"Honestly, I couldn't help myself," she replied. "You were being a little bitch, so I had to teach you a lesson."

"You did," Pravus replied. "That you can't be trusted…and that you're a black-hearted villain who deserves to rot in my dungeon for the rest of your miserable little life!"

"Wait, so she attacked you?" Chauncy asked, trying to process this. "Because of me?"

"I'm afraid so," Templeton confirmed. "Many lives were lost to the violence of her dread serpent Fang."

"All because your father couldn't keep his serpent in his pants," Pravus pointed out.

"Indeed," Zella agreed. She turned to Imperius then, who was eyeing her with a cold blue stare. "We meet again Fanny," she greeted.

"That's Imperius *Fanning* to you," Nettie interjected. "Show some respect kid."

"Respect?" Zella inquired, arching an eyebrow. "To the man who started this whole mess in the first place?"

"What're ya talkin' about, hussy?" Nettie demanded.

"Huh?" Valtora asked, her expression immediately going innocently blank.

"Not you!" Nettie snapped. Valtora relaxed, clearly relieved.

"Who do you think told my husband to travel through the Gate to Borrin all those years ago, hmm?" Zella asked, crossing her arms over her chest. "Who gave him directions to a certain magic shop in Southwick? A Little Magic, if I recall."

Chauncy blinked, frowning at Imperius.

"You did?" he asked the man. Imperius hesitated, then nodded. "I did," he confessed.

"And so my loving husband – who'd never strayed before – went off to do Imperius's bidding, being a good little wizard of the Order. And…" she gasped, putting a hand to her mouth. "Who did he meet there…but an adorable, sweet little blonde that seduced him into making…" her eyes went to Chauncy, "…you."

Chauncy just stared back at her, dumbfounded.

"He had a little tryst, a single night's affair," Zella mused. "And after coming there, he came back to the Order…and confessed everything. Every sordid little detail."

"But…why have him go to Southwick?" Chauncy asked Zella. She eyed Imperius.

"Why indeed, oh Imperial Fanny?" she inquired.

"Imperial Fanny?" Harry interjected.

"He's an imperialistic ass," Zella explained.

"Oh," Harry murmured. "Good one."

"Shut up Harry," Nettie hissed.

"Tell them," Zella urged. "Why oh *why* did you send my poor husband to A Little Magic?"

"I didn't know at the time," Imperius replied. "But it was to meet Chauncy's mother…and conceive Chauncy."

"And there you have it," Zella declared. "He confesses the whole thing. My marriage ruined, my husband estranged…all because of Imperius Fanning, the great bestower of destinies. The face of the Order of Mundus."

"Aw, thanks Impy!" Valtora exclaimed, beaming a smile at him. "I wuv my widdle Chauncy-poo," she added, giving Chauncy a sideways hug. "Even if he abandoned me and Chaos to die falling down that waterfall," she added rather unnecessarily, but also quite accurately.

"Um…sorry," he replied, scratching the back of his head. "I sort of panicked."

"Sort of?" Nettie asked.

"I'm not a good Chosen One," he confessed.

"So I've come to learn," King Pravus interjected.

"But he's adequate," Valtora argued. "He defeated The Dark One, and saved magic!"

"He helped," Pravus corrected.

"In any case," Zella interjected. "After the whole debacle, your mother ascended to become a Magus…and my husband, still pining for her, decided to join her instead of staying with me."

"That was his choice," Imperius stated. She glared at him.

"His *choice?*" she blurted out. She gave a bitter laugh. "The only choice he made was to choose to listen to *you*," she argued. "He knew he could've ascended for decades, but he stayed human for *me*."

"Zella…" Imperius began.

"Until *you* ruined my life," Zella interrupted, pointing right at him. "You took my husband away from me, Imperius. The Order did. And then you had the gall to kick me out."

Imperius gave her a cold glare.

"And now it's quite clear our decision was correct," he replied.

"I would never had done what I did if you hadn't started it," she retorted.

"A true wizard of Mundus would never have been able to commit the atrocities you did," Imperius shot back.

"Good people can be pushed to do bad things," she countered. "Besides, who's to blame?" she added before he could reply. "None of this would've happened if *you* hadn't done what *you* did. You're responsible for all of it, Imperius. My marriage. My reaction. Even the destruction of poor little Pravus's tower and the deaths of his people."

Imperius grimaced.

"I didn't know the ramifications of my actions," he said in his defense. "My magic prevents worse-case-scenarios from happening…and I assure you from experience, whatever happened because of what I did pales in comparison to what would have happened if I hadn't."

"How convenient that we'll never know," Zella sneered.

"Trust me," Imperius began, but she scoffed.

"Never again," she declared.

"So anyway," Nettie interjected, putting her hands on her hips. "I get that you guys don't get along. But what exactly are we *doing* here?"

"Whatever Fanny wants you to do, as usual," Zella muttered.

"All he told us was that you were gonna kill Chauncy," Nettie stated. "And we know that's not gonna happen, unless you kill him with kindness."

"True," Zella admitted.

"So…wait a second," Chauncy told Imperius. "You told me Zella was going to end my world. By killing me."

Imperius cleared his throat.

"I did," he conceded.

"But she isn't going to," he pointed out.

"So you were wrong!" Valtora added, gleeful at the thought of knocking Imperius down a peg. "I thought you said you were *never* wrong."

"Nonsense," Imperius replied. "My *gut* is never wrong. But my interpretations of why it's telling me to do things sometimes is."

"So your gut wanted us to do what we did, and end up here and now," Chauncy stated. "Why?"

Imperius paused.

"I don't know," he confessed.

"I do," Zella offered, raising a hand. Imperius frowned.

"You do?" he asked.

"Well it's obvious, isn't it?" Zella replied. Everyone stared at her.

"Um…not really," Chauncy said.

"Not at all," Nettie agreed. Everyone nodded, having no idea why they were there. Except for Gavin, who spoke up.

"I think I know what she's inferring," he stated. Everyone turned to him. "From her perspective, Imperius's magic destroyed her life, by giving her husband a destiny that didn't include her. So naturally, she would see this reunion as an opportunity to fulfill *her* destiny."

"And what's that?" Nettie asked. Gavin reached for the scabbards of his golden knitting needles, his jaw set firm.

"To destroy Imperius Fanning," he answered. "And the Order of Mundus."

Zella broke out into a grim smile, clapping her hands slowly.

"Bra*vo* Mr. Merrick," she congratulated. "You've deduced my master plan."

And with that, she tossed her hair back, draping it over Shackles…and suddenly her hair wrapped around the golem's arms…and tore them right off.

"What the…!" Chauncy blurted out.

Zella's hair whipped around, shoving Shackles off the edge of the beach, sending him tumbling down to the ocean below. Then her hair seemed to melt into her scalp, vanishing there and leaving only a tattoo of hair behind. And – utterly bald – Zella Trek lifted her arms to her sides, smirking at them all.

"Thank you all for bringing me here," she told them. "Now that I've found a new love – and a new best friend – I've only one more wrong to right. And that's to kill you, Fanny…and destroy the Order of Mundus. The wizards of the world will no longer dance to the Order's tune, doing their bidding generation after generation. We'll find our *own* destinies…and be free of your tyranny at last!"

And with that, Zella attacked.

# Chapter 40

It started with great hair.

Zella's hair-tattoo sprung back out of her scalp in long, luscious black locks, moving of its own accord like innumerable tiny serpents. The tattoo on her back came next, springing midnight-black wings that spread outward magnificently. She smiled at Imperius then, the kind of smile that a predator gives its prey. An indication that the prey's life was about to end, and what's more, that the predator was going to enjoy forcing that particular transition.

"Everyone get ready," she told…well, everyone. "Attack on my command!"

"Wait, what?" Chauncy asked.

"Attack Imperius on my command," she repeated. "If we all strike together…"

"We're not attacking him," Chauncy interrupted.

Zella blinked.

"Why not?" she asked.

"He's not a bad guy," Chauncy explained.

"Haven't you heard a word of what I've said?" Zella inquired. "He's a controlling, manipulative member of the Order."

"Well I don't know about all that," Chauncy countered. She looked at him as if he were quite stupid.

"Don't you understand?" she pressed. "You've been Imperius's pawns all along! He's how the Order controls you!"

"I mean maybe so, but…"

"Do you seriously want to be this guy's obedient little slave?" she continued incredulously.

"Slaves to the Fanny," Harry noted, nudging Nettie's. She glared at him.

"Shut up Harry," she hissed. Zella looked around at the others.

"Do you all really want to be pawns of some old wizard's club?" she pressed. "They're using you to control the world! And all you're doing is bowing and scraping to obey them, as if it were some sort of honor to do their bidding!"

"We're two of those 'old wizards' you're talkin' about," Nettie told her. Zella looked taken aback.

"You are?"

"Oh ya," Nettie confirmed.

"Sure are," Harry agreed.

Zella's expression hardened, and she turned back to Chauncy.

"Are you really going to take *their* side?" she asked. "Are you going to be a good little slave, Chauncy? Or are you going to take your destiny into your own hands?"

"Well, um…" Chauncy began, glancing at the others. Who didn't help him one bit. "See, the thing is, before Nettie and Harry came for me, my life was terrible," he told her. "There was no magic at all. They taught me that my destiny was to be a wizard, not to do any one particular thing."

"Except to save magic and defeat The Dark One," Valtora pointed out.

"Except that," Chauncy agreed sheepishly.

"See?" Zella exclaimed. "That's what they do, making you do their bidding!"

"Well, so far it's gotten me a fancy wizard's cloak, magic, an awesome wife, a new child, a renewed purpose in life, some great friends, and…well, just a great life in general," Chauncy pointed out. "So all in all, I have to say I'm pretty pleased."

"That's how it always starts," Zella countered. "They draw you into their trap with honey…then spring it on you later." She shook her head at him. "They did it to me," she added. "They'll do it to you."

Chauncy glanced at Imperius, who just stood there, eyeing him. He turned back to Zella.

"Um…" he began, then paused. Then shrugged. Zella rolled her eyes, turning to Gavin.

"Surely *you* understand," she told him. "You were a powerful man once. You don't want to be a slave to the Order, do you?"

Gavin considered this for a moment.

"A wise man once told me that I was living a life of transactional relationships with compulsion to profit from them," he answered. "And that this was my relationship to myself. Always doing things to get things from others or myself." He smiled at her. "I was never more of a slave than when I was powerful," he mused. "Now that I've given my power away, I'm free."

"Okay," Zella stated. "Whatever. You still haven't answered my question."

"I don't think the Order is interested in controlling people," Gavin told her. "They're interested in the opposite. Magic dies when it's controlled," he added. "But the natural human tendency is to control things. I suspect the Order exists to counteract mankind's compulsion to control each other, so that magic can still exist in the world."

Imperius smiled at Gavin, inclining his head.

"You've come a long way in a short time Mr. Merrick," he told Gavin. Gavin smiled back.

"Just Gavin will do," he replied.

"So is *no* one going to help me here?" Zella interjected, clearly flabbergasted by everyone's response. She turned to Valtora. "What about you?" she asked. "We're evil besties!"

"I mean yeah," Valtora replied. She put a hand on Chauncy's shoulder. "But my bestest bestie is Chauncy, so I'm with him."

Zella stared at her incredulously…and then threw up her arms.

"Fine!" she exclaimed. "I'll do it myself."

"Can't let you do that," Nettie told her. "You mess with the Order, you mess with me."

"And me," Harry added.

"And me," Gavin piped in.

"And me!" Valtora exclaimed exuberantly. "So like, watch out." Chauncy smiled, but didn't say anything. So Valtora nudged him. "Come on Chauncy," she prompted.

"Um…and me I guess," Chauncy replied. Valtora gave him a look.

"Wow, so heroic," she grumbled.

"He really is a weak Chosen One," King Pravus observed.

"Not so much weak as unsure," Templeton countered gently. "Nothing a bit more success can't cure."

Valtora took a sharp breath.

"He rhymed!" she hissed, nudging Chauncy. "Are you a wizard?" she asked Templeton.

"Enough!" Zella snapped, and everyone's head snapped around to face her. She glared at them all. "If you're not with me, you're against me!"

265

"Ooo, see that?" Valtora asked Chauncy excitedly. "That's like *classic* supervillain shit right there. Anyone who says that is *totally* evil."

"Shut up!" Zella commanded.

And with that, she *really* attacked.

\* \* \*

Zella brought both of her hands up as if to flip everyone off…and instead, brought the sides of her forearms together in front of her. This joined two halves of a tattoo on her forearms…a tattoo of a great big demon-bull head. A fully colorized tattoo, in fact, one remarkably detailed…and about to get even more so.

For the demon-bull's eyes flashed bright red…and then it burst from her forearms as a *real* demon-bull, charging right at Imperius!

Who vanished into a puff of blue sparkles right before the bull hit him.

The demon-bull slammed head-first into the transparent dome surrounding the Isle of Mundus, making a loud *DONG* as it did so. One that reverberated powerfully across the dome's huge surface. Chauncy covered his ears, backing away from the awful sound quickly…and stepping right off the edge of the beach.

"Crap!" was all he had time to blurt out.

He plummeted toward the water far, far below, the wind howling with a steadily higher pitch as he gained speed. His staff vibrated in his hands…which reminded him that it existed. And its existence reminded him – for the umpteenth time – that he was, in fact, a wizard.

"Vertical vault!" he cried, thrusting downward mightily.

His descent reversed, and he shot upward shockingly fast, blasting above the shore. He realized that his staff must have absorbed far more wind than he'd realized…a fact that would make his attacks with it formidable indeed. He spotted Zella and the raging bull facing off against his friends, and set his jaw firmly, winding up for an epic staff-swing. One he executed with a grunt, aiming right at the demon-bull.

"Blasted bull!" he exclaimed…not before, but *after* the swing. For by the time the bull or Zella heard it, it would be too late.

The blast of wind struck the bull with the power of a gosh-darn hurricane, sending it flying into the dome with another loud *DONG*. Unfortunately, it also struck his friends, though indirectly. Still, its power was formidable enough to send the bull and everyone else flying…even Rocky and Harry, and the dragon, who happened to have its wings spread a bit at the time. And Zella Trek, of course. And while the dragon and Zella – with her tattooed wings – could fly, everyone else could not. So instead, they ricocheted off the dome, then flew over the edge of the floating island, falling to the ocean far below.

Chauncy watched as his friends plummeted to their certain doom, fully realizing that even with his staff, he couldn't save them all.

"Oh," was all he could say as they fell screaming to their deaths.

* * *

Gavin watched as Chauncy tripped over the edge of the beach, yelling "crap!" as he fell. Gavin reached for his knitting needles, pulling them free from their sheaths and rushing to the edge. But before he could come to the rescue, Chauncy came to his own, shooting upward with remarkable speed by the power of his magical staff.

*Well done*, he thought. For though Chauncy had gotten himself into that pickle in the first place, it wasn't the mistake that Gavin focused on, but the solution. And Chauncy had solved his problem almost instantly, which was an admirable act.

Gavin saw Chauncy fly far overhead, then wind up his staff for a formidable swing. Which was another mistake, considering an arcing wind blast would be too broad an attack to hit just the enemy. And when the wind ricocheted off the dome…

That's when the blast struck Gavin, sending him flying into the dome. He ricocheted off with a *DONG*, nearly dropping his knitting needles. He managed to hold on to them, even as he flew over the edge of the shore, the great ocean chasm appearing below him.

And all around him, his new friends flew through the air just like him.

He made a quick calculation, then touched the ends of his needles together, triggering them to produce yarn between them. Then he chucked one of the needles at the underside of the island, and the other a ways below Nettie, who was farthest away, with everyone else somewhere in-between them, luckily enough. The length of yarn between the two needles grew longer as the needles flew farther apart, and Gavin grabbed on to that yarn with both hands, holding on for dear life.

He watched as the knitting needle passed underneath Nettie, then snapped his fingers. It was the magical way to recall his needle…and it flew back toward him to do just that, making a big loop of yarn behind it. Which Nettie fell onto, conveniently enough…just as he'd planned.

Then, with a thought, he connected with the yarn in his hands, that single thread that, when woven, created the fabric of its own particular universe. A single strand woven over and under itself, such that each portion supported the others. A metaphor for life, for human interconnection…and for reality itself.

He smiled, willing the yarn to knit itself, and so it did.

It wove with near-instantaneous speed, forming a massive net. One that caught every last friend within it…and from which Gavin now hung.

The knitting needle he'd recalled smacked back into his hand with a *thwack*, and Gavin threw it up at the underside of the rapidly retreating island just as hard as he could. And, Gavin being quite strong still…and the knitting needle being magical in nature…it flew at the island with terrific speed, embedding itself into the rock.

The two strings of magical yarn stretched, slowing the net's descent…and then they went taut. And a moment later, the yarn rebounded like a trampoline, sending everyone flying back upward.

"Nettie, water elemental!" Gavin cried. But she had already grabbed her Wetstone, taking its water and shaping it into a rapidly-expanding orb. One that engulfed them all, even as they flew ever-upward toward the island. She shaped it into a great big water elemental, creating a hollow chamber inside that everyone flowed into. Gavin's head burst through the floor of that chamber, and he sucked in a deep breath of air, smiling at Nettie, Harry and everyone else as their heads popped through the surface.

"Not bad kid," Nettie told Gavin, inclined her head. He inclined his head back.

"Not bad yourself," he replied.

"All right," Nettie stated. "Let's go kick some ass."

* * *

Nettie felt her stomach flip-flop as her water elemental reached the peak of its flight. Which just so happened to be a bit below the lip of the shore, problematically. But a problem was just something waiting to be solved; focusing on the solution rather than the problem was the secret to doing so.

So Nettie merely extended one of the water elemental's arms above its head, stretching it out to the shoreline's edge. Then she froze its fingers just as they closed on the shoreline...and then the entire arm. With an overlying skin of water to connect it reliably to the rest of the elemental, of course. This allowed her to send more water flowing from the elemental's hand onto the shore...which pulled the elemental up to it.

Within moments, the huge elemental was standing at the shore, towering over Zella Trek. Her bull was gone, having very likely drowned in the ocean far below.

"All right Zella," Nettie declared, crossing the elemental's arms over its chest. "Playtime's over."

"I don't think so," Zella replied with an irritating smirk. "I'm just getting warmed up honey. You ain't seen *nothing* yet."

"Harry?" Nettie called out, turning to eye her husband. He took off his glasses, blowing on them to get the water off, then put them back on.

"Yes angel?" he replied.

"Can you kick that tatted-up tart's ass already?" she asked. He broke out into a shit-eating grin.

"Thought you'd never ask," he replied.

\* \* \*

Harry felt himself get sucked underwater from the hollow chamber in Nettie's water elemental, and held his breath, watching as he flowed rapidly through one of its huge, watery arms toward the shore below. He waited until his feet touched the sand – and the watery hand separated from him – before taking a breath in. Then he took off his glasses, blowing on them again, and returning them to his face.

Only then did he look about, spotting Zella Trek near the dome protecting the Order of Mundus, in the process of absorbing her inky black wings into her back. He grinned, even giving her a little wave.

"Hey there," he greeted.

"Hey yourself," she replied.

"Where'd your bull go?" he inquired, looking around. She glared at him, and he chuckled.

"I don't want to fight you Harry," she warned.

"Well that's good," he replied.

"But I will if I have to," she added. "Don't make me hurt you, Harry."

"Another evil classic!" Valtora shouted from with the water elemental behind Harry. "Go Zella!"

"Idiot!" Nettie snapped at Valtora. "Whose side are you on?"

Harry chuckled again, kicking off his shoes and feeling his feet sink into the sand. Mostly ground-up seashells and such, meaning calcium carbonate. Along with a smattering of many other minerals, of course. A tough material to connect with, sand. So many separate little pieces that didn't wanna stick together. Unless they got wet, of course.

Which, thanks to Nettie's elemental, they were. No coincidence there; Harry and Nettie had been together so long that they knew just what to do for each other.

"Ready?" Harry asked Zella. She smirked.

"Come and get me Harry."

And with that, Harry connected with the calcium carbonate underfoot, and more importantly, with the dilute solution of the mineral dissolved in the water Nettie had provided. Calcium carbonate wasn't particularly soluble under neutral or alkaline conditions, but it was soluble enough for his purposes. Even this dilute solution connected the grains of sand together as a single unit, one that allowed Harry to feel the sand wherever that solution spread. And to bring them together in his favorite kind of rock: a sedimentary conglomerate.

*Wait for it*, he told what he'd created.

At the same time, he stuffed a hand in his pants pocket, fingering a piece of steel he kept there. Just in case.

As he did this, Zella's left shoulder tattoo separated from her skin, rising to form a giant eyeball that floated beside her. This was also a colorized tattoo, unlike her wings and her hair; the eyeball had a blood-red iris and pulsing blood vessels, and an optic nerve dangling like a grim ponytail behind it.

"Say hello to Bloodshot," she told him.

"Doesn't look bloodshot to me," he noted. And indeed the eyeball didn't.

And then a beam of blood-red light shot out of the thing's pupil, striking Harry in the belly.

The beam was, to his surprise, surprisingly hot. Hot enough to burn through some of the wood chips mixed in with the pebbles on his vest. And then through the brown shirt underneath to strike his skin.

Had he not connected with the steel in his pocket, Harry was sure the beam would've gone right through him. As it was, it only heated things up a bit.

The beam winked out, leaving a hole burned in the flesh in front of the eyeball's pupil. This oozed blood…until it healed up as Harry watched. Which didn't make much sense, considering that part of the eye didn't have a blood supply.

"So Bloodshot's filled with blood," Harry guessed.

"How observant," Zella replied, looking pleased that Harry hadn't died. But a bit miffed that he didn't seem surprised.

"And he shoots people," Harry continued. "That's why you called him Bloodshot."

Zella rolled her eyes.

"Are we going to talk or are we going to fight?" she inquired.

"I'd rather talk."

"Pound sand," she replied…and her long black hair whipped forward, wrapping around Harry's neck and torso…and around his wrists and ankles. He was lifted up from the sand, then slammed down on his back on the beach. Over and over again.

Harry chuckled…until he was thrown backward over the edge of the levitating Isle of Mundus.

That's when his sedimentary conglomerate burst into action, rising from the beach and extending a big arm out to catch Harry. It carried him back to the beach, and he rose stiffly to his feet at the beach's edge…with big ol' thirty-foot-tall conglomerate golem – or ConglomerGolem – standing beside him.

"Anything else you want me to pound?" he asked. With a shit-eating grin. She glared at him.

"No thanks," she replied. "You're not my type."

"What's your type?" he inquired.

"Alive," she answered.

"Fucking *badass* line, bestie!" Valtora shouted from within the water elemental.

"Shut up idiot!" Nettie snapped. And then plunged Valtora below the surface of the water for a bit to enforce it.

271

"Your golem there looks wet," Zella noted, eyeing Harry's creation. "You know what happens when wet rock is superheated?"

"Well," Harry began.

"This," Zella interjected.

Bloodshot shot another crimson beam from its pupil, this time striking the ConglomerGolem…and instantly vaporizing the water inside of it. Which caused that water to expand almost instantly into a gas. Which was, of course, the very definition of an explosion.

It struck Harry in the side, sending him hurtling violently up and away from the golem…and far, far away from the edge of the floating island. Instead of panicking – which never did anyone any good anyway – he simply connected with the fabric of his shirt, becoming like fabric himself. He felt himself ripple madly in the wind, then settle down as he slowed, to a gentle fluttering down.

*Sure could use a good wind*, he thought as he floated a good hundred feet from the island's edge. But the only one who could give him that was either chance…or Chauncy.

* * *

Chauncy had been tested by many an emergency in the last year or two. And as has been mentioned before, it is common knowledge that in an emergency, there are not two, but three options: run away from danger, run toward it, or freeze in place. Each time danger had reared its ugly – or in this case, painfully beautiful – head, Chauncy had chosen the third option. So, being nothing if not consistent, he did it again.

By watching in horror as his friends plummeted to their certain deaths…all because of him.

"Oh," he'd blurted out, while flying backward and upward in the air. And was immediately seized by a sense of shame. For a hero would've recovered rapidly from their mistake, and rushed to save their loved ones from a watery grave. By the time it registered that his beloved wife and son were about to die, it was too late. "Shit," he added.

He reached the apex of his flight, and decided right then and there that he'd join them. By doing nothing at all, as usual…and falling to his death in the ocean far, far below.

Then, to his surprise, he saw a giant red net appear seemingly out of nowhere catching his doomed friends and family within it. And un-dooming them, to his profound relief. Soon after, a rapidly

272

expanding sphere of water exploded outward from Nettie, forming a huge water elemental whose massive legs plunged into the ocean below. It reached up for the edge of the Isle of Mundus, grabbing it and freezing, then hauling itself up. And soon after, deposited none other than Harry on the beach.

But relief soon turned to shame, and Chauncy contemplated continuing with his plan to die of it. But the thought of abandoning his poopy-dooz – and poor little Chaos Little – stopped him. And prompted him to the surest cure for helplessness: action.

He thrust his staff downward and backward to slow his fall, and to bring him back toward Harry, who was busy being thrown violently backward by Zella's magical hair. Chauncy was about to come to the old man's rescue when Harry rescued himself...with a big arm made of what appeared to be sandstone shooting out of the beach to catch him. It brought Harry back to the beach before Zella, and belonged to a big golem that sprouted from the sand beside Harry. A giant eyeball levitating at Zella's side shot a beam that struck the golem, shattering it into a bajillion pieces.

And that, dear reader, brings us back to the present.

Chauncy saw Harry blast sideways...and then promptly act like a big piece of fabric, flattening and fluttering in the wind. Chauncy burst into action, thrusting repeatedly to fly up to Harry, grabbing him and thrusting again. This time toward Zella Trek, and the big eyeball floating at her side. He landed on the shore with a *whump*, and Harry turned back to his usual self, nodding at Chauncy with a smile.

"Thanks," Harry said.

"Sorry for nearly killing everyone," Chauncy apologized. Harry just chuckled, slapping him on the shoulder.

"Well well," Zella declared, eyeing them both. "Look who's come back for more."

"I'll come as many times as it takes," Chauncy vowed, holding his staff before him.

"I as well!" Tip chimed in.

"I certainly hope so," Zella quipped. Chauncy grimaced.

"Surrender," he commanded.

"Or what?" Zella inquired, arching an eyebrow. "You're going to stop me, Chauncy?"

"Probably not," Chauncy conceded. "But my friends will. A wise old wizard once told me that the best rocks of all were sedimentary," he declared. "They're really a bunch of rocks glued together...and together, we're more powerful than you."

Zella clapped, which usually meant applause. But the way in which she did it was profoundly belittling.

"Nice monologue darling," she replied. "But monologues only allow the other side to..."

And with that, the big floating eyeball shot a beam of light at Chauncy's left arm. Which made it disappear. In that it left a blackened, smoking stump at his shoulder.

"Oh," he mumbled, staring at it.

"Chauncy!" Valtora cried from within the water elemental. "Tookums, get me and Rooter down there!"

Rocky did so, leaping out of the elemental's hollow chest-chamber and landing with a *whump* in the sand. Rocky rushed to Chauncy's side, then set Rooter down beside him. Rooter's plant started to glow...

...and then a beam of blood-red light shot out of the giant eyeball, obliterating Rooter.

"Noooo!" Rocky roared. He charged at Zella, leaping at her and the eyeball floating beside her. Her hair whipped forward, wrapping around Rocky's ankle and yanking it sideways. He tripped over himself, landing face-first in the sand...and the giant eyeball shot him with its terrible beam, burning a hole in his upper back.

"Shmookie!" Valtora gasped, rushing after the poor giant. Chauncy grabbed her by the wrist...or at least he tried to. For his free hand had no wrist, because it didn't exist.

"No!" he shouted. "She'll kill you!"

A dark figure emerged from Zella's back then: her doppelganger Inkling. It lunged at Valtora, tackling her to the ground. Chaos was squashed between the two, and shrieked in surprise and pain.

"No!" Chauncy cried.

"I didn't want to hurt you darling," Zella told him. "But you made me do it."

"Don't call me that," Chauncy snapped, glaring at her. "I hate you!"

"Now," she replied. "But you'll learn to love me, Chauncy. We'll get past this. All you need to do is stop fighting for the wrong cause."

"The Order would never do this to us," Nettie argued from her perch within the water elemental. The elemental blasted water from its palm, aiming for Zella's magical eyeball. It shot its horrible red light at the same time…and the water turned instantly to steam, exploding in a shower of boiling water and gas.

Chauncy *screamed* as he was boiled alive, falling to his hands and knees in the sand. The pain was beyond agony, instant and unbearable.

He heard Valtora scream, and Harry grunt, and Nettie shouting something from behind and above. But the shrill cry of Chaos was most horrible of all.

"Son!" Chauncy cried, struggling to his feet. He couldn't see out of his left eye, for it'd been burned beyond all hope. And awful blisters were growing on his remaining hand, the skin beet red. Valtora too was burned, though with the doppelganger atop her, she'd been spared the worst. But Harry had been tied up completely by Zella's magic hair, and the giant eyeball had vaporized much of Nettie's elemental. Rocky was lying motionless in the sand, a horrible crater burned into his back. And poor Rooter was utterly gone, save for a piece of his plant that'd survived the eyeball's attack.

Zella's doppelganger tore Chaos from Valtora's wrap, bringing the boy to Zella. Who stood there before them, her arms crossed over her chest. She gazed down with pity at Chauncy, extending a hand to him…even as strands of her hair wrapped around poor Chaos's neck.

"Join me Chauncy," she urged. "The Order will only use you. With me, you'll be free from their tyranny…and I'll always love and protect you."

"Let my son go!" Chauncy ordered. "I swear, if you hurt him…"

"I don't want to hurt anyone my dear," Zella replied. "You're the ones who attacked me."

"Actually, you attacked us first," Chauncy pointed out.

"Only because you betrayed me."

"By disagreeing with you?" he pressed.

"Correct," Zella agreed. "If you truly supported me, you'd agree with me."

"Another classic evil line," Valtora mused. Then her expression hardened. "Now seriously, give me back my baby, or I'll kill you bitch."

"Surrender or the baby dies," Zella replied. And with that, her hair tightened around poor Chaos's neck. Such that his face turned beet-red.

"Stop it!" Chauncy cried, lunging toward her. The hair around Chaos's neck drew even tighter, and his face turned a deep purple.

He gasped and coughed, then gave a horrible, strangled sound. One that made Chauncy lunge at them, the need to save his only son overwhelming any sense of self-preservation.

"Any closer and I'll crush his throat," Zella warned. Chauncy froze, terror gripping him. For Chaos went limp, his eyes rolling in the back of his head.

"No!" he shouted. "Please!"

"Let that poor baby go, you monster!" Nettie shouted.

"You know my terms," Zella replied. "Surrender, and join my side. Help me destroy the Order of Mundus…or the baby dies."

# Chapter 41

King Pravus the Eighth found himself blown away.

A most unexpected blowing, that came not from the front, but from behind. And promptly shoved him headlong into the dome surrounding the Isle of Mundus. His face smashed into it, ricocheting off with a *DONG*. The biggest *dong* his face had ever had the occasion to raise, in fact. He flew backward, the beach zooming by beneath him. Until it was no longer beneath him, because the ocean was. Still he hurtled backward, having struck the dome just so, until he plunged into the waterfall far beyond. Its ice-cold water engulfed him, shoving him instantly downward with terrible speed…and driving him deep, deep underwater at the bottom, where he was surrounded by utter blackness.

Which was *irritating*.

He felt his descent stop, pressure building in his ears. It didn't hurt, by virtue of his kingly uniform and crown, but still, the sensation was remarkably uncomfortable. Which only served to fuel his irritation. So as soon as his descent stopped, Pravus swam upward through the water using a vigorous breaststroke, eventually reaching the surface. A few yards from the roaring waterfall, whose chilly spray assaulted him. Far above, he saw the rocky bottom of the levitating Isle of Mundus…and a big water elemental hanging from its edge. A hundred or so feet ahead, he spotted the fire dragon leaping from the water, flapping its huge wings to stay above its violently churning surface.

Pravus frowned, scanning the water quickly.

"Templeton?" he called out. "Templeton!"

But his dear, sweet cousin was nowhere to be found.

"Templeton!" he shouted, his voice booming across the water. But compared to the roar of the waterfall, its volume was woefully small. Fear gripped him, an emotion he'd rarely had the occasion to experience. "Dragon!" he cried.

The fire dragon whipped its head around to eye him.

"I fear Templeton is in trouble," Pravus declared. "Can you help me save him?"

The dragon snorted...then splashed down again, lowering its neck into the water and stretching it out next to Pravus. He climbed aboard – no easy feat with its slippery red scales – then managed to scooch down to the saddle. He sat astride this, then patted the dragon's back.

"To Templeton!" he urged.

The dragon flapped its wings, rising from the water. Then it made a wide circle around the perimeter of the watery canyon, gaining altitude as it did so. The dragon – and Pravus – searched the water below...until Pravus spotted a dark shape in the water ahead and to their right.

"There!" he cried, pointing the way. The dragon dove downward, plunging a clawed forelimb in the water...and when it flew upward from the surface, none other than Templeton himself was clutched within. "Cousin!" Pravus exclaimed in horror. For Templeton was lying limply in the dragon's clutches, his face a dreadful blue hue. "To the surface!" Pravus commanded. "Far away from danger!"

The dragon complied, bringing them 'round the far side of the Isle of Mundus and depositing them on the narrow strip of beach before the dome there. Pravus rushed to Templeton's side, kneeling before him and cupping his poor cousin's face in his hands.

"Templeton!" he called out, slapping his cousin's cheek. At first lightly, then a bit harder. But Templeton just stared off at nothing, his face that terrible shade of blue. "Wake up!"

But to Pravus's utter horror, Templeton did not.

\* \* \*

Gavin Merrick was wading within Nettie's water elemental – along with Nettie and Valtora, Rocky and Rooter, when he saw Zella's floating eyeball obliterate Chauncy's left arm, leaving a blackened stump at the poor man's shoulder.

"Chauncy!" Valtora cried from within the water elemental. "Tookums, get me and Rooter down there!"

Rocky did so, leaping out of the elemental's hollow chest-chamber and landing with a *whump* in the sand. Rocky rushed to Chauncy's side, then set Rooter down beside him. Rooter's plant started to glow...

…and then a beam of blood-red light shot out of the giant eyeball, obliterating Rooter.

"Noooo!" Rocky roared, charging at Zella and the eyeball, leaping at them. But Zella used her magical, inky hair to trip the giant…and the eyeball shot a smoking hole in Rocky's back with its deadly red beam.

"Shmookie!" Valtora gasped, leaping down onto the sand, then rushing up to the poor giant. But Zella's Inkling doppelganger emerged from Zella's back, tackling Valtora to the sand.

"Gavin, we're up," Nettie prompted, pointing one of the elemental's watery palms at Zella. "The Order would never do this to us," she yelled at Zella…right as she made the elemental shoot a blast of water at the floating eyeball. At the same time, Gavin tapped the ends of his knitting needles together to form yarn between then, then flung one of his knitting needles right into that water stream. All it needed to do was stick into the eyeball's flesh, and Gavin would be able to…

That's when the eyeball shot its horrible red light once again…right into the elemental's stream.

The stream – and the elemental's entire arm – vanished in a violent explosion of steam and boiling water, obliterating the chamber within which Nettie and Gavin floated. Gavin hurtled sideways, the world rotating madly around him. Then he felt himself hit the sand, the air blasting from his lungs. He gasped, coming to a stop on his belly in the sand.

The entire left side of his body was in agony, burned by the superheated water. He couldn't see out of his left eye, nor hear from that ear. It was as if they didn't exist.

He grunted, focusing not on what he'd lost, but what he had. And what he had was a pulse…and therefore, a chance to save his friends.

Gavin rose to his feet, seeing Nettie lying on the sand a few yards away, burned badly. Her face was filled with blisters, almost unrecognizable now. He stopped before her, but she shooed him away.

"I'll live," she told him. "Go do something smart."

Gavin nodded, turning his remaining eye on Zella. Chauncy was absent one arm, and Harry trapped in Zella's hair. Valtora's doppelganger had managed to grab Chaos…and as Gavin watched, Zella wrapped a few strands of her hair around the baby's neck, choking him.

279

"Surrender or the baby dies," Zella warned.

"Stop it!" Chauncy cried.

"Any closer and I'll crush his throat," Zella warned...even as Chaos went limp, his eyes rolling in the back of his head.

"No!" Chauncy pleaded. "Please!"

"Let that poor baby go, you monster!" Nettie shouted, struggling to her feet. She fell back onto the sand, crying out in pain.

"You know my terms," Zella replied. "Surrender, and join my side. Help me destroy the Order of Mundus...or the baby dies."

Gavin reached down for his knitting needles...then realized he no longer had them. Not that they would be much good now. He stared at Chaos, the baby's little face going from red to purple to a dark blue...gritting his teeth.

*Think!*

But it was hopeless. Though he was a wizard now, and had once been perhaps the most powerful man in the world, neither his magic or his money could help him now.

*Money!*

He blinked, then reached into the pocket of his knitted uniform, the one at his chest. And retrieved a single golden coin...the one that his dear wife Marie had given him on their wedding day.

*Now you'll never run out of beautiful things,* she'd told him.

*I don't need gold,* he'd replied. *I have you.*

Gavin wound up, then chucked the golden coin not at Zella or her doppelganger. Not even at the floating eyeball with its deadly light. But at Chaos Little.

The coin struck the baby in the head...turning him instantly into gold. And by extension, the doppelganger...and Zella's strands of hair. She cursed, separating herself from her hair at the last minute, before she too was turned to gold.

And, as pure gold, Chaos couldn't die...or even be strangled. It would buy them time...and right now, that's what they desperately needed.

Gavin snapped his fingers, triggering the coin to fly back to his hand.

"Well *done* Gavin," Zella congratulated. Gavin chucked his coin at the eyeball...but it dodged out of the way, shooting its deadly beam at Gavin's legs. Which vaporized instantly below the knees, forcing him to fall onto his stumps on the sand. He toppled forward onto his chest with a *whump*, grunting with the impact.

"Nice try," she told him, smirking at his attempt…and eyeing the ruined side of his face. "You were trying to make it an eye for an eye, weren't you Gavin?"

Gavin didn't reply, grimacing at the horrible pain in his leg-stumps. Zella turned her gaze to Chauncy.

"You have a choice, Chauncy," she stated. "Join me, or continue this foolishness. As I said, I have no desire to hurt you or your friends."

"But you did," Chauncy retorted miserably.

"Because you made me," Zella countered.

"Everything you've done is because you wanted to," Chauncy argued. "I didn't make you do a thing."

"You're wrong Chauncy," Zella replied evenly. "But I don't want to argue anymore. Join me or fight me. It's your choice."

* * *

Pravus grabbed Templeton's limp body by the shoulders, shaking him.

"Templeton!" he urged, shaking him harder. "Wake up!"

But Templeton just laid there, water dribbling from the corner of his lips, his face blue, his eyes dead.

"No!" Pravus cried, tears dripping down his cheeks. "Don't leave me, sweet Templeton!"

He sobbed, making a fist and slamming it down on Templeton's chest. Water spurted out of Templeton's mouth with the impact, and Pravus blinked. An idea came to him then…that Templeton might still be drowning. Not because of an ocean around him, but an ocean within.

Pravus slammed his fist upon Templeton's chest again, and more water came spurting out. Pravus turned his cousin on his side, then laid down beside him, spooning him. He wrapped his arms around the man, clasping his hands at Templeton's lower chest. Then squeezed…and squeezed again, with violent, sudden jerks. More water spewed from Templeton's mouth, until no more water came. Pravus rolled away, then stood up…but despite this, Templeton didn't breathe again.

In desperation, Pravus lowered his lips to Templeton's, crushing them against his cousin's. For if Templeton wouldn't breathe, by the gods Pravus would do it for him.

281

He blew in Templeton's mouth, seeing his chest rise and fall. Then he blew and blew and blew again…until at last, to his utter amazement, Templeton gasped, then coughed!

"Templeton!" Pravus cried, watching as his cousin's face went from blue to pink. Templeton's eyes focused on Pravus, and he smiled gorgeously.

"Hello cousin," Templeton greeted. "What happened?"

"I believe that Chosen One Chauncy blew us off the island," Pravus guessed. "You nearly drowned, so we brought you back up to the island and I've revived you."

"Revive me? How?" Templeton asked.

"By blowing in your lungs," Pravus replied. Which was not how Pravus would have preferred to blow Templeton, but still.

"The breath of life!" Templeton declared, his eyes twinkling with delight. "Thank you, dearest cousin," he added. "I'm forever in your debt."

"There are no debts between us," Pravus retorted gently. "For the joy I feel by helping is more payment than helping cost."

"Wise words indeed," Templeton agreed, sitting up. "You're crying!" he realized, eyeing Pravus's wet cheeks.

"Tears of sorrow turned to tears of joy," Pravus assured him. "I was afraid you were taken from me forever."

"It'll take more than a dip in the sea to steal me from your side," Templeton declared valiantly. "But come cousin, we have work to do! For there's foul play afoot, and we can yet save the day!"

"Then let us engage in heroic play," Pravus replied at once, helping Templeton to his feet. Templeton grimaced, rubbing his sore chest.

"Did we do chest day recently?" he inquired.

"I'll explain later," Pravus replied. "Come, sweet Templeton!"

And at once, they mounted the fire dragon, bidding it to fly back toward Zella Trek. For while the Chosen Ones were trying their best – to varying levels of success – to defeat the dastardly villain, it was up to Pravus to save the day.

The fire dragon soared over the dome protecting the Isle of Mundus, and ahead Pravus spotted Zella and the Chosen Ones. To his dismay, the Chosen Ones were in dire straits, most of them horribly injured. Indeed, as he watched, a giant floating eyeball beside Zella shot a beam that vaporized Gavin Merrick's legs below the knees, forcing the poor man to fall to his belly in the sand.

"Breathe fire!" Pravus prompted his dragon, standing up in his saddle. He made the motion to draw his magical sword from his back, and it appeared in his hands at once. The dragon swooped down and breathed a narrow cone of fire on Zella and the eyeball…and Pravus leapt off the dragon, plummeting toward the two. The fire engulfed him, but with his magical, kingly uniform it did him no harm.

He lifted his great golden sword up, then brought it down with all his might…just as he landed before the floating eyeball.

* * *

Chauncy watched in disbelief as fire engulfed Zella and the giant eyeball…and then King Pravus himself landed behind the eyeball with a magnificent *whump*. And an equally magnificent chop with his massive golden sword…one that cut the great, deadly eyeball perfectly in half.

The two halves separated, falling to the sand. Blood and clots gushed out of its halves, coagulating in the heat of the fire, while some of it poured onto Chauncy's feet, soaking into the sand.

"Ew," he blurted out, making a face.

The fire cleared, revealing a charred, split eyeball…and a perfectly intact Zella Trek. For she'd sprouted her inky wings and used them to shield herself, charring her armored feathers but leaving herself unharmed. She turned to face Pravus, who posed before her in the most magnificent, manly, heroic posture Chauncy had ever witnessed.

"Surrender, villain!" he commanded, his voice booming mightily. He held his sword out menacingly, its deadly golden metal gleaming in the sun.

"Wo*wee*," Chauncy breathed.

The dragon landed to one side of them, Templeton climbing down from its back…and drawing a long fencing blade.

"Your villainy has met its end," the man declared. "For our blades are guided by righteous hearts…that yet beat with love for our friends!"

"Well *said* Templeton!" Pravus exclaimed.

"From the depths of my soul, my liege," Templeton replied zestily.

"Are you done?" Zella inquired, putting a hand on her hip and looking quite bored with them.

"Nearly so," Pravus answered. "Surrender or die!"

"You took the words right out of my mouth," she replied. And then she reached out, touching her golden doppelganger. Which should have turned *her* to gold, but instead, the Inkling was drawn back into Zella's skin…and then came out again, not gold, but inky black once again.

The doppelganger leapt at Pravus and Templeton, and Templeton lunged forward with an expert thrust, impaling it through the chest. Then Pravus followed up with a magnificent slash of his own oversized sword, decapitating the Inkling in a spray of black blood.

"Ha!" Pravus exclaimed…just as Zella drew the halves of Bloodshot back into her skin, letting the eyeball out again. It blasted Pravus with its deadly beam, striking him in the face.

Pravus flew backward with the force of the beam, tumbling in the sand and rolling to a stop a good thirty yards away. Templeton hobbled after him…and Zella turned to Chauncy. She drew her gilded Inkling hair back into her scalp, then let it out again, inky black…and sent strands of it to wrap around Chauncy's neck, pulling him toward her. He struggled in vain against this, digging his heels in the sand. But it was no use.

She brought him all the way to her, so their faces were inches apart. And smiled mischievously, a twinkle in her purple eyes.

"Now now darling," she chided. "You've been a naughty boy. But I forgive you Chauncy. We can still be together."

"I don't want you!" he retorted.

"I'm conflicted," Tip piped in.

"Shut *up* Tip!" Chauncy snapped. Zella smirked, eyeing Tip through Chauncy's robe, then meeting Chauncy's gaze again.

"Looks like *someone* still wants me," she purred, giving Tip a touch. Chauncy tried to pull away.

"Not conflicted anymore," Tip announced. "I'm all yours Zella."

"How could you say that?" Chauncy demanded.

"What can I say?" Tip replied. "I see myself in her."

Chauncy was about to retort when he was struck with a sudden feeling. The same feeling he'd had when he'd gazed down at Chaos during their first walk together…and saw Chaos looking back up at him. He blinked, then looked at Zella. *Really* looked at her. Her purple eyes, gorgeous lips. Her magical tattoos. A wizard just like him, who found magic in ink. Who lived differently, and had been abandoned by Chauncy's father, just like he had, in a way. Hurt like he'd been hurt.

Zella was just reacting in a different way, with villainy instead of heroic play.

Chauncy smiled at her, suddenly realizing what it was he had to do.

"I see you in myself," he declared. "And I see myself in you."

Then he leaned in, giving her a kiss.

She stiffened in surprise, then melted into it, even giving him a bit of tongue in return. Which was when Chauncy brought his left hand to her cheek, cupping it gently.

And at that moment, he felt a *shift*...and was suddenly Zella Trek, kissing his former self.

Chauncy drew backward, making a face...and Zella – now in his body – blinked, looking utterly confused.

"What...?" she blurted out, stumbling backward.

"Wow Chauncy," Valtora grumbled, glaring at Zella. Chauncy smiled.

"That's not Chauncy," he countered. "I am."

Valtora blinked, then her eyes widened...and she gasped.

"Chauncy!" she blurted out. "You...?"

"Switched bodies with her," Chauncy confirmed. "Which means she doesn't have any magical tattoos, because I don't."

"Which means she's like, super weak and pathetic!" Valtora concluded.

"Um...right," Chauncy grumbled. And grabbed Zella's staff – or rather, *his* staff – from her hands before she could think to use it. His Inkling hair was still wrapped around his Chauncy-body, trapping it in place anyway.

"I am *so* confused right now," Tip declared.

Chauncy chuckled, then frowned, eyeing the eyeball floating beside him. On a whim, he decided to touch it, willing it to return to his skin. And lo-and-behold, it worked, seeming to melt back into its customary place, a mere tattoo once more. Which was odd, because tattoos weren't magical to him...at least not in the way that they were to Zella. He shouldn't be able to use her magic.

Unless...

Anyone could use Chauncy's Staff of Wind once he made it. Perhaps Zella's tattoos were similar, in that her magic was in creating them and bringing them to life...but once they existed, they could be drawn out and put back into her skin at will. For the magic wasn't in the storing or retrieving, but in the act of creation.

"What now?" Valtora asked.

"I can empty her skin of tattoos," Chauncy offered, "...and then switch bodies again so..."

"Die, villain!" a heroic voice cried from the side. Chauncy turned, seeing King Pravus and Templeton hobbling awkwardly at him, swords poised to strike!

"No!" Valtora cried. The two men paused, and Valtora quickly explained what was going on.

"They're lying!" Zella blurted out. "*I'm* Chauncy!"

"No you're not," Chauncy retorted.

"You're really not," Valtora agreed. Pravus frowned, eyeing Chauncy, then Zella, critically.

"Then answer me a question," he told Zella. "Why didn't Valtora want to go to a banquet in her honor after defeating The Dark One?"

Zella blinked. Then stammered.

"She knew there'd be speeches and parades and toasts and polite applause," Chauncy answered with a smile.

"And tiny forks and shit," Valtora added with a smile of her own. Pravus eyed Zella, turning his blade on her.

"Your deceit is unmasked, vile villain," he declared. Then he paused. "What now?"

"I was going to drain all of her tattoos, then switch bodies again," Chauncy explained.

"An excellent plan," Templeton concurred.

"And here I thought you were a terrible Chosen One," Pravus mused. "Simply the worst, really. You almost killed poor Templeton here with your indiscriminate blast."

"Sorry," Chauncy offered.

"But you mostly made up for it by him not dying," Pravus continued. "And by neutralizing Zella Trek at the last minute."

"Thank you," Chauncy replied. "I..."

"...after most of your friends were gravely or mortally wounded," Pravus continued, eyeing Gavin and Nettie. And Rocky, who was stirring, but still had a big hole in his back. And Rooter who'd been vaporized save for a portion of his plant. And Chauncy's body, which was still missing an arm.

Chauncy grimaced.

"I take it back," Pravus stated. "You really are a terrible Chosen One."

"Not terrible," Templeton countered. "But perhaps barely adequate."

"At the razor's edge of inadequacy," Pravus compromised.

"Indeed," Templeton agreed.

"So anyway," Chauncy grumbled. "Guess I'll get rid of these tattoos."

"Wait," Valtora interjected. "I have an idea."

"What's that?"

"Switch bodies with me," she requested. Chauncy blinked.

"What?"

"*Do* it already," Valtora insisted, walking up to him. He shrugged, then touched Valtora with his left hand, focusing on seeing himself in her. Which was far easier than seeing himself in Zella, save for Tip's particular perspective, which was the reverse. He felt a *shift*, and then he was in Valtora's body…and Valtora was in Zella's. Her eyes widened, and she looked down at herself, breaking out into a huge smile.

"Aww *yeah*," she exclaimed.

"Why did you…" Chauncy began.

"Now switch bodies with yourself," Valtora interrupted. He blinked. "Just do it," she urged. Chauncy shrugged, touching his body's cheek…and switching with Zella. Which meant that he was now back in his own body, and Zella was in Valtora's.

"Why'd you…?" Chauncy began.

Valtora shushed him, then made a frowny-face, scrunching her eyebrows together. And suddenly her left hand turned to solid diamond, with a slight purple hue.

"Ha!" she exclaimed, opening and closing her diamond fingers.

And promptly spun around, punching Zella right in the frickin' head.

Zella's head snapped to the side with a *crack*, and she fell to the beach, her limbs spasming rhythmically. Then she stopped moving, staring blankly outward at nothing at all.

"Bitch," Valtora spat. And then spat on her.

"Oh," was all Chauncy could say.

"Huh," Harry said.

"Well," Pravus stated. And didn't quite know what else to say.

"You um…just punched your body," Chauncy notified Valtora. Who ignored him, kneeling down to check a pulse. Her smile broadened, and she stood again.

"Whelp, she's dead," Valtora declared.

# Chapter 42

Chauncy stared at the dead body of his fiancée – the love and light of his life, the woman he'd planned on spending the rest of his life with – in utter disbelief.

"What did you *do?*" he blurted out, turning to Zella. Or rather, Valtora in Zella's body.

"Well *duh*," Valtora replied. "I murdered her. Obviously."

"How could you do that!?" he demanded.

"Diamond fist," Valtora replied, displaying hers. "Doesn't take much of a punch either, honestly." She put a hand on her hip, eyeing the corpse with satisfaction. "Awesome, right?"

"But you just killed your own body!" he pressed.

"Yeah, but this one's *so* much better," she replied, running her hands over the more intriguing parts. "And I'm gonna bedazzle the *shit* out of it, just you wait."

"I'll wait," Harry offered, appearing quite intrigued.

"I'll pass," King Pravus piped in.

Chauncy had to admit that he was intrigued as well, not that he could admit it out loud. Even Peter was clearly up for waiting, as evidenced by the fact that he was obviously up…and waiting.

"Besides, I know you like it better," Valtora told Chauncy, crossing her hands over her chest and giving him a look that dared him to disagree.

"Poopy-dooz," he began. But Tip barged in.

"He totally does," the demon declared. "It isn't even a contest, really. Something about those tattoos and those purples eyes, and those incredible, luscious…"

"Shut up!" Chauncy blurted out, covering Tip with his hand over his robe.

"He's kind of a dick sometimes, isn't he?" Gavin quipped.

Everyone turned to stare at the man, Nettie with her mouth agape.

"Did you just make a joke?" she asked. Gavin smiled.

"I guess I did," he replied. "What can I say? I'm a wizard now," he added. "Work wasn't working for me, so now my work is play."

"A rhyme!" Valtora hissed, giving Chauncy a significant look. Which proved that she was in fact herself and not Zella.

"Guess you are a wizard," Nettie conceded. She smiled. "Welcome to the team," she added.

"Happy to help," Gavin replied. "It's the least I can do after everything you did for me." He turned to Chauncy. "Especially you, Chauncy."

"Well I don't know about that," Chauncy replied.

"You gave me a chance," Gavin insisted. "A second chance. And you showed me the Cave of Wonder so I could find the most valuable treasure of all."

"Knitting needles?" Nettie inquired, eyeing his holsters dubiously.

"Myself," Gavin corrected.

Chauncy smiled, for he knew precisely what Gavin was talking about. That was, he suspected, the path of every wizard-to-be. The journey to the Great Wood, then to the Cave of Wonder, and sometimes even to the summit of Mount Thrall...well, it was more than just a physical journey. A trip from point A to point B. No, it was a well-worn path to finding oneself. To rediscovering oneself, the person that the demands of society and so-called adulthood had kidnapped and hidden away.

He didn't have to say so to Gavin, of course. They understood each other at a glance. As all wizards did, having had the courage and luck to make the journey to being different again...by being more themselves than everyone else.

Chauncy smiled at the man...and then watched as Rocky got up, gently cupping Rooter's plant in his hands. The stone giant shook his head miserably, tears dripping down his blocky cheeks.

"Roooo...ter," he moaned.

And then something strange happened.

A glow appeared in the plant's remaining roots, traveling up its stem and leaves. That light shone on Rocky...and the hole in his back healed before their very eyes.

"Gasp!" Valtora gasped. "Rooter's still alive!"

"Let me see," Harry requested. Rocky handed Rooter to Harry, who frowned...and moments later, a medium-sized rock came out of the ground. "From deeper down," Harry explained when everyone gave him a questioning look. And with that, he fashioned a new golem-body for Rooter, one just like his old one. "It's gneiss," Harry said.

"Rooter!" Chauncy exclaimed, his heart soaring. Rooter smiled at them adorably, waving a little hand.

"So *coot*," Valtora gushed, clasping her hands before her heart.

"Can you heal everyone?" Chauncy requested. Rooter nodded at once, his plant-head bobbing cutely.

"Aww!" Valtora exclaimed.

With that, Rooter was passed around, healing each friend in turn. So that Nettie's burns were mended, Gavin's legs regrown, and Chauncy's left arm whole again. They even tried healing Valtora's body, despite her protestations. Which didn't work, To Valtora's immense satisfaction.

"Chaos!" Valtora blurted out, rushing to her baby resting in the sand. For he was still solid gold.

"I'll change him back," Gavin offered, producing his golden coin. He went up to Chaos and tapped the baby gently, returning him to flesh. And with a few shrieking breaths, his purple face pinked right up. Still, not taking any chances, Chauncy had Rooter try healing the poor kid. After which Valtora cradled Chaos in her arms, rocking him back and forth.

"Well," Chauncy declared with relief, after kissing Chaos's cheek. "It looks like we did it."

At that moment, Imperius appeared before them in a burst of blue sparkles, his twisty staff in hand. He eyed them all with a proud smile…even Valtora, who he must've recognized despite being in Zella's body.

"Impy!" Valtora gasped, rushing up to him and giving him a hug. Thereby verifying her identity once again. Imperius tolerated this, then pulled away, eyeing Chauncy.

"Very clever Chauncy," he congratulated. "You did well."

"Thanks," Chauncy replied, grinning like an idiot. All his life he'd hoped to have a great, powerful wizard like Imperius tell him such a thing. And now that it was happening, it was a dream come true.

*I did it*, he told himself, struck with the sudden feeling that he'd arrived. Sure, he hadn't come up with the idea to neutralize Zella by switching bodies with her right away, and had nearly died trying to do it the typical way. But as it turned out, his magic wasn't just to put stuff into stuff – and then pull it out again – but also to see things differently. Doing things the way everyone else would do them wasn't magical at all, it seemed. And every time he'd won the day, it'd been by seeing himself in others. With Zarzibar, then with The Dark One…and now with Chaos and eventually Zella.

"Zarzibar!" Chauncy blurted out, remembering the lich. He slapped himself in the forehead. "We could've used him to beat Zella!"

"Oh," Valtora replied. "Oops."

"You really aren't great Chosen Ones," King Pravus grumbled, shaking his head.

"Well, time to go," Imperius interjected, patting his belly. Which was really quite small for something so powerful. Thus showing that size wasn't everything…although Peter would probably disagree.

"Your gut's telling you that?" Valtora asked.

"It is," he confirmed with a wink. "I'm hungry."

"Oh."

"Goodbye all," Imperius stated. "I trust I'll see some of you again, and perhaps sooner than you might expect."

"Is *that* what your gut tells you?" Valtora pressed. He smirked.

"That's correct."

With that, he vanished in a burst of blue sparkles, which fell lazily to the sand.

"Wo*wee*," Chauncy breathed. For Imperius was in every way the wizard he imagined wizards would be.

"Well, I suppose," Nettie said, smoothing out her shirt. "Better get going. Already been away from the Order for too long." She turned to Harry. "You ready?"

"Sure," Harry answered.

"Already?" Chauncy asked, his face falling. Nettie smiled, patting him on the shoulder.

"I know kid," she replied. "Never seems like long enough, does it?"

"That's for sure," he agreed. The time they spent together was never quite what he wanted it to be, always ending abruptly and far too soon. "See you again in a bit?"

"You betcha kid," she agreed. "We'll be around, won't we Harry?"

"Long as I get to see her," Harry replied, gesturing at Valtora. Who beamed at him.

"Aww!" she gushed, leaping at him and giving him a big hug. She might as well have leapt on a statue, for Harry didn't budge at all. He hugged her back, giving Nettie an eyebrow-waggle while he did so. Nettie rolled her eyes, then turned back to Chauncy.

"Give 'er here kid," she told him, leaning in for a hug. He hugged her back, then pulled away. Nettie turned to Valtora. "You too Momma," she added.

"I'll miss you," Valtora promised, wiping away a tear.

"Must've got a few too many head injuries recently," Nettie replied. "'Cause I'll miss you too." She disengaged, hugging Rocky, then Rooter, and even Peter. Then she turned to Gavin. "All right," she told him. "Come on."

Gavin paused, then leaned in for a hug. Nettie hugged him back – for a bit longer than Harry found reasonable.

"You guys want a room?" Harry quipped.

"I might," Nettie replied, "…but I'm sure he doesn't."

"Don't know what yer missing," Harry told Gavin with a twinkling wink. Gavin ignored them both.

"I'll miss you too Harry," he stated. Harry chuckled, extending a hand, and Gavin shook it. And then winced, breaking away.

"Quite the grip," he stated, shaking his hand out.

"Like iron," Harry agreed.

"A man after my own heart," King Pravus stated. Chauncy blinked, having forgotten that the man was still there. "I'm afraid Templeton and I must be off as well," he declared. "Have to run a kingdom after all. Thanks for helping to defeat Zella Trek."

Nettie rolled her eyes at that, mouthing "helping."

"Want us to kneel?" Harry asked.

"I ain't doin' it," Nettie replied.

"I'd rather shake your hand," Pravus stated, extending a hand to Harry. Harry took it…and then squeezed. Pravus squeezed back, his massive forearms bulging, veins popping out of his skin. Harry's eyebrows went up, and he grinned, squeezing harder. Pravus smirked, his forearms seeming like they'd pop out of his flesh.

"Damn," Gavin breathed.

"Damn *sexy*," Valtora agreed.

At length, Harry did Pravus the honor of releasing his grip, and the men both inclined their heads at each other.

"You're the strongest I've met," Pravus declared.

"Same to you," Harry replied. "Got a grip like a vise."

"Deadlifts," Pravus explained. "Hook grip."

"They take away before they give," Templeton mused ruefully, stretching stiff legs.

"Indeed," Pravus agreed. "Had it not been for post-leg day, we would've surely defeated Zella ourselves."

"A likely scenario," Templeton concurred. "Leg day was her most powerful ally!"

"Uh huh," Nettie grumbled.

"Need a ride back to Borrin?" Pravus inquired of Chauncy and Valtora. "We know the way."

"Um…sure," Chauncy answered. "Actually, that'd be great." For, stuck on a floating island in the middle of a massive hole in the ocean, it wasn't clear how they'd get back otherwise.

"Very well," Pravus replied. "Come when you're ready." He turned to his cousin. "In any case, back to the dragon sweet, dearest Templeton?" Pravus prompted.

"A scenic flight home!" Templeton replied zestily. "I'd offer a race like the last time, but…"

"A race you'll have again!" Pravus declared. "For it is not the rate at which we run that matters, but the struggle past the resistance of our pain!"

With that, both men took off. Or rather, they hobbled awkwardly across the sand toward the dragon, with a symphony of groans, at times slipping and falling in the sand. Everyone watched them go in bemused disbelief. Chauncy was quite sure he'd never met a pair quite like them. He couldn't imagine what it'd be like being around them all the time, but he supposed it would be exhausting.

"That's the second time they rhymed," Valtora noted, her hands on her hips. "They *have* to be wizards!"

"At what, lifting weights?" Chauncy asked.

"Uplifting power," Harry noted.

"Shut up Harry," Nettie grumbled. "Nobody wants to hear your dumb jokes."

"Well I do," Harry countered.

"That's 'cause you're a nobody," she explained. He chuckled.

"I love you like nobody's business," he replied. A reply that earned him a reluctant smile…and a not-so-reluctant kiss.

"Aww," Valtora cooed. "I hope we're like that one day," she told Chauncy.

"I think we already are," he replied.

Valtora strapped Chaos to her chest, after removing her wrap from her dead former body. Then she leaned over the corpse, putting a hand on its cheek.

"Saying goodbye?" Chauncy inquired. She gave him a look.

"Hell no," she replied. "We're taking it with us."

"Um…what?"

"We're totally taking it with us," she repeated. "I wanna keep it."

"To bury it?"

"To *keep* it," she repeated.

"But…it'll rot," Chauncy pointed out.

"Not anymore," she countered proudly. "I bedazzled it. Now it'll *never* decompose. Like those flowers back home I told you about, remember?"

Chauncy did remember, at least that she'd threatened to bedazzle *his* corpse after he died. So that she could have his preserved corpse forever like a mannequin at the shop.

"I don't think…" he began.

"Good," she replied. "You shouldn't." And it was clear from the look she gave him that this wasn't up for debate. So it was that she had Rocky pick her corpse up and haul it toward the waiting dragon. Everyone else followed behind, including Harry and Nettie, who apparently decided to see them off. Valtora reached out to hold Chauncy's hand, and he smiled, taking it. While ogling her new body, then feeling a bit ashamed that he was doing so.

"This is gonna be *fun*," Tip declared…and started to wake up, to Chauncy's dismay.

"Sorry poopy-dooz," he said.

"Pfft," she scoffed. "That's totally why I switched bodies," she explained. "Now you can be more attracted to Zella and it doesn't matter, 'cause she's *me*."

"Pretty clever," Harry mused.

"Pretty psychotic," Nettie retorted.

"I *am* pretty and psychotic," Valtora declared. "I'm a psycho homicidal hussy *bitch*. So like, watch out and shit."

She executed one of her patented hair-tosses then. Or at least she tried to. For she was bald.

"Well crap," she swore. Then she frowned, scrunching up her face.

"Looks like that's what she's doin'," Harry noted.

Suddenly the tattoo of hair on Valtora's scalp sprung outward, giving her a full head of luxurious black hair. She smiled in triumph, executing a hair-toss again…and this time, it was to spectacular effect. Whether or not everyone slowed down to experience it, or time itself had slowed down, Chauncy might never know. But *damn*.

"And I'm up," Tip announced. Accurately, to Chauncy's embarrassment.

They reached the dragon, which had a rope ladder hanging from its right side. Gavin began the long climb up, and then Rocky and Rooter. Chauncy paused then, glancing at Peter.

"Um…how's Peter going to come?" he asked.

"I'll help," Valtora replied. "One more for the road, Petey?"

"I mean on the dragon," Chauncy clarified, blushing a bit.

"Have to ask the dragon first," Valtora told him. "Needs to be consensual."

"I mean how's Peter going to ride the dragon home!" Chauncy blurted out, blushing furiously now.

Peter snorted…and Nettie came to his rescue, sending a fine mist of water Peter's way. It revealed a rainbow…and Peter jumped through it, vanishing from sight. Chauncy regarded this feat, then gestured for Valtora to climb up next. Which she did. Chauncy took the rear, doing his best not to ogle Valtora's rear on the way up.

"Look at my *butt*," Valtora ordered. So, having been given explicit permission, Chauncy did.

Then, with King Pravus's mighty dragon mounted, they soared to heights previously unknown. And that is how Chauncy, Valtora, Chaos, and their dear friends were at long last taken home.

# Chapter 43

Upon his return to Cumulus, King Pravus the Eighth found his castle's repairs well under way. With his kingdom once again secure, and the various logistics of its repair being handled by capable, if dreadfully boring, hands, he was finally able to do what *he* wanted to do. Which of course was to go to the gym.

So it was that he found himself stepping through the great double-doors into the gymnasium he'd designed, with his dear cousin Templeton faithfully at his side. It was ridiculously early in the morning, the sun still sunken below the horizon. Which meant of course that the gym was empty save for them.

"Good to be home, isn't it?" Templeton mused with a smile on his lips.

"Good indeed," Pravus agreed.

"What day is it today?" Templeton inquired. And Pravus knew that his cousin didn't mean what day of the week. For as any avid lifter knew, weeks were not divided into days but body parts.

"Seeing as our last workout was leg day, I say we do shoulders, biceps, and triceps," Pravus replied.

"Skull crushers?" Templeton proposed.

"You read my mind, dearest cousin," Pravus replied.

They went at once to one of the flat benches, and Pravus grabbed a fifty pound barbell, setting it near the head of the bench. Then he laid down, sliding backward until the bar was touching the top of his head. He grabbed the barbell with an overhand grip, and lifted it in swinging motion, making sure his upper arms didn't move more than a smidge.

"Perfect form," Templeton declared, even as Pravus brought the bar slowly back to tap the top of his head. And as usual, Pravus did twenty total reps, focusing on maintaining his form throughout. When he was done, he set the bar down, and Templeton took his turn.

"Marvelous," Pravus purred, eyeing Templeton's form…in more ways than one.

Pravus's thorough study of anatomy had taught him many things about the human arm. The triceps made up two-third's of the upper arm's diameter, and the long head of the triceps was the largest of the tricep's three parts. The skull crusher was the perfect exercise to stress this particular part, and thus was critical in developing the beefiest of upper arms. Sadly, most lifters neglected to do this exercise, focusing on their biceps to grow their arms. Thus they barely filled out their sleeves, while Pravus simply *burst* out of his.

When Templeton was done, he returned the barbell to its proper place, as any proper and considerate lifter would do. Which, unfortunately, was the minority of gym-goers. An important lesson to learn early on was that the majority of humanity was disappointingly disappointing. It was a lesson the gym had taught Pravus well.

"Two hundred?" Templeton inquired.

"A good start," Pravus replied.

With that, he commenced with lifting this much heavier weight, with precisely the care he'd given earlier. Each repetition done properly and safely, and never to the point of failure. The risk of injury was too great to take, the idiotic urge to optimize one's muscular growth a terrible thing indeed. For in the end, it hardly mattered whether the journey to the peak of one's potential took a year or two longer. To climb a mountain, one merely had to continue to put one foot in front of the other…and take care not to fall.

In this way, Pravus had surpassed those who'd compulsively destroyed their bodies taking risk after risk. And he'd done so without any serious injuries whatsoever, ensuring he would be able to continue to enjoy his passion well into the future.

He finished his set, then watched Templeton take a turn. And after a few more sets, they'd stimulated quite enough, and it was time to move on.

They commenced with the lateral deltoid flies, and then the bicep curls of course. And then the most important – and overlooked – exercise of arm day: the face-pull. An exercise that, in Pravus's opinion, should be done every time someone went to the gym. For without it, one risked long-term shoulder pain beyond imagination.

When at last their workout was done, the two returned to the castle by way of a three-mile run. Pravus found himself drawn to the part of the castle still under repair after Fang's attack, and he stopped there with Templeton at his side, watching as the construction experts worked. They were lifting heavy stone and mortaring them to a new wall…and for some reason Pravus had the sudden urge to help. For building a castle was not unlike building one's muscles; one brick at a time.

So, being king, he would do what he wanted, optics be damned. He eyed Templeton.

"Fancy erecting my tower, dearest cousin?" he inquired.

"It would make a wonderful finisher," Templeton replied with a smile. Pravus smiled back, struggling to contain himself.

"Indeed it would," he agreed. "Come, Templeton!"

"At once, my liege!" Templeton replied.

They rushed forward to help the workers, who were flabbergasted at their monarch's presence, much less his desire to help. And they watched in amazement as their king lifted stone that normally took three men to heft, doing so with ease…and with flawless body mechanics, naturally. Indeed, more than a few of these workers were so inspired by Pravus that they vowed to join him in the gym the very next day.

That was the power of magic, to so inspire others to want to experience it. For a man or woman who had a magical relationship with the world stood out among those who did not. It didn't matter so much whether that relationship was with weights, or water, or earth or yarn or beautiful things. Whatever it was, those who witnessed it found themselves struck in a primal place, a forgotten part of their hearts. A place of wonder, of possibility. Not in a particular accomplishment, but in a way of being.

So, by being so completely himself, Pravus was an inspiration to everyone else.

This, he realized as he continued to work, was perhaps the real function of leadership. Not so much to order around as to inspire. For the throne gave him the power of command, allowing him to compel others to do his will, willingly or not. But by being willing to jump in and do the work himself, he set an example for others.

That was the lesson his most recent adventure had given Pravus. That everyone had their place in his kingdom, whether high or low or somewhere in between. But as king, he could not be content to rule merely from the safety of his throne. No, he had to show his people that he was willing to jump in the fray…whether by leaping off a fire-breathing dragon to slay a great big serpent, or by traveling to a mystical island to stop its vile master. He couldn't – and shouldn't – do everything himself, as his near-defeat by The Dark One had taught him. But every once and again, he should jump on in, and show his people that though he was above everyone else, that at the same time, nothing was beneath him. And while his people would still have to kneel in his presence, it was worth far more when they wanted to...because he'd earned it.

# Chapter 44

After returning home to Southwick – and leaving Rocky and Gavin behind – Chauncy and Valtora fell back into their regular routine. Or rather, their routine with Chaos added to the mix. The little bastard changed things a bit, and took center stage far more often than Chauncy would've liked. Being the loudest and thus least pleasant member of the family, Chaos was at times quite the handful. But as long as Chauncy and Valtora took care of each other – and themselves – first, everything would be alright.

As such, they rarely required Rooter's aid, though they'd taken the little golem home with them for a bit. At least until they could be sure they wouldn't kill the poor kid by accident or sudden unexpected rage.

So it was that Chauncy found himself waking up one bright, sunny morning, three days after returning home. He yawned, then rubbed his eyes, then stretched…and turned to find two gorgeous purple eyes staring at him. Not Valtora's, but Zella Trek's.

"Gah!" he blurted out, flinching away.

She cackled, sounding very much like the evil wizard she was.

"Never gets old," she mused, grinning at him. "Can't believe you still fall for it."

"I was with your old body for a long time," Chauncy said in his defense. "It's going to take more than a couple of days to get used to this."

"I hope I never do," Tip mused, having already gotten up even before Chauncy had. Tip was an early riser, it seemed. Valtora eyed the demon.

"You look stiff, Tip," she told him. "Need a massage?"

"Please do," the demon replied.

But before she could, her eyes widened, and she let out a horrified gasp.

"We slept all night," she exclaimed. He frowned.

"And?" he asked. Then it occurred to him precisely what that meant: that Chaos hadn't woken up. "Uh oh," he blurted out, terror striking him.

"Whelp, he's dead," Valtora declared.

They both leapt out of bed, rushing to the baby's crib at the far end of the room. To Chauncy's relief, Chaos was *not* dead, but rather sleeping peacefully. Still, Chauncy watched like a hawk for the rise and fall of his little chest just to be sure.

"Whew," Valtora breathed, shaking her head. "Scared the shit outta me."

"Me too," he admitted. "Guess he slept through the night."

"They do that?" she asked.

"I mean I don't know," Chauncy replied.

They both watched the baby for a while longer, pondering this unlikely event. No, not unlikely…*magical*. For even though they were full-fledged wizards, they'd both discovered that no magic was more powerful than a good night's sleep – and of course a belly full of food – at least when it came to the subject of one's mood.

Tip stared at them both, clearly vexed.

"Massage?" he reminded Valtora impatiently.

"Oh, right," Valtora replied.

With that, she commenced with making good on her offer, and it wasn't long before Tip was fast asleep. This meant Chauncy could focus on other things…which, after making sure one more time that Chaos wasn't dead, meant cooking breakfast for his poopy-dooz.

Down to the kitchen he went, donning his chef's apron and nothing more. Thus commenced the sizzling of the ol' sausage and eggs. It wasn't long before the sublime scent of breakfast summoned Valtora downstairs, with a now-awake Chaos in her arms. She went right to Grandma Little's old kitchen table, one that Chauncy refused to replace with something newer. For every time he sat down at it, it reminded him of his breakfasts with her. He heated up some tea for himself, and then served breakfast, sitting down opposite Valtora.

"Titty pop!" she declared, and did just that, releasing the part in question and pressing Chaos to it. Which shouldn't have worked, of course, considering that Zella's body hadn't given birth. But such was Valtora's magic that in bedazzling these particular parts – among others – she'd given them the magical ability to make milk.

"Breast," Chauncy corrected, for it was only proper. Still, he stared in a way that was anything but proper. For as he'd said before, he still hadn't gotten used to the idea of Valtora in Zella's body. Her new body had been plenty captivating before, but having bedazzled it, Valtora had truly outdone herself. And Zella. And every other woman in Southwick…and perhaps the world…for that matter.

Chauncy sighed, smiling happily. For despite their latest harrowing journey, everything had turned out alright. His family was safe and sound, and he finally believed in himself. Not just as a wizard, but as a father. He was hardly perfect at either, and with time, would hopefully improve. But at least he could say he was adequate…which at the moment, was good enough for him. He'd spent so much of his time as a wizard beating himself up for not being better than he was, and it hadn't helped one bit. So instead, he'd decided to enjoy getting better rather than punishing himself into it. And most importantly, to enjoy the wizard – and the father – that he was right here, right now.

For taking joy in being a father – in spending time with his son – was the surest way to be a good father, regardless of the mistakes he made along the way. After all, the biggest mistake of all would be to *not* enjoy being a father to his son.

Valtora finished eating at about the same time that Chaos did, and they both burped in unison.

"Thank you baby," she told Chauncy, leaning over the table for a kiss. Chauncy stood and kissed her…and as usual, her kiss turned dangerous. The kind of kiss that could wake a demon mod from a well-deserved slumber…and did.

"Mmf," Tip groaned. And promptly fell back asleep.

Their breakfast had, Chauncy got ready for work, going back upstairs to put on some underwear – from the special drawer, of course – and his wizard's robe. Then he went downstairs, smiling at Valtora, who'd strapped Chaos to her chest.

"Ready m'Lady?" he inquired.

"Ready m'Lord," she replied. "Grab thine staff and be off!"

Chauncy did so, opening the door for her, and earning a curtsey for his efforts. He did a little bow in return, then followed her out, locking the door behind him. They went down the steps to the sidewalk, turning right as per their routine. Hand-in-hand they went, not so much walking as strolling. For being in the presence of his love and his son was precisely where Chauncy wanted to be. As such, the stroll *was* his destination…and thus with every step he took, he'd already arrived.

That, he supposed as they made their way toward the city center, was the point the Cave of Wonder had tried to teach him. Those endless fields of grass he'd traversed hadn't merely been to frustrate or confuse him. For when everywhere was identical to everywhere else, no matter where he went, he was in the same place. And that was here and now, the only time and place where magic could be found.

Perhaps more importantly, no matter where or when he was, he was with himself. The magic of life was *his* relationship with the world...one that no one else could ever quite share. A fact that he hoped he could somehow teach his future students, for his magic school was due to open very soon now. There was no book or rubric that could impart such understanding, but perhaps there was another way. One that didn't involve the typical journey through the Gate to the Great Wood, then down the Cave of Wonder.

At length they reached the courtyard in the city center. As they neared the statue of Archibald Merrick, Chauncy let go of Valtora's hand in preparation for her ritualistic punching. But to his surprise, she passed the statue without her customary violence.

"Um...?" he asked, stopping and turning to face her.

"Hmm?" she replied. He gave her an odd look.

"Aren't you going to, you know," he asked, then pantomimed a left hook.

"Nah," she answered. "Gavin's one of us now."

They continued across the courtyard toward A Little Magic, and Chauncy took the time to contemplate this change. He supposed it made a kind of sense. After having hoarded magic, then nearly destroyed it, magic had in turn saved Gavin. An act of forgiveness in a way...just as Valtora had shown in not beating the likeness of Gavin's grandfather. And as Gavin had shown Valtora in forgiving her for murdering his wife.

"Wanna place bets?" Valtora asked, giving him a mischievous smile. He frowned.

"Hmm?"

"About Mrs. Thimblethorp," she explained. "I bet she totally kicks the bucket this week."

"Poopy dooz," he chided. "Come on now."

"In fact, I bet it's today," she continued. "Let's up the ante," she added. For they usually bet a silver coin. "Something *big*."

"Honey..."

"Place your *bet* already," she insisted.

"Fine," he sighed. "I bet no."

"Ooo, prizes!" she said. "What do we get if we win?"

Chauncy shrugged.

"I'll do that thing you like if *you* win," she promised. "And if *I* win, you have to do what *I* want."

"What's that?" he inquired. Her smile broadened.

"You'll see."

"Does it involve death or permanent injury?" he pressed.

"I mean, not to your *body*," she replied.

"Fine," he decided. "It's a bet."

"Promise?" she pressed. Which should have worried him.

"Promise," he agreed.

They reached the end of the courtyard, then crossed the street, walking toward the front door of the shop. Chauncy found himself gazing up at the large sign above the entrance: "A Little Magic," it read, with the word "Little" larger than the others. It was, he realized now, not just a play on words, but a metaphor for Grandma Little's favorite saying: "Littles do a lot."

"That we do," he murmured, smiling at the sign. For his mother was Light incarnate, his father Space itself. And he was a wizard of some repute...and the father of Chaos to boot. He'd saved magic and put The Dark One in his place. And by seeing himself in his mortal enemy, he'd defeated her as well, stopping her from attacking the Order of Mundus with a body-switching spell.

For a shopkeeper from Borrin, it wasn't bad at all. Littles *did* do a lot...and Chauncy only wished that Grandma Little was still alive to see what he'd done.

He sighed, reaching the door and unlocking it, then ramming it open with his shoulder. He proceeded to gallantly gesture for Valtora to go through first, as was only proper.

"After you m'Lady," he stated. She went inside, and he followed behind. Valtora went to the broom closet to get his broom, and took his staff in return. With that he commenced with the ritual of the sweeping, rounding up innumerable dust bunnies and evicting them from the shop. With a considerable amount of gusto, he might add, making great sweeping motions punctuated by various heroic declarations. Then, his task complete, he sank to one knee, bowing before his love.

"It...is done," he gasped, clutching at his chest with his free hand.

"My *hero*," Valtora gushed. "Let me take thy weapon so that thou canst claim thine reward!"

He did so, and she returned the broom to its proper place. They sat side-by-side behind the counter then, and Valtora eyed Chauncy with a devilish grin.

"What?" he asked, struck with a pang of fear. For when Valtora gave him devilish looks, it meant she was up to no good. And no good generally meant a fair amount of bad. In lieu of reply, something emerged from her back: an Inkling woman...Zella's doppelganger, in fact. "Oh!" he blurted out, nearly tipping out of his stool.

"Shh," Valtora scolded. And with that, the Inkling crouched below the counter. What happened next was precisely what he'd hoped and feared might happen. He issued his customary complaints, but in the end it was to no avail. For such was the Inkling's prowess that his reward was rapidly claimed. He giggled involuntarily, then shot Valtora a glare. But she only smiled sweetly back at him.

"How was that?" she asked.

"The best," he confessed. And it was true. Valtora's smile broadened.

"Good," she replied. "I've been practicing."

Chauncy smiled back at her...and then frowned, suddenly quite concerned with what that might have entailed. But before he had a chance to ask, there came a *dong*.

"Welcome to A Little Magic!" Chauncy greeted automatically, with an equally automatic Grandma Little smile. To his surprise, none other than Mr. Schmidt came in to the shop. An elderly man, tall and thin, his back bent with age, and possessed of thick glasses over which he peered – or rather leered – at Valtora. "Mr. Schmidt," Chauncy said, trying not to wince. For the creepy old man had once been a regular at the shop, until Chauncy'd refused to sell his special lotion. "What're you...um, doing here?"

"Heard you were bringing back the lotion," Mr. Schmidt replied. Chauncy frowned.

"Huh?"

"Addie told me," the old man explained. "Before you went on your little trip."

It took Chauncy a moment to recall the particulars of why Addie might've had that impression, and he blushed, shooting a glare at Valtora.

"When's it coming back?" Mr. Schmidt demanded. While continuing to leer at Valtora. In even more creepy a way than he'd looked at Valtora's original self.

"I'm afraid Addie was misinformed," Chauncy replied apologetically. "We're not bringing it back."

"What?"

"Not bringing it back, sorry," Chauncy told him. Mr. Schmidt turned to look at him – for the first time since entering the shop – and the look was not a pleased one.

"It's not right what you did to poor Valtora," he chided, pointing a knobby finger at Chauncy. "Shame on you!"

With that, Mr. Schmidt harrumphed, leering at Valtora one more time before exiting the shop. With as disappointed a *dong* as the last time he'd done so. Chauncy sighed, feeling a familiar frustration. For as far as everyone in Southwick was concerned, he'd ditched his fiancée after the birth of their son, and had replaced her with a very naughty-looking woman. One covered in tattoos and quite provocatively dressed and endowed. He'd of course attempted to tell people the truth, but few agreed to listen, and those who did listen rarely believed him. Thus Chauncy had to live with the fact that most were silently judging him for having left his former love for another woman…and for having a kinky predilection for women with diamond left hands.

*Dong!*

The door opened, and this time it was none other than Mrs. Gilson, one of his most loyal customers. In fact, she'd been coming to A Little Magic since before Chauncy'd been born. He gave her a big smile, rushing around the counter to come to her aid. For despite using a cane, she had a hard time getting around.

"Good *morning* Mrs. Gilson!" he greeted, taking her arm. "What can I do for you today?"

"Not a thing," she answered, yanking her arm away. And glaring at him, or so he assumed. With the elderly, it was hard to tell the difference between a glare and a peer. His suspicion was confirmed when she slapped his hand, then pointed an arthritic finger at him. "For shame!" she snapped.

"Um…pardon?" he asked. She shifted her finger-point to Valtora.

"Leaving your poor fiancée for this…*harlot*," Mrs. Gilson spat, eyeing Valtora's tattoos with particular disgust. "How *could* you Chauncy?"

307

"Actually, a harlot's a whore," Valtora pointed out. "I just drew on my skin."

"Now now Mrs. Gilson," Chauncy began in his defense, "…you see, I…"

"Your grandmother would turn in her grave if she knew what you were up to!" Mrs. Gilson declared, raising her cane high in the air. And promptly tipping over. Chauncy caught her before she fell, righting her. And earned another slap across the hand for his heroics.

"Mrs. Gilson, I can…"

"And taking your poor son away from his mother!" the old woman stated, looking utterly aghast. She gasped, covering her mouth in horror, then her poor heart. Her jowls trembled as she glared at him. "You're a *monster* Chauncy. A monster!"

With that, she turned about, shooting Chauncy one last glare before *click-clacking* out of the shop. Chauncy watched her go, then sighed, slumping into his stool.

"Great," he muttered. "Just great."

"They'll come around," Valtora reassured him. Chauncy gave her a look.

"Yeah right," he muttered. "Everyone in town thinks I'm a…"

*Dong!*

Another customer entered the shop, and Chauncy braced himself for what was to come. But to his surprise, it was none other than Addie. His automatic A Little Magic smile transformed into a genuine one, for Addie was always welcome in his shop. She gave a little smile back, to his relief.

"Hi Chauncy," she greeted. Then her gaze went to Valtora, and she did a double-take, freezing in place. "Um…?"

"Hi Addie," Valtora greeted, even giving a wave. With her diamond hand, which glittered in the sunlight. Addie frowned.

"Who…?" she asked, glancing back at Chauncy.

"It's Valtora," he told her. "She just looks different."

"Got a new body," Valtora informed Addie. "You likey?" she asked, standing up to display it.

"I…I mean I do," Addie replied. "The tattoos are…a lot," she added.

"Badass, right?" Valtora asked. Addie grimaced, eyeing Chauncy.

"What can I do for you today, Addie?" he inquired.

"Oh, nothing," she replied. He frowned.

"Is there anything you'd like to buy?" he pressed.

"Um…that's not really why I'm here," she confessed.

"You're not here to tell me what a horrible person I am, are you?" he pressed. "No one in town seems to believe Valtora's still Valtora."

"Oh goodness no," Addie replied. She hesitated, then reached into her purse, pulling out a rod. A medium-sized silver rod with a small purple crystal at its head. Chauncy immediately recognized it, for she'd bought it from him over a year ago. It was magic, of course, having the power to absorb courage from the people around her and give that courage to her. Upon wielding it, her posture shifted, and she stood up quite a bit straighter, her eye-contact becoming more direct.

"It's Mrs. Thimblethorp," she declared solemnly. "She's dead."

Chauncy's eyes widened in horror, and Valtora stood bolt upright from her stool.

"YES!" Valtora exclaimed, pumping her fist in triumph. Addie blinked, and Chauncy stared at Valtora in horror.

"Honey!" he gasped.

"Ha!" Valtora cried, beaming at him. "I win!"

"Honey, a dear beloved friend has just died!" he protested.

"Well *yeah*," Valtora replied. "But I mean it wasn't like she didn't have it coming."

"What?!"

"She was *old*," Valtora explained, making a face. "*Too* old if you ask me."

"You can't be too old!" he shot back.

"She wanted to die," Valtora insisted, putting her hands on her hips. "She even told us, remember?"

Chauncy frowned, recalling that she had, in fact, told them that. "Oh."

"So she got what she wanted," Valtora concluded with a smug smile. "So I'm right. And I win our bet."

"Your…bet?" Addie interjected. Valtora nodded happily.

"We make a bet every week that this is the week Mrs. Thimblethorp will kick the bucket," she explained. Chauncy buried his face in his hands, suddenly wishing that he could join Mrs. Thimblethorp in the act of bucket-kicking.

"You do?" Addie pressed incredulously, turning her gaze to Chauncy. Chauncy kept his face in his hands, trying desperately to get his heart to stop.

"Yup," Valtora confirmed. Addie stared at them for a bit longer, then shook her head.

"That's *highly* inappropriate," she chided.

309

"We're not good people," Valtora explained. And clearly had no shame whatsoever at admitting it. Addie considered this.

"You are," she countered. She gave a guilty smile. "Sometimes I have bad thoughts too," she added. "But unless I touch this rod, I don't have the courage to admit them."

"Speaking of which," Valtora replied, nudging Chauncy, "…you owe me my reward."

"Huh?" he asked, lifting his face from his hands. Valtora smiled at him, then eyed Addie. Then turned back to him. Then eyed Addie again. Then waggled her eyebrows. And then made an "O" with one hand, and…

"No!" he blurted out, slapping her hands down.

"Your reward?" Addie asked Valtora. Who walked out from behind the counter, leaning in to whisper in Addie's ear.

"No!" Chauncy cried in horror, but it was too late. Addie's eyes widened, and she covered her mouth with one hand. "Addie, I…"

"When?" Addie asked.

"Tonight work for you?" Valtora asked. "I'll take your kids at my house."

"That works," Addie agreed.

"You've got him 'til noon tomorrow," Valtora added. "Morning sex is the *best*."

"Honey!" Chauncy protested.

"If he wusses out, just have him hold your magic rod," Valtora recommended. "He's wanted this for like, *decades* and shit."

"We both might need to hold it," Addie confessed.

"Come by after dinner," Valtora told her.

"See you then," Addie replied. And with that, she left the shop with a *dong*, and the promise of another later on. Chauncy lifted his face from his hands, shooting Valtora a vicious glare.

"No," he told her.

"Yes," she replied.

"No!"

"Yes!"

"I'm not doing it," he announced, crossing his arms over his chest. And attempting a jawline-ripple. Which had absolutely no effect whatsoever, to his dismay. He could hardly hope to out-jawline-ripple Valtora, who practiced in front of a mirror several times a day.

"You promised," she reminded him.

"Well I break my promise," he retorted.

"You can't!"

"I can too," he countered. "We're not good people, remember?"

"Fine," Valtora replied. "Then you get to take care of Chaos every day and night for a week."

Chauncy blinked.

"Excuse me?"

"You heard me," she told him. "A whole week. Make it *two* weeks for being a dick about it."

Chauncy stared at her, then at Chaos. Then back at her. She raised an eyebrow at him.

"After dinner?" he asked.

"Right," she confirmed.

Chauncy sighed, his shoulders slumping. He stared at the door of the shop glumly, the vim and vigor he'd felt that morning gone. For while the magic of magic was here and now, his mind had been cast into the future. And the future was where anxiety lived, and dread, and all sorts of other terrible things. Most of which he was feeling right now.

"Well, I have to say I'm having a simply *marvelous* day," Tip proclaimed.

"Shut up Tip," Chauncy grumbled. And to his relief, the magical mod did just that.

*Dong!*

The front door opened yet again, and this time it was none other than Ginny Smithers who stepped in. A distinguished-looking man in his eighties, wearing a sharp-looking white suit...and a white tie, and white shoes, and white hair to match. He was the owner of the second and third floors of the shop...and thus, the man who was selling the second floor to Chauncy for the magic school. He fixed Chauncy with an apologetic look.

"Hello Chauncy," he greeted. "Have you heard the terrible news?"

"About Mrs. Thimblethorp?" Chauncy guessed. Ginny Smithers nodded gravely.

"Indeed," he replied. He put a hand to his heart. "She was a dear friend," he declared. "A woman with a wonderful heart. A tragedy that her daughter died last year. I suspect Mrs. Thimblethorp died of a broken heart."

"Um...right," Chauncy replied. For, as he recalled, Mrs. Thimblethorp's relationship with her daughter had been less than ideal.

311

"Nah," Valtora said cheerfully. "She wished her daughter had never been born. Hated her guts."

Mr. Smithers blinked.

"I mean, that's what she told us anyway," Valtora continued.

"And you are…?" the old man inquired.

"Valtora," Chauncy answered. "She switched bodies using my magic. It's a long story."

"Ah," Mr. Smithers replied, looking not at all convinced.

"What can I do for you today?" Chauncy asked.

"It isn't so much what you can do for me, but what has been done for you," the old man answered. "Mrs. Thimblethorp happened to be a rather wealthy woman. And you may be correct regarding her relationship with her late daughter."

"We totally are," Valtora confirmed.

"The lawyer on the third floor happens to be in charge of executing Mrs. Thimblethorp's will," Ginny Smithers told them. "Her daughter died a year ago, and she doesn't have any other family."

"I see," Chauncy replied.

"But she did leave something for you," he continued. He reached into his suit pocket then, retrieving a long white envelope and handing it to Chauncy. "Go on," he prompted.

Chauncy frowned, opening the letter and withdrawing what appeared to be a check. A check, in fact, with numbers on it, addressed to him. And as he studied these numbers, he found that they'd been arranged in such a way as to represent one large number. A *very* large number.

"Oh my," he breathed, reading said number. And then reading it again.

"She was quite fond of you," Ginny Smithers stated. "It came with a letter," he added. Chauncy blinked, then reached into the envelope again, finding a folded-up letter within. He unfolded it, then started to read.

*Dear Chauncy,*

*I do hope this letter finds you and your wonderful family well. And me well and dead, otherwise you really shouldn't be reading this.*

*When I heard that you'd gone off on another adventure, I suspected I wouldn't last the time 'til your return. I only wish I could've met that dear child of yours before you'd gone! I hope that it's a child that's easy to love, so that it'll be a joy to do so rather than a chore.*

*I've lived a long life, and I wish it'd been a great one. But alas, unlike you, most of my adventures have been in my head. I'm afraid I waited for just the right time to take a chance, only the time I waited for never came. It was always there in the present...the only place I didn't look for it. A fate far worse than death, to realize this when one is too old to start the life they were always looking forward to.*

*I've accumulated a great deal in not spending it, just as I accumulated my years. After seeing the life your adventures have given you, I realized what I had to do: support your magic school, in hopes that you convince others not to do what I did, living their life waiting to live.*

*Good luck, dear Chauncy. Enjoy what you have while you have it. And teach others to do the same. I'm no wizard, but if there's one thing I've learned in all my time, it's that there's magic in a life lived to its fullest, as I never lived mine.*

*I simply adore you,*
*Betty Thimblethorp*

Chauncy swallowed past a sudden lump in his throat, his vision blurring with tears. He reread the letter, then folded it with utmost care, replacing it in the envelope.

"Thank you," he murmured. Whether to Ginny Smithers or Mrs. Thimblethorp, he wasn't sure. But he felt in that moment most grateful for what he'd been given, far more for the letter than any numbers.

"That should cover the cost of the dance studio and far more," Mr. Smithers stated. "She must have truly loved you, Chauncy."

"More than I ever knew," Chauncy replied. And he felt a bit guilty that he hadn't spent more time with poor Mrs. Thimblethorp, knowing now how she regarded him.

"I'll see you next week," Ginny Smithers stated, "...for the grand opening of your school. Until then," he added.

"Goodbye," Chauncy stated. And with that, the man left.

Chauncy sighed, feeling quite out of sorts. The day had just begun, after all, and already so much had happened. Such was the life of a wizard, he supposed. A life where more things happened in a day than happened for regular folks in a year. Indeed, he'd lived more in the last year and a half than he had in the thirty years prior. Thanks to Nettie and Harry…and of course, his poopy-dooz.

"Gimmee," Valtora ordered, snatching the check from the counter. She studied it…and her eyes widened. "Oh *fuck* yeah!" she cried, thrusting her diamond fist up in triumph. "We're *rich!*"

"We were rich before the money," he pointed out. She paused, then lowered her fist.

"That's true," she conceded. She smiled at him, then snuggled up to his shoulder.

"Love you poopy-dooz," he told her.

"Reowr," she replied.

Chauncy blinked, then realized the reply had come not from Valtora, but from his lap. He looked down…and saw ZoMonsterz there. He was in the midst of petting her; for how long he'd being doing so, he couldn't be sure. She purred contentedly, gazing up at him with purple-pink eyes.

Loving eyes. *Sexy* eyes.

He flinched, then relaxed, smiling ruefully.

"I don't think I'll ever get used to that," he confessed.

"She loves you *so* much," Valtora said. "Just like Mrs. Thimblethorp. And me."

"Aww," he replied.

"And Addie," she added, quite unnecessarily. He grimaced.

"About that," he began.

"Two weeks if you pull out," Valtora warned.

"I won't," Tip promised.

"Shut up Tip!" Chauncy snapped.

"She *does* want one more kid," Valtora told him. "She never had a boy."

"Honey!"

"You can count on me," Tip reassured.

"Can we change the subject already?" Chauncy pleaded, having had quite enough of this nonsense for a day.

"Fine," Valtora replied. "Wanna get hitched?"

Chauncy blinked.

"Huh?"

"I know you want to get married and stuff," she said. "So let's just do it already."

"You really mean that?" he asked, daring to hope. "I thought you said it was just legal bullshit."

"That's the whole point," she replied. "Then you legally have to give me half of that sweet-ass check."

He rolled his eyes at her, and she cackled. Then she held his hand.

"I mean it," she insisted. "If you want to get married, I'll marry you."

"Do *you* want to?" he asked.

"I want you to be happy," she answered. "So if it makes you happy, I'll be happy to do it."

"Alright," he agreed. "Should we set a date?"

"Today," she replied. He blinked.

"Today?"

"Before dinner," she stated. He frowned.

"But...I thought..."

"Then you can go off with Addie," she explained. "And I can spend tomorrow reclaiming you."

"But..."

"Then I'll have a great story to tell people," she continued, clearly getting into it now. "How you like, totally cheated on me on our wedding night with your childhood crush!"

"Valtora!"

"You think they hate you now," she continued with a chortle. "Just *wait*."

"Enough," he pleaded. "Please."

And to his relief, she ended this particular conversation. With a sudden frown.

"Well crap," she muttered.

"What?" he asked, dreading what was coming next.

"I forgot my engagement ring on my corpse," she explained. "I'll have to go home and get it before we go to the justice of the peace."

"Oh," Chauncy replied. For Valtora, ever a woman of her word, had brought her former body home, bedazzling it to preserve it for all eternity. They'd kept it in the guest room, of all places. Valtora justified it by planning to make use of it whenever company decided to invite themselves over and try to stay the night. An effective deterrent, Chauncy had to admit...and an equally effective way to rid themselves of "friends" they didn't want. It'd been a bit much that Valtora had hung the corpse from the rafters above the would-be-guest's bed, however.

Another customer entered the shop then, and to Chauncy's relief, his day took on a more normal rhythm. Such that he

315

completely forgot about what was to come later that day. He enjoyed the moment instead, talking with his customers and showing them his wares. And showing off Chaos as well. For the customers who didn't come in just to tell Chauncy how horrible he was came in to see the baby instead. And, seeing how Chaos had prettied up quite a bit during their adventure, these customers didn't have to lie when they called him cute. A fact that disappointed Valtora, for she'd really hoped to catch people not telling the truth.

So it was that Chauncy found himself enjoying his day, with Valtora and Chaos at his side. And when Chaos cried, they dealt with it together, performing the triple-check each time. Indeed, Chauncy found that by working together – and by living moment-to-moment instead of harboring expectations for the future – Chaos was far easier to endure.

There'd been a whole lot of chaos recently, and not just Chaos Little. Chauncy's rod had a demonic mod, and his wife had changed bodies with his supervillain stepmom, with which he had relations each night. And what's more, his father was Space and his mother was Light. But when all was said and done, Chauncy felt quite alright. For as much as chaos had added difficulty and uncertainty to his life, it'd given far more than it'd taken.

Indeed, after a quarter-decade of orderly drudgery, spending almost every day with his well-worn routine, chaos had arrived in the guise of Harry and Nettie, and had utterly changed Chauncy's life. It'd struck again when Valtora had been caught in a little white lie, and The Dark One had come to reclaim her. And now a third time, in the guise of Zella Trek…and the birth of Chaos himself.

Yes, chaos was something jarring when it came, and seemed to ruin just about everything. But for those with the courage and wisdom to see the value of a little chaos in their lives, what joy and happiness – and magic! – it could bring.

Chauncy's life had been darn near perfect before this whole adventure, or so he'd thought. Now it was differently perfect, if far more complicated…and he found himself quite content with the change that ludicrously inappropriate magic had brought.

# Epilogue

Imperius Fanning sighed, easing himself into his comfortable old chair at his desk in his tower. One of the tallest – and crookedest – towers in the Castle Mundus. He gazed out of the window beyond the desk, looking beyond the courtyard far below with its levitating benches, and even beyond the slight sheen that marked the translucent dome surrounding the Isle. He looked, in fact, all the way to the waterfall falling beyond it, a never-ending flow of the ocean to the ocean below.

Why he'd chosen to watch it, he hadn't a clue. And it didn't matter one bit that he didn't. Imperius had learned to be quite content in merely experiencing, without the constant compulsion to review.

A life unexamined was the finest life of all, though few could manage to live it. For it was ever the habit of humans to examine, then examine that examination, then examine that examination of that examination, and so on. Thoughts about thoughts that brought one further from the here and now.

The one place where magic could be found.

He stared idly at the falling water for a while, then turned his gaze on a whim to the books resting on the bookshelf to his left. He found his gaze slipping off their spines like so many slippery slopes, to land on his scrying orb resting on its shelf. It was a perfect orb of clearest crystal, allowing him to remotely view most anything he requested it to display. And upon retrieving it – on yet another whim – his gut told him to display not Chauncy, but Valtora.

So, trusting his gut, he did.

She was sitting on her front porch with Chauncy, sipping some tea with one hand while carrying Chaos in the other. And with another whim, Imperius focused not on Valtora, but on *him*. A still mildly ugly-looking baby, but with sharp blue eyes that studied his mother intently.

Then the baby turned...and looked directly at Imperius.

Imperius blinked, furrowing his brow. For this sometimes occurred when gazing through his scrying orb, that people seemed to be looking back at him. A trick of coincidence, at least in every prior case. But in this case, it really did seem that Chaos was focusing directly on him.

So he shifted his head to the left…and lo-and-behold, Chaos's eyes followed him.

Imperius conducted this experiment a few times more, and each time Chaos proved capable of following him. The child *was* looking at him…through the scrying orb…which was proof positive that there was magic afoot.

"That's impossible," Imperius muttered, his brow furrowing further. For scrying orbs were supposed to be one-way things. Not even a skilled wizard should be able to pry on a prying wizard scrying. But Chaos was, so impossible it was apparently not.

Imperius set down the orb, the image of Chaos winking out. Or rather, that's what *should* have happened. For it was only activated by his touch and his thoughts. Which meant that Imperius was quite alarmed indeed when Chaos's image remained, those blue eyes still staring right at him.

"Stop it," Imperius scolded, glaring at the baby. Which did nothing at all. So on a whim, he banged his hand on the bookshelf. Chaos startled, and the image winked out. But this hardly gave Imperius peace of mind. For it occurred to him that he didn't know whether Chaos had startled because of the sudden movement of his hand…or whether he'd heard the bang. One wasn't *supposed* to be able to hear things through a scrying orb, at least not this particular one. But Chaos had already broken the rules, so Imperius supposed anything was possible.

He frowned, sitting back down in his chair and eyeing the orb whilst stroking his beard.

"Chaos Little," he murmured. He sighed then, resting his hand on his gut. And his gut, he found, was at peace. Which was in direct opposition to his mind, which was awhirl with thoughts. Flitty, flighty things, thoughts. And while they were the work of his mind – or rather, *were* his mind – he paid them no mind. His mind would make up his mind about what'd happened without him having to get in its way.

So instead, he turned to gaze out of his window again, beyond the desk, and the courtyard and the sheen of the translucent dome far beyond. At the waterfall falling beyond it, a never-ending flow of the ocean to the ocean below. An orderly process, according to the nature of nature. To those who understood its ways, there was no surprise at all. But order was by its nature orderly, and chaos was quite another thing.

Imperius's gut grumbled uneasily, and his eyes widened. A chill ran down his spine, goosebumps rising on his arms. He experienced this, then leaned back in his chair, taking off his hat and running a hand through his long white hair.

"Well then," he murmured, rubbing his uneasy belly. It calmed quickly, for in having provided punctuation for his revelation – and exclamation mark to his enlightenment, so to speak – it needed do nothing else. Not for a while, anyway. Whatever it was that chaos would bring, wouldn't happen for quite some time.

Still, it was clear that one day – and this day would be upon him sooner than rather than later – chaos would rear its head. And on that day, Imperius would have to travel back to Borrin, to a little magic shop called A Little Magic.

For it was well known that, as mushrooms begat mushrooms and trees begat trees, that wizards tended to beget wizards. And in a similar way, Chaos would bring chaos when the time came, and the Order of Mundus…and Imperius himself…would have to be ready.

So, dear reader, we come to the end of this particular tale, of Chauncy's particular world coming to an end. As luck would have it, its end merely marked the beginning of a new world for him, one with a new wife with a new body, a new child, and a new perspective on his life. For he was a wizard of some minor repute, merely adequate, which was perfectly fine. For though he would've preferred to be an ultra-powerful wizard, being adequate meant being enough, and – having enough – he didn't really need anything else.

So instead of struggling with trying to be more, he simply enjoyed being what he was. And in that way, made it far more likely he'd become what he wanted to be. For being true to being oneself was the surest way to fulfill one's destiny.

And so, alas, we find ourselves once again repeating the beginning at the end. For as I mentioned before, that, dear reader, was how the end of Chauncy's world began. But also ended, and began anew.

So now, dearest reader, we'll take a break for a bit. But fear not, for Chauncy's story is not even close to being complete. There are far more tales of inappropriate magic to tell, and I promise you'll get to read them, at some later date anyhow. In the meantime, it will have to suffice for you to enjoy the *here* and *now*.

The following is an excerpt from

# The Magic Collector

Book 1 in the Magic of Havenwood series

# Prologue

A year after his young son Xander's death, a painter set about to do something terrible.

He set his old wooden easel in the center of his studio, a good-sized room on the second floor of his home. A home once filled with love and a beautiful wife, with friends that visited almost daily. Now it was abandoned. Everyone else had moved on after Xander's death.

Everyone but him.

The painter gathered his paints and paintbrushes, mixing his colors carefully. Then he placed a large canvas on the easel, and got to work.

He outlined a shadowy head, then a body. A hand stretching out, reaching for him...even as it fell away, deeper into the canvas. Then deep, dark blue water that filled the entire canvas, save for the very bottom. On this he painted the edge of a wooden raft, slick with puddles of water.

And in the reflections of these puddles, he painted children running toward the edge of the raft, faces struck with desperation...and horror.

At the very surface of the water, around the shadowy figure reaching for him, he painted violent ripples that expanded outward. As if something had just plunged beneath the surface.

The painter stopped, the pain too unbearable to continue.

He went to the small window in his studio then, one overlooking a wide expanse of backyard. And beyond that, a lake. Moonlight splashed over the water in ghostly silver ripples, the sun having long since buried itself below the horizon. He lowered his chin to his chest, closing his eyes.

*I'm sorry son.*

Tears trickled down his cheeks, dripping onto his paint-smudged shirt. He turned back to the painting, walking up to it and stretching his hand out to the figure reaching for him. If he'd only been a minute earlier, he could have…

*Stop it.*

He took a deep breath in, centering himself. Then he put brush to canvas, forging onward.

He filled in the dark figure's details. An eight-year-old boy's bare chest, a pair of blue shorts. Skinny legs and bare feet. A head of short brown hair, large brown eyes.

Frightened eyes. Desperate, filled with terror…and hope.

The painter almost stopped again, his guts twisted with grief. More tears blurred his vision, and he wiped them away, pushing past his feelings. No…*using* them. He painted as if possessed, the story of the painting flowing from his heart and through his brush, so that it might find life on his canvas.

A mouth open in a silent scream, bubbles of air rising from it in a horrible torrent. Life-giving air leaving the boy, rising to the surface even as he sank deeper into the deadly lake.

The painter cried out then, a tortured sound that filled the studio. But still he painted, the strokes at times angry, then bitter. Loving, then guilty. Every stroke a memory, an emotion. Every layer of paint a layer of his soul.

And then, at long last, as the sky outside began to brighten, the sun promising to peek above the waters of the lake any moment now, the terrible deed was done.

The painter stood before his work, studying the painting carefully. His son Xander, reaching out to him, fingers seeming to leap off of the canvas. A painting so vibrant it almost seemed real.

He stared at his son's face, twisted with horror, desperate to be saved…and extended one hand toward his son's, reaching for the boy. His fingertips touched the canvas, pressing against it. He blinked in surprise, not expecting the resistance, and withdrew his hand.

*It's not real.*

He stared at the boy's face, that angelic face. A face burned into his memory. Trusting that his father would always be there, that if anything bad happened, daddy would save him. But daddy hadn't been there. Daddy hadn't saved him.

The painter's eyes went to the bottom right of the painting, at the surface of the raft. Then they dropped to the palette in his left hand...and to a fine-tipped paintbrush lying on the floor nearby.

He swallowed in a dry throat, his heart starting to race.

*It's not real,* he reminded himself.

But he found himself kneeling down, reaching for the paintbrush. His hands trembled as he stood, dipping the tip of the brush into the white splotch of paint on his palette.

He faced the canvas, his whole body quivering now, his heart hammering in his chest.

Taking a step forward, he leaned over, pressing the tip of the brush against the canvas. Before he could change his mind, he cried out, signing his name in quick, sure strokes, each letter perfectly executed.

A gentle breeze caressed him from behind.

He stood then, staring at the painting. And in that moment, he didn't care about the consequences. Didn't care about what might happen to him. He felt a sudden sense of peace...a feeling he hadn't felt since...

The painter smiled, reaching out to the painting again, his fingertips touching the canvas.

And passing right *through* it.

He felt a familiar warmth in his fingers, spreading to his hand as he plunged it into the painting. A warm, pulsing sensation, along with a subtle tingling, as if his hand had started to fall asleep. His wrist vanished into the painting, and then he felt his hand touch something warm and soft.

A palm.

He drew a sharp breath in, then pressed his own palm against it, marveling at the resistance. Then he hesitated, but only for a moment. Reaching in further, he went past the palm, feeling his fingers wrap around a small, bony wrist.

He closed his eyes, taking a deep breath in...and pulled.

# Chapter 1

*BAM!*

Bella jerked upright with a start, her eyes snapping open. She realized she was sitting at her desk at school…and that a hand had slammed down on her algebra book, jolting her out of a particularly pleasant daydream. Bella stared at the hand, following it upward. An almost skeletal wrist poking out of a black sleeve. A scrawny neck. And the face of a dreadfully thin, middle-aged woman staring down at her, pale lips pursed in disapproval.

"*What* did I tell you about daydreaming in my class, Miss Brown?" the woman inquired. Bella stood up straighter, warmth spreading across her cheeks. Everyone in the class was staring at her…and a few were snickering.

"Sorry Mrs. Pittersworth," she mumbled. Mrs. Pittersworth lifted her hand from Bella's book, crossing her arms over her chest. She held Bella's gaze for a moment longer, then turned away, walking back to the front of the room. Bella let go of a breath she hadn't realized she'd been holding, wiping sweaty palms on her thighs. She felt the eyes of her classmates still on her, and pretended to ignore them, glancing at the clock on the wall.

She sighed, groaning inwardly.

For while her daydream had seemed to go on for hours – a silly fantasy involving a mushroom forest and a sparkling lake, with dragons flying in the air all around her – only five minutes had passed in the real world. And there were far too many more to go before the last class of the day was over.

*Tick, tock.*

Bella stared at the black hands of the clock on the wall as Mrs. Pittersworth droned on. The hands made no sound in real life, but in her imagination they rang loudly between each dreadful pause in their movements, celebrating every hard-earned step in the laborious passage of time.

*Tick, tock.*

Mrs. Pittersworth paced in front of the classroom, reciting almost verbatim from the textbook she held. But try as she might, Bella couldn't focus on what Mrs. Pittersworth was saying for more than a minute or so. She found her mind wandering again, and soon her eyelids grew heavy.

*Focus,* she scolded herself.

Bella sighed, opening her notebook. On the left page were various algebra problems, and on the right a half-finished sketch of a dragon standing next to a sixteen-year-old girl. The girl was Bella herself; slender, with chocolate-colored skin and long, curly black hair pulled back into a ponytail. Big brown eyes and arched eyebrows. Jeans and a loose sweater…the clothes Bella was wearing now. The dragon was one she'd drawn hundreds of times before, if not thousands. It was no ordinary dragon, the ones with pretty golden scales and elegant wings and such. No, this dragon had no scales whatsoever. Or much in the way of flesh for that matter. It was a skeletal dragon, pinpricks of ghostly light glimmering from deep within in its eye sockets. Bony wings spread outward magnificently from its back, skeletal fingers connected by inky-black skin. The dragon stood between the girl and a menacing figure; a tall man cast entirely in shadow, wielding a long, slender sword that glowed with an eerie light.

She gazed at the dragon – *her* dragon – for the moment forgetting the tortuous passage of time.

"Now, if you turn to page fifty-seven," Mrs. Pittersworth instructed, her voice practically quivering with anticipation, "…you'll find your very first quadratic equation!"

Bella glanced at her textbook, flipping to the appropriate page. Not because she was particularly interested in what it had to say, but because she didn't want to get caught not paying attention again. The last thing she needed was another day of detention. It was obvious that teachers knew how absolutely awful school was; the worst punishment of all was to give you more of it.

*Tick, tock.*

She turned to gaze out of the tall, narrow windows to her left. Stately trees stood in a sea of grass, their red and orange leaves fluttering in a slight breeze. The year was dying, its long, cheery days – and the freedom they'd brought – but a wistful memory now. Dark, dreary days were ahead, cold and devoid of life, with no end in sight.

Bella sighed again, returning her attention to her dragon. She picked up her pencil and started filling in a few details. Long bone-colored horns atop its head. Short spikes on each vertebra of its spine. Each finger and toe terminating in a deadly black claw. And, as always, a heart-shaped ruby amulet embedded within its long breastbone.

Bella hesitated, then drew a jagged crack in the center of the ruby, touching her chest with her other hand. She felt the same amulet there, resting against *her* breastbone.

"Bella?"

She barely heard her teacher, continuing to draw, finishing her dragon's tail. It was long and thin, curling around its feet.

"Bella!"

She jerked her head up, staring at Mrs. Pittersworth from across the room. Mrs. Pittersworth stared right back, her hands on her narrow hips. She did *not* look pleased.

"Are you doodling again?" her teacher snapped. Bella grimaced. There was no point in lying; Mrs. Pittersworth would march right up and snatch the notebook away to see for herself.

"Yes Mrs. Pittersworth," she mumbled.

"Show me," Pittersworth commanded, extending a hand. Bella sighed, grabbing her notebook and getting up from her desk, walking dejectedly to the front of the class. She heard snickering from her classmates.

"Here," she muttered, handing the notebook over. Mrs. Pittersworth studied the drawing, her lips pulled into a thin, disapproving line. Then she handed Bella the notebook, crossing her arms over her chest.

"Do you think you'll be able to make a living doodling *dragons*, Bella?"

More snickers from the back of the classroom.

"No Mrs. Pittersworth," Bella mumbled, lowering her gaze to her feet.

"Then I suggest you pay attention during class," her teacher counseled. "Look at me when I talk to you!"

Bella lifted her gaze reluctantly.

"How many times have I warned you Bella?" Mrs. Pittersworth demanded. "And still you don't listen. So now we'll be spending some quality time together at detention."

Bella nodded mutely, walking back to her desk and slumping back into it.

"Weirdo," someone whispered from behind.

Bella felt her cheeks grow warm, and did her best to ignore the eyes she knew were on her. She glanced at the clock, its hands seeming to move even slower than before.

*Tick, tock.*

She gave a heavy sigh, turning her attention to her algebra book and doing her best to listen to her teacher. Time stretched outward before her, a veritable infinity of drudgery. First school, then a job, forever a slave to the clock. Always waiting for something better. For a tiny sliver of freedom at the end of the day, where she could finally be herself…without anyone yelling or snickering at her for it.

She'd been so close, a mere twenty minutes away. But now there would be many more *ticks* and *tocks* before she was finally free of the clock.

* * *

Bella plodded up the spiral staircase toward the third floor of her apartment building, her overstuffed backpack threatening to pull her backward and send her tumbling down the stairs. A heavy sigh escaped her, the weight on her shoulders both literal and figurative. For though she had finally managed to escape that horrid prison they called high school, she was not truly free from its clutches. A monstrous amount of homework was waiting for her, cackling from its lair within the dark recesses of her backpack.

It offered a grim choice: a quick death by yanking her down the stairs with its awful weight, or the slow, painful disintegration of her soul.

She chose the latter, trudging along until she'd reached the third-floor landing. A dull brown door greeted her, the paint scuffed and peeling. Stepping up to it, she knocked precisely thirteen times, in the rhythm she'd long since memorized.

There was no answer.

She counted to herself, reaching thirty-three, then knocked again, seven times.

"Yes?" a deep, muffled voice inquired from beyond the door. She recited the following passage:

"A dragon circle,
White and good,
Will one day rise
For Havenwood."

There was a *click* from beyond the door, followed by a *thunk,* then another series of *clicks.* The door swung open, revealing a short, narrow hallway beyond...guarded by an old man. He would've been tall if the weight of time hadn't bent his spine. Time had been similarly cruel to his short curly hair and haphazard beard, draining them of their color until they were stark white. He wore a ratty brown sweater and gray sweatpants that'd grown far too big for him...the same ones he'd worn yesterday, she noted with dismay. His dark brown skin was lined with wrinkles, only his eyes carrying the spark of life. They peered at her from behind golden spectacles, then past her to the stairwell beyond.

"You're late," he accused in a deep, rich baritone, the kind of voice that could fill a room and send chills down your spine. "Are you...?"

"I'm alone Grandpa," she confirmed wearily, pushing past him and into the hallway beyond. She kicked off her shoes, setting them neatly against the wall, then slid her backpack off, letting it fall to the floor with a *thump.* Grandpa shut the door quickly, re-engaging the ridiculous number of locks he'd installed on it.

"Did anyone follow you?" he asked, turning from the door and putting his hands on his hips. She sighed.

"No Grandpa."

"Did you see any police?" he pressed.

"*No* Grandpa," she repeated, rubbing her aching shoulders. "You met that friend of yours again, didn't you," she accused. He was always like this afterward.

"You're sure you didn't see any..."

"Grandpa!" Bella exclaimed exasperatedly. His shoulders slumped.

"Fine," he mumbled. He eyed her for a moment. "Caught doodling again?" he guessed.

"Yeah."

"Show me," he requested, holding out a hand. She sighed, kneeling down to rummage in her backpack. She found her notebook, handing it to him. Grandpa flipped to the proper page with a practiced hand, peering over his spectacles at it. "Hmm, it's good," he admitted.

"Mrs. Pittersworth didn't think so."

"Bah," Grandpa scoffed, giving her a look. "Only concern yourself with what people who *think* think," he counseled. "Believe me, they're few and far between."

Bella smiled at that. Grandpa had a low opinion of most people, Mrs. Pittersworth included. He often mused on how he'd spent the first part of his life trying to make friends…and the remainder trying to get rid of them. He must've done a good job, seeing as how he only had one friend left in this world…and Bella, of course. He could stand to have more, she knew. As it was, all he did was sit at his desk and write books that he wouldn't let anyone read. He left their tiny apartment a few times a year at most, even paying their downstairs neighbor to go grocery shopping for him. It was profoundly unhealthy if you asked her, but trying to get Grandpa to change was like smashing her head repeatedly against a brick wall: the only thing she got out of it was a splitting headache.

"Guess I'll be in the dining room," she sighed, grabbing her backpack by one strap and lugging it out of the narrow hallway and across the living room. "Did you eat today?"

"Doing what?" Grandpa inquired, ignoring her question. Which meant he hadn't.

"Grandpa," Bella scolded exasperatedly, stopping to glare at him. "You have to eat!"

"Doing *what?*" he repeated.

"Hard labor," Bella answered, continuing into their small dining room and tossing her backpack atop the old wooden table there. She began extracting her books.

"No no," Grandpa retorted, following her and grabbing her by the arm. "You can do that nonsense later. I want to show you something."

"Grandpa," she complained wearily. "I really need to get this done. And *you* need to eat something. I made you that chicken you like last night, remember?"

"Later, later," he insisted. "Come," he added, dragging her back into the living room. She sighed, allowing herself to be led toward one of the three small bedrooms in their little apartment. She spotted Grandpa's old wooden desk in the living room, set against the far wall. His notebooks were stacked haphazardly upon it, with framed drawings of mushrooms of all kinds displayed at the desk's edges, sketches Bella had drawn for him. She loved mushrooms, but not eating them. There was something magical about things that thrived in dark places.

She slowed, staring at the desk. There was something…*off* about it. She frowned, then realized what it was.

There was a painting hanging above it. A very large painting.

She stopped, studying it. Nearly as tall as the ceiling and a good three feet wide, it was of a graveyard bathed in ghostly moonlight. Tombstones rose from the dank earth like rotted teeth, and before these lay a body sprawled on its belly over the dirt. A naked body with dead eyes staring right at her.

"Oh god!" Bella gasped, bringing her hand to her mouth. "Grandpa!"

It *was* Grandpa…an eerie likeness of him, anyway. Grandpa followed her gaze, his eyes lighting up.

"Do you like it?" he inquired. "My friend painted it for me."

She didn't have to ask which friend, of course; he only had one. She'd never met the man, and strongly suspected she never would.

"He painted you dead in a graveyard," she stated. He nodded happily. "You sure he's your friend?" she pressed.

"Well, we did have a bit of a falling out years ago," Grandpa admitted, scratching his short beard. "He sort of ruined my life, actually. But he's doing his best to make it up to me."

"Huh."

"What do you think of it?" he pressed.

"I like everything except my naked dead Grandpa staring at me."

"I'll take that as a compliment."

"Tell me you didn't pose for this," she pleaded, eyeing him warily. He gave her a look that was far too innocent. "That's it, I'm shampooing the carpet," she grumbled.

"I laid on some towels," he reassured her. "And threw them in the wash," he added hastily.

"Just…why, Grandpa?"

"Well, my naughty bits were on them, you see, and I…"

"The *painting* Grandpa."

He chuckled, then regarded the painting for a quiet moment.

"It helps remind me of what's coming," he answered at last. "And that every beginning has an end…and every end a new beginning."

"There you go, being all mysterious again," Bella muttered. Grandpa was always saying things like that.

"I'm a writer," he replied matter-of-factly, as if that explained it. It was his excuse for just about everything he did.

"You're really going to keep that up there, aren't you?"

"Just be glad I wasn't on my back," Grandpa replied with a wicked grin, waggling his bushy eyebrows. She pretended to retch, and he laughed. "Come on sweetheart," he urged, pulling her toward one of the bedrooms again. "I want to show you something."

"I think I've seen enough," she retorted. But she let herself be led, and they entered the small spare bedroom Grandpa used as a storage room. To her surprise, it'd been cleaned out…and at the far end of the room stood a wooden easel, a fresh canvas sitting upon it.

She drew a sharp breath in, her eyes widening.

"Happy birthday sweetheart," he declared, gesturing at the easel. She just stared at it, her mouth agape. She closed it with an audible *click*.

"How…?"

"I had the neighbor get them," Grandpa explained.

"Grandpa, this…" Bella said, shaking her head. She gave him a big hug, wiping sudden moisture from her eyes. "Thank you Grandpa."

"You're welcome."

They disengaged, and she walked up to the easel, running her fingertips over the rough canvas. For the first time that day, she felt a burst of excitement. A spark of life. He'd gotten her *everything*…the easel and canvas, a palette, brushes, and boxes and boxes of paints.

"You always said you wanted to be a painter like your mother," Grandpa reminded her, gazing at the gifts with a satisfied smile. "And if you want to *be* something…"

"You have to *do* it," Bella recited.

"Right," he agreed. "I thought we'd start you off with acrylics."

"This is great," Bella murmured, shaking her head slowly. She turned to Grandpa then, her hands on her hips. "How much did it cost?"

"I've been saving," he stated rather defensively.

"I counted our money last week," she retorted. "We barely had enough for rent!"

"I've been saving," he insisted. "I put some cash away." Her eyebrows rose.

"You hid money from me?"

"I wanted it to be a surprise," he explained. "You only turn sixteen once you know."

"Is this why you haven't been eating?" she pressed. He grimaced, but held his ground.

"We can afford it," he insisted. "We *have* to afford it. Yes this cost a lot, but not following your dreams will cost you far more."

She sighed, dropping her hands to her sides. The thought that Grandpa had gone hungry, lying awake at night starving…and all for her…was heartbreaking. But it was clear that he was absolutely delighted with the result, his eyes twinkling with excitement. She gave a reluctant smile, and Grandpa beamed back at her. She stepped up to him, giving him another hug.

"Thanks Grandpa."

He gave her a squeeze, then pushed her away gently, gesturing at the canvas.

"Go on," he urged. "Try it out!"

She turned to the easel, stepping up to it. Then she hesitated. The pristine whiteness of the canvas was suddenly intimidating, a perfect emptiness that she could only ruin.

"I don't know…"

"Of course you don't," he agreed. "You've never painted before."

"Can you teach me?" she asked. He scoffed.

"I'm a writer, not a painter."

"But I don't know what to do," she pointed out.

"Well it's easy," he replied. "Squeeze some paint on this," he instructed, pointing to the wooden palette, "…then dip your brush in it. Then wipe your brush on the canvas."

Bella shot him a withering glare, crossing her arms over her chest.

"Thanks for the tip," she grumbled.

"Have fun!" he exclaimed, walking out of the small room and closing the door behind him. She stared at the door for a long moment, then turned to give similar treatment to the canvas.

Its perfect emptiness was vast, an unconquerable wasteland. She stepped up to it slowly, feeling overwhelmed. The thought of doing homework was suddenly far preferable, and she turned back to the door, opening it.

And found Grandpa standing there, arms crossed over his chest.

"What's wrong?" he demanded.

"I…don't know what to paint."

He relaxed visibly, a smile lighting his features.

"Ah, of course," he replied, leading her back to the easel. "Terrifying, isn't it?" he added, gesturing at the canvas. "A blank page is the artist's most dreaded enemy." He wrapped a bony arm around her shoulders. "I feel the same way when I'm writing."

"Really?"

"Oh yes," he confirmed. "That perfect blankness! Untouched. Pure!" He looked down at her with a conspiratorial smile, his eyes twinkling. "Ruin it."

She blinked, and his smile broadened.

"Go on," he urged.

"What?"

"Ruin it!" he cried, grabbing the package of paintbrushes and tearing one free from its window of plastic wrap. He grabbed a tube of acrylic, squirting it directly onto the brush, then presenting it to Bella.

"But…"

"No buts!" he retorted, shoving the brush into her hands. He pointed at the canvas. "Destroy!"

Bella hesitated, eyeing the canvas. Then she stepped forward, looming over it. She glanced back at Grandpa, who made violent slashing motions with one arm, as if conducting a mad orchestra. She smiled reluctantly, facing the canvas.

And brought the paintbrush down upon it, violating its perfection with an angry black gash.

"Ha!" Grandpa cried in triumph, beaming at Bella. She broke out into a bigger smile, eyeing her handiwork. The canvas was utterly ruined.

"*Now* you can paint," he declared.

"But…what if it's bad?"

"Oh, it *will* be," Grandpa answered matter-of-factly. He gestured to the right of the easel then, at an enormous number of canvases stacked on top of each other, forming a tower that threatened to touch the ceiling. He pointed to the top of it. "This one will be too," he added. Then he pointed to the canvas at the bottom of the stack. "But *this* one, ahhh…I can't wait to see it!"

Bella must have looked entirely unconvinced.

"You'll be terrible," he assured her. "Even your mother was at first. And she ended up being the second-best painter I ever met."

"But…"

"Just paint," he interjected. "When you're done, I promise I'll devour that delicious meal you made me." Then he turned about, leaving the room and shutting the door behind him again.

Bella sighed, trudging up to the easel, then glancing down at the tubes of acrylic paint set neatly in their packaging to her left. She knew full-well that Grandpa really *wouldn't* eat until she'd filled the canvas with paint. He'd clearly lost weight this month, and couldn't afford to lose much more. They were barely getting by on him selling his stories.

She sighed again, looking down at the paintbrush in her hand. Suddenly she felt silly wasting her time painting. There was a mountain of homework she still had to do, after all. She had to do well in school to have a chance at getting a good job…one that would let her take care of both of them. Mrs. Pittersworth had been right, of course; Bella would never make a living doodling.

But she couldn't *not* paint, not after what Grandpa had sacrificed to get this for her.

"Just paint, huh?" she mumbled to herself. She took a deep breath in, squaring her shoulders and focusing on the blighted canvas. "All right Bella, you can do this."

And with that, she got to work, proving herself utterly and horribly wrong.

*The Magic Collector is available on Amazon, iTunes, and Audible!*

Printed in Great Britain
by Amazon

24106418R00199